The Financial Times Guide to Investing for Income

FT Prentice Hall
FINANCIAL TIMES

In an increasingly competitive world, we believe it's quality of thinking that gives you the edge – an idea that opens new doors, a technique that solves a problem, or an insight that simply makes sense of it all. The more you know, the smarter and faster you can go.

That's why we work with the best minds in business and finance to bring cutting-edge thinking and best learning practice to a global market.

Under a range of leading imprints, including *Financial Times Prentice Hall*, we create world-class print publications and electronic products bringing our readers knowledge, skills and understanding, which can be applied whether studying or at work.

To find out more about Pearson Education publications, or tell us about the books you'd like to find, you can visit us at

www.pearsoned.co.uk

The Financial Times Guide to Investing for Income

Grow your income through smarter investing

David Stevenson

**Financial Times
Prentice Hall
is an imprint of**

Harlow, England • London • New York • Boston • San Francisco • Toronto • Sydney • Singapore • Hong Kong
Tokyo • Seoul • Taipei • New Delhi • Cape Town • Madrid • Mexico City • Amsterdam • Munich • Paris • Milan

PEARSON EDUCATION LIMITED

Edinburgh Gate
Harlow CM20 2JE
Tel: +44 (0)1279 623623
Fax: +44 (0)1279 431059
Website: www.pearsoned.co.uk

First published in Great Britain in 2011

© Pearson Education Limited 2011

The right of David Stevenson to be identified as author of this work has been asserted by him in accordance with the Copyright, Designs and Patents Act 1988.

Pearson Education is not responsible for the content of third party internet sites.

ISBN: 978-0-273-73565-6

British Library Cataloguing-in-Publication Data
A catalogue record for this book is available from the British Library

Library of Congress Cataloging-in-Publication Data
Stevenson, David.
  The Financial times guide to investing for income : grow your income through smarter investing / David Stevenson.
     p. cm.
  Includes index.
  ISBN 978-0-273-73565-6 (pbk.)
  1. Investments. I. Title.

  HG4521.S758 2011
  332.6--dc22

2011009437

10 9 8 7 6 5 4 3 2 1
15 14 13 12 11

Typeset in 9pt Stone Serif by 30
Printed by Ashford Colour Press Ltd., Gosport

To Vanessa, Rebecca, Zac and Jake!

Contents

Publisher acknowledgements

We are grateful to the following for permission to reproduce copyright material:

Figures

Figures 1.2, 1.5 from Numis Securities Investment Companies Research; Figures 1.1, 1.3, 1.4 from Moneyfacts, www.moneyfacts.co.uk; Figures 1.6, 1.8, 1.9, 1.10, 1.11, 3.5, 3.6, 3.7, 3.8, 3.9, 3.10, 4.6 from *Equity Gilt Study*, Barclays Capital (2008); Figure 1.7 from Bank of England, www.bankofengland.co.uk/mfsd/iadb/notesiadb/wholesale_baserate.htm; Figure 2.2 from LV= Asset Management; Figures 3.1, 3.2 from www.bondscape.net; Figure 4.2 from *Credit Suisse Global Investment Returns Sourcebook 2009*, Credit Suisse (Dimson, E., Marsh, P. and Staunton, M. 2009); Figure 4.3 from *Credit Suisse Global Investment Returns Sourcebook 2011*, Credit Suisse (Dimson, E., Marsh, P. and Staunton, M. 2011); Figure 4.4 from *Equity Derivatives (EDS): Dividends 18 May 2009, Significant upside to 2010 and 2011, Euro ETOXX 50 Dividends*, BNP Paribas Research Report (Shiller, R); Figure 4.5 from Standard & Poor's; Figure 4.12 from *S&P Europe 350 Dividend Analytical Contacts, S&P Research Paper*, Standard & Poor's (Soe, A.M. 2008); Figure 5.1 from http://www.whitelist.co.uk/_images/january_2010_WL.pdf; Figures 5.2, 5.3, 5.4, 5.5 from *Where to find income? Investment companies offer diversity and security of income*, Numis Securities Investment Companies Research (Cade, C. *et al*); Figure 8.1 from *Lifetime Asset Allocations: Methodologies for Target Maturity Funds*, Ibbotson Associates Research Paper (Idzorek, T. 2008).

Tables

Table 1.3 from *Daily Press Email*, Killik & Co; Tables 1.4, 1.5 from Numis Securities Investment Companies Research; Tables 1.1, 1.2, 2.1, 2.2 from Moneyfacts, www.moneyfacts.co.uk; Tables 2.3, 2.4, 2.5 from www.premiumbondcalculator.com; Table 3.1 from *Equity Gilt Study*, Barclays Capital (2008); Table 3.4 from Standard & Poor's; Table 3.6 from Gemini

Investment Management Ltd; Table 4.1 from *Equity Derivatives (EDS): Dividends 18 May 2009, Significant upside to 2010 and 2011, Euro ETOXX 50 Dividends*, BNP Paribas Research Report (Shiller, R.); Tables 4.2, 4.3, 4.4, 4.5 from *S & P Global Strategies Report*, Standard & Poor's (2009); Table 4.7 from Rob Davies, The Munro Fund, www.themunrofund.com/; Table 4.9 from *S&P Europe 350 Dividend Aristocrats*, Standard & Poor's Research Paper (Soe, A.M.); Table 5.4 from http://www.whitelist.co.uk/_images/january_2010_WL.pdf; Table 5.7 from *Where to find income? Investment companies offer diversity and security of income*, Numis Securities Investment Companies Research (Cade, C. *et al*); Tables 5.9, 5.10 from www.split-sonline.co.uk/, with the permission of Morningstar; Tables 7.1, 7.2 from *Barclays Capital Equity Gilt Study 2009*, Barclays Capital (2009); Table 8.3 from www.trustnet.com, Trustnet is the UK's largest source of retail funds data including detailed factsheets for a range of investment vehicles, alongside portfolio analysis tools and qualitative research from a highly qualified editorial team.

Text

Box on page 37 from http://www.direct.gov.uk/en/MoneyTaxAndBenefits/Taxes/TaxOnSavingsAndInvestments/DG_4016453 under the terms of the Click-Use Licence; Quote on page 48 from 'Where to park a windfall', *The Sunday Times*, 14 March 2010 (Montagu-Smith, N.), Nina Montagu-Smith / The Times / nisyndication; Box on page 64 from Gemma Goodman; Box on page 129 from *S & P Global Strategies Report*, Standard & Poor's (2009).

In some instances we have been unable to trace the owners of copyright material, and we would appreciate any information that would enable us to do so.

1

The basics – risk, yield and structure

Income matters

This book is the result of a straightforward moment of revelation, a tiny epiphany. As an investment journalist I'm used to writing about weighty issues that prey on the minds of supposedly smart people who work in banks and asset management houses – is inflation about to make a comeback, can we trust the central bankers to properly manage volatile asset markets? These translate into relatively straightforward actions within the investment world, such as buying gold if you believe inflation is about to shoot up or selling government bonds if you think government's haven't got a handle on sovereign risk.

But a great many investors, though curious about this 'weighty' stuff, aren't actually that bothered by all this smart talk. What they care passionately about is squeezing out an income from their investments to pay for a huge range of things including their retirement, payments to their children at university or frankly anything that requires a monthly or quarterly cheque. This small revelation is of course no great surprise to the managers of massive investment management houses who have spent countless decades building empires around marketing funds that offer a 'reliable' income, with a headline percentage featuring prominently in the billboard advertisement. But for investment journalists it is a revelation as we assume that investors are really only interested in 'growing' their investments, at best, and preserving their capital at worst. Income is useful as a tool for building models that can calculate the fair value of an investment – analysts at big stock broking houses use the dividend paid out by companies as the basis for many valuation models – but basically it's just a small building block on the path to capital growth.

This book is a reminder that for many people income is an end in itself. A few years ago I attended a focus group for a large investment house and found myself astonished at the wide range of ordinary 'punters' who were interested in income, in one shape or another. I'd expected the older investors in retirement to be desperate to build a sustainable income but I was surprised just how interested the younger investors were in generating an income. In particular I found myself astonished by the mid-twenty-something investors who carefully scrutinised the dividend payouts of large companies – I'd rather lazily assumed that they'd be desperate to talk exclusively about finding the elusive, racy tenbagger stock that shot up tenfold in price. Instead they wanted to know whether GlaxoSmithKline could afford its dividend over the next ten years.

Hopefully this book will address many of those concerns, worries and aspirations. I'm aware that Financial Times/Prentice Hall has already published books on planning for retirement which feature a heavy dose of commentary on income. I'm also aware that there are a great many good books on bonds and income investing, and personal finance books full of worldly wisdom about cutting costs and finding the right savings accounts. All of these serve a purpose but I hope you find this book equally as useful if only because it has at its core a slightly wider purpose, namely to provide a comprehensive overview of all the investment options open to investors looking for a sustainable income over the long term, ranging from ordinary high street savings accounts through to complex structured products built on derivatives and an understanding of equity markets.

Investing for an income

Investing for an income needs, of course, to be focused, most importantly, on generating that **income**, be it on a monthly, quarterly or annual basis. But it also needs to be about **investing**, a term that we all believe we're familiar with except when it comes to how we implement an 'investing' strategy. Go online to Princeton's dictionary and you'll find the definition of investing summarised as follows: 'the act of investing; laying out money or capital in an enterprise with the expectation of profit'. For the vast majority of investors that 'enterprise' is investing in a fund or profit, and

the key word for me in this discussion is capital

the profit will consist of either capital growth or income. But the key word for me in this discussion is **capital**, which is the result of many years of hard work and dedication (unless of course you've inherited it all from a rich aunt!). Your labour produces its own income, most of which is consumed by expenses, living expenses that include housing, food, transport and a nice holiday every once in a while. What's left over is the residual, your savings, which hopefully accumulates over time to produce a big enough pot of capital so that you can deploy it into an investment.

Once you've decided to deploy that capital into an investment, you're forced to make a decision – how much risk are you willing to take for your reward or return? Many investors live in a wonderful make-believe world where they believe that they generate super-sized returns – for income or capital growth – without taking extra risks. But there's a simple equation that holds true over many hundreds of years of study – that you only ever accrue great returns by taking equally great risks. Economists have another way of putting it – there are, apparently, no free lunches in the money world. Or as one anonymous US economist put it:

> There is an old joke, widely told among economists, about an economist strolling down the street with a companion when they come upon a $100 bill lying on the ground. As the companion reaches down to pick it up, the economist says, 'Don't bother — if it were a real $100 bill, someone would have already picked it up.'

If it's obviously a profitable idea you can thus be sure that either a) it's a con or b) it is a good idea that has already been spotted by a million and one other investors who have piled into the investment and pushed up the price. In the real world, investment is defined by the trade off between risk and return and investors have no other choice than to make a judgement about that balance once they decide to employ their capital for (hopefully) productive investment use.

But as the expectation of future returns slowly weaves its way into your thinking (and your expectations of future returns), a new beast emerges. Capital, or should we say the deployment of that capital, encourages heady expectations of future returns which eventually translates itself into greed which in turn encourages excessive risk taking. Warnings go ignored, and eventually that capital is put at jeopardy by foolish decisions. A wonderful 10 or even 15% income or return may be many times above that of the market average but your greed drives you to take the risk.

Sadly many such schemes and products come with a bitter aftertaste as the investors in Bernie Madoff's investment schemes discovered. The hedge fund tycoon turned convict churned out steady 10–20% returns year in, year out, which many investors relied upon as a source of income to fund them through retirement. But history teaches us that even the very best fund managers have bad years, so a fund manager who is nearly always churning out predictable sums is clearly doing something pretty extraordinary. History also teaches us that anyone offering something that's consistently doing better than the rest of the 'pack' is probably up to no good, i.e. cooking the books or indulging in a bit of performance puffing so that they can take in more money. In fact the Madoff debacle was a classic Ponzi fraud scheme which involved very little superior skill except in the hoodwinking department and destroyed many investors hard-earned capital.

This terribly sad episode reminds us of another key aspect examined in this book – sustainability and capital preservation. Generating an unsustainable income eventually forces the depletion of your capital as many split capital fund investors realised at the turn of this century. These complex creatures were built around the traditional investment trust structure and involved investing in equities with the subsequent returns 'split' up into different share classes. The capital growth of these equity investments plus the dividend cheques received were parcelled out to a combination of income, zero dividend and capital share investors. The zero dividend investors were promised a defined return of between 5 and 10% per annum for a period of time, rolled up into a final payment payable when the fund wound up or went into what's called 'redemption'; in effect they received a defined income that was made at the very end of the fund's life. The income investors received the income payments derived from the dividend cheques plus some of the capital growth, with yields well above the market average. Whatever profits remained after these two had had their share was paid out to the capital shareholders who in effect had an option on the fund managers generating great returns from the underlying investments. If both the income and zero dividend investors got 5% apiece per annum, and the manager managed to produce 15% per annum, the capital shareholders got the remainder for a very small initial outlay.

This split returns structure can and does work much of the time but back at the start of this century things started to go terribly wrong. Split capital fund managers started promising ever bigger income payments off the back of booming stockmarkets. Money flooded in and fund managers started believing their own hype and committed the cardinal sin of then believing other fund managers' hype. This resulted in these managers investing in each other's split capital funds, the end result of which was a myriad pattern of cross shareholdings, all built on bullish (positive) equity stockmarkets. Obviously the income shareholders receiving their generous dividend income didn't seem too bothered but it was clear to all and sundry in the investment analysis world that things were about to go horribly wrong if markets suddenly soured. And sour they did as the tech bubble imploded, dragging global stockmarkets down with them! Suddenly all those myriad cross holdings produced what scientists called a feedback effect – as one fund reported big losses, other funds with holdings in that fund also reported losses. Confidence collapsed, investors started selling all classes of the shares, assets under management fell, costs as a proportion of total funds under management shot up (the pool of available investments to charge against was falling) and the whole edifice came crashing down. Many investors with a requirement for income lost nearly everything and the capital shareholders with their 'options' on future growth were wiped out.

It would be nice to report that since then investors have avoided such obvious examples of stupidity, but we know of course that this sadly isn't true. The complex mortgage-backed securities catastrophe in the USA is just another variant on the same structured, split capital fund, with similarly disastrous results. Volatility of markets has shot up and barely a year or two seems to go by without some crash or disaster. This massive uncertainty has encouraged investors to focus on the need to preserve capital, even if fund managers and advisers promise some wonderful 'high income/high return' scheme. The bottom line here is perhaps obvious – that investors need to understand risk, and they need to understand how they can measure the ability of the borrower or investee company/fund to pay back their principal as well as the income or growth. This book will talk incessantly and in great detail about risk and capital preservation.

But this book will also keep returning to another lesson learnt from Madoff and the split capital debacle – simplicity works. If you can't understand it and your adviser can't really explain it, there's probably a very good chance that it will go wrong eventually. This is not to say that everything that is complex is inherently dangerous, as there are a great many clever investments that defy the most simple explanation yet produce impressive returns. But these complex products are probably best left to experts, professionals and the really adventurous types who relish digging under the bonnet of a system, figuring out how the profits engine works and are willing to take on board extra risk for the promise of extra returns. The vast majority of ordinary investors are better off using simple

simplicity shouldn't
also imply wilful
ignorance of the wider
context of investing

to understand products, accounts and investments, which are easily available, easy to trade in, and easy to withdraw should needs dictate. But simplicity shouldn't also imply wilful ignorance of the wider context of investing – the legendary US investor Peter Lynch (one of the greatest fund managers of all time, based at Fidelity) always invoked his fans to kick the tyre of the relatively simple businesses he invested in so that they understood what they were getting themselves involved with. Lynch wanted his legion of private investors to do some hard work on this simple investment idea – analyse the investment, understand how the business made a profit, visit the company if it had a high street presence, and, crucially, understand the wider business environment. It's the contention of this book that investors looking for an income also have to do the same 'leg-work' in understanding what they're putting their money into.

That understanding will take many different forms. This book will introduce you to many different relatively simple structures that produce an income, but hopefully you'll also learn a great amount about the broader context of both investing and the wider economy. Choosing a savings investment product for instance is a relatively simple process but it does involve some hard work scanning the market, understanding the (usually small) risks involved, and working out what impact changes in either the inflation rate or interest rates will have on your investment idea. In the next section we'll sketch out the current wider macro-economic context to savings, income and investment and introduce the reader to long-term trends in both inflation and the cost of capital (otherwise known as the interest rate). We'll then move on to a quick dash through the history of how income-producing investments have been structured over time, before finishing with a canter through some basics of investment structure, notably the idea of duration, the risk spread, volatility and the absolute need to diversify your investment portfolio.

The Fall of the House of Income

As I write this book, we live in extraordinary times for income investors. In the next chapter we'll look at the work of research company Moneyfacts, an organisation that dominates the research into everything from savings rates through to relatively complex pension fund products. In particular it focuses its work on income yields (the rate of income compared to the sum invested, and expressed as a percentage) or in common language the plain old interest rate, with much of the most fascinating analysis contained in a publication called the *Moneyfacts Treasury Report*. I have in front of me the latest report – from summer 2010 – and all I can say is that it makes terrible reading for investors seeking a sustainable, high, long-term income. The report looks at savings trends and contains a number of what I think are fairly self-explanatory graphs and tables.

Figure 1.1 sums up the terrible rate of return from simple no notice savings accounts – the rate has crept up from 0.68% in summer 2009 to the princely sum of 0.73% this year.

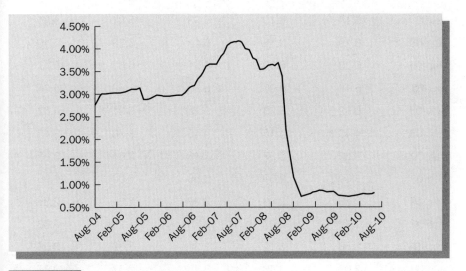

Figure 1.1   **Average no notice savings rate**

Source: Moneyfacts

Table 1.1 delves into a little more detail and looks at the rates paid to investors in savings bonds, ranging from one-year bonds through to five-year bonds. Back in September 2008 a one-year bond paid the princely sum of 6.28% whereas a five-year bond paid a slightly more humble 5.17%. Flash forward two years and that one-year bond pays a miserly 2.59% whereas the five-year bond now pays 4.10%. All of these rates are an improvement on the interest rate paid to no notice account savings account investors (which are next to nothing, as of writing) but these term bonds do require an investor to lock up their savings, with no access, for periods lasting between one and five years. Sadly these rates also tell a wider story. They suggest that the banks and building societies that issue them expect interest rates to remain low for a relatively long period of time.

Table 1.1 Average fixed rate bond rates (%)

	1-year bond	2-year bond	3-year bond	4-year bond	5-year bond
Jan-08	6.00	5.75	5.66	5.80	5.08
Feb-08	5.66	5.44	5.28	5.43	4.76
Mar-08	5.63	5.19	5.14	5.48	4.75
Apr-08	5.66	5.39	5.24	5.47	4.84
May-08	5.87	5.62	5.42	5.55	5.04
Jun-08	5.92	5.77	5.51	5.69	5.05
Jul-08	6.14	6.10	5.93	5.81	5.31
Aug-08	6.19	6.19	6.13	5.80	5.40
Sep-08	6.28	6.09	6.01	5.63	5.17
Oct-08	6.18	5.96	5.80	5.53	5.06
Nov-08	5.82	5.33	5.25	5.31	4.62
Dec-08	4.49	4.15	4.13	3.76	3.48
Jan-09	3.62	3.37	3.46	3.64	3.33
Feb-09	3.00	2.89	3.08	3.09	2.95
Mar-09	2.78	2.83	2.98	2.89	2.86
Apr-09	2.79	2.97	3.13	3.25	3.08
May-09	2.86	3.12	3.30	3.39	3.36
Jun-09	3.04	3.40	3.48	3.57	3.77
Jul-09	2.98	3.34	3.52	3.72	3.74
Aug-09	3.15	3.64	3.84	4.12	4.38
Sep-09	3.22	3.74	4.05	4.18	4.64
Oct-09	3.23	3.75	4.08	4.19	4.77
Nov-09	3.18	3.75	4.16	4.26	4.77
Dec-09	3.12	3.73	4.14	4.30	4.69
Jan-10	3.07	3.72	4.05	3.99	4.56
Feb-10	2.97	3.67	3.91	4.18	4.60
Mar-10	2.88	3.51	3.86	3.85	4.55
Apr-10	2.83	3.40	3.72	3.98	4.37
May-10	2.72	3.30	3.63	4.03	4.35
Jun-10	2.64	3.19	3.53	4.07	4.27

Table 1.1 Continued

	1-year bond	2-year bond	3-year bond	4-year bond	5-year bond
Jul-10	2.62	3.16	3.52	4.02	4.12
Aug-10	2.52	3.13	3.50	4.05	4.02
Sep-10	2.59	3.19	3.52	4.01	4.10
Oct-10	2.62	3.22	3.51	4.01	4.10
Nov-10	2.62	3.18	3.46	3.73	3.99
Dec-10	2.66	3.19	3.45	3.74	3.92
Jan-11	2.61	3.17	3.59	3.74	4.06

Source: Moneyfacts

Figure 1.2 explains much of the logic behind these low rates. It shows the
interest rate levied on banks that want to lend money to each other for
three months. The measure is widely regarded as the barometer for the

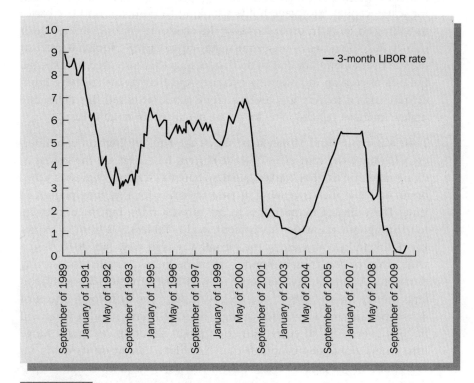

Figure 1.2   **Three-month LIBOR rate**

Source: Numis Securities Investment Companies Research, Datastream

cost of capital in the UK and currently shows a rate of 0.71%, down from 1.27% last year (Summer 2009). These are extraordinarily low rates and tell us a very simple story that can be summed up in the following equation:

Quantitative easing = misery for income investors

This book isn't a treatise on current economic policy or a primer on how to kick-start moribund, debt laden national economies but the current worldwide efforts by central bankers to encourage economic activity are currently having, and will continue to have, profound effects on the returns that investors can expect from their capital. Put simply, in a recession, investors flee from risk, cut their exposure to risky assets such as equities or loans and build up their cash reserves.

in a recession, investors flee from risk

That build-up of cash may preserve their capital but it saps the real economy of resources to grow. Factories needing new extensions sit waiting for scarce capital. Mortgage holders looking to trade up, find the banks unwilling to lend. In order to boost the economy central bankers flush money into the system – hence the quantitative easing – so that banks can use the cash to lend out. But to do that 'easing' they also need to make the holding of cash an unrewarding exercise. And that means crushing interest rates down to very low levels – some economists call this deliberate policy 'financial repression' as savers are penalised for holding cash.

Table 1.2, again from Moneyfacts, shows the Bank of England base interest rates since the start of 1979 – the current base rates are the lowest in living memory! Central bankers are desperate to kick-start depressed economies and that means keeping interest rates low for very long periods of time. Their chosen main tool is to use interest rates, but the effects are felt throughout the wider investment world. Table 1.3 is from stockbrokers Killik and Co and shows the income yields in early July 2010 from a wide range of government bonds (otherwise known as gilts) for varying durations. Astonishingly (for this writer, at least) investors are willing to lend money for 30 years to the US government for an income return of 3.90% per annum. I say astonishingly because I have no idea what will happen over those 30 years – inflation might shoot up, we might lunge into a new global depression or the USA might default on its debts. Or everything might be a lot rosier than it is today. The point is that we just don't know, and that uncertainty over future returns must have a price in investors' minds: I would simply suggest that 3.90% is a low price for what must be some chunky risks! Perhaps equally importantly one could note that the cost of borrowing that money over those 30 years by the US government had actually gone down by not far under 1% (actually 74 basis points or 74/100th) over the previous year!

Table 1.2 Bank of England base interest rates (1979–)

Date	BBR(%)	Date	BBR(%)	Date	BBR(%)
05-Mar-09	0.50	18-Sep-01	4.75	08-Mar-96	6.00
05-Feb-09	1.00	02-Aug-01	5.00	18-Jan-96	6.25
08-Jan-09	1.50	10-May-01	5.25	13-Dec-95	6.50
04-Dec-08	2.00	05-Apr-01	5.50	02-Feb-95	6.75
06-Nov-08	3.00	08-Feb-01	5.75	07-Dec-94	6.25
08-Oct-08	4.50	10-Feb-00	6.00	12-Sep-94	5.75
10-Apr-08	5.00	13-Jan-00	5.75	08-Feb-94	5.25
07-Feb-08	5.25	04-Nov-99	5.50	23-Nov-93	5.50
06-Dec-07	5.50	08-Sep-99	5.25	26-Jan-93	6.00
05-Jul-07	5.75	10-Jun-99	5.00	13-Nov-92	7.00
10-May-07	5.50	08-Apr-99	5.25	16-Oct-92	8.00
11-Jan-07	5.25	04-Feb-99	5.50	22-Sep-92	9.00
09-Nov-06	5.00	07-Jan-99	6.00	17-Sep-92	10.00
03-Aug-06	4.75	10-Dec-98	6.25	16-Sep-92	12.00
04-Aug-05	4.50	05-Nov-98	6.75	05-May-92	10.00
05-Aug-04	4.75	08-Oct-98	7.25	04-Sep-91	10.50
10-Jun-04	4.50	04-Jun-98	7.50	12-Jul-91	11.00
06-May-04	4.25	06-Nov-97	7.25	24-May-91	11.50
05-Feb-04	4.00	07-Aug-97	7.00	12-Apr-91	12.00
06-Nov-03	3.75	10-Jul-97	6.75	22-Mar-91	12.50
10-Jul-03	3.50	06-Jun-97	6.50	27-Feb-91	13.00
06-Feb-03	3.75	06-May-97	6.25	13-Feb-91	13.50
08-Nov-01	4.00	30-Oct-96	6.00	08-Oct-90	14.00
04-Oct-01	4.50	06-Jun-96	5.75	05-Oct-89	15.00

▶

Table 1.2 Continued

Date	BBR(%)	Date	BBR(%)	Date	BBR(%)
24-May-89	14.00	29-Jul-85	11.50	05-Nov-82	9.00
25-Nov-88	13.00	15-Jul-85	12.00	14-Oct-82	9.50
25-Aug-88	12.00	19-Apr-85	12.50	07-Oct-82	10.00
08-Aug-88	11.00	12-Apr-85	12.75	31-Aug-82	10.50
18-Jul-88	10.50	29-Mar-85	13.00	18-Aug-82	11.00
04-Jul-88	10.00	21-Mar-85	13.50	02-Aug-82	11.50
28-Jun-88	9.50	28-Jan-85	14.00	14-Jul-82	12.00
22-Jun-88	9.00	14-Jan-85	12.00	08-Jun-82	12.50
06-Jun-88	8.50	11-Jan-85	10.50	12-Mar-82	13.00
02-Jun-88	8.00	23-Nov-84	9.50	25-Feb-82	13.50
18-May-88	7.50	20-Nov-84	9.75	25-Jan-82	14.00
11-Apr-88	8.00	07-Nov-84	10.00	03-Dec-81	14.50
17-Mar-88	8.50	20-Aug-84	10.50	09-Nov-81	15.00
02-Feb-88	9.00	10-Aug-84	11.00	14-Oct-81	15.50
04-Dec-87	8.50	09-Aug-84	11.50	01-Oct-81	16.00
05-Nov-87	9.00	12-Jul-84	12.00	16-Sep-81	14.00
26-Oct-87	9.50	09-Jul-84	10.00	11-Mar-81	12.00
07-Aug-87	10.00	27-Jun-84	9.25	25-Nov-80	14.00
11-May-87	9.00	10-May-84	9.00	03-Jul-80	16.00
29-Apr-87	9.50	15-Mar-84	8.50	15-Nov-79	17.00
19-Mar-87	10.00	07-Mar-84	8.75	13-Jun-79	14.00
10-Mar-87	10.50	04-Oct-83	9.00	05-Apr-79	12.00
14-Oct-86	11.00	15-Jun-83	9.50	01-Mar-79	13.00
22-May-86	10.00	15-Apr-83	10.00	08-Feb-79	14.00
21-Apr-86	10.50	15-Mar-83	10.50		
08-Apr-86	11.00	12-Jan-83	11.00		
19-Mar-86	11.50	29-Nov-82	10.00		

Source: Moneyfacts

Table 1.3 Income yields in early July 2010 from range of government bonds

Government bond	Yield today in %	Change on week in basis points or 100ths of 1%	Change year to date in basis points
UK 2 Year Gilt	0.77	4.20	–54
UK 10 Year Gilt	3.33	–5.40	–68
UK 30 year Gilt	4.12	–11.00	–29
German 2 Year Gilt	0.67	10.30	–65
German 10 Year Gilt	2.57	–4.40	–82
German 30 Year Gilt	3.26	–9.40	–85
US 2 Year Gilt	0.63	–2.36	–51
US 10 Year Gilt	2.94	–17.00	–89
US 30 Year Gilt	3.90	–16.74	–74

Source: Killik and Co.

But it would be wrong to simply blame the government, central banks and base rates. There are of course other factors at work too. Figure 1.3 shows the gross savings here in the UK as a simple measure – you'll notice that over the past few years the sheer quantity of savings has shot up. This simple graph tells you that we, the British, are saving more than ever. The bottom line? The supply of savings has increased.

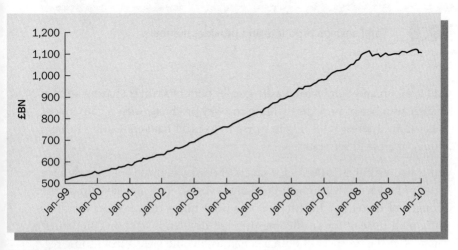

Figure 1.3   Retail savings: balances outstanding

Source: Moneyfacts

Figure 1.4 shows us the flip side of this increase in supply. The number of financial institutions offering savings products has dramatically declined – this graph shows the number of savings products and product providers. It clearly shows that since the beginning of 2010 the supply of banks and building societies willing to offer products has collapsed. This would tend to imply that the demand for those massively increased savings has decreased.

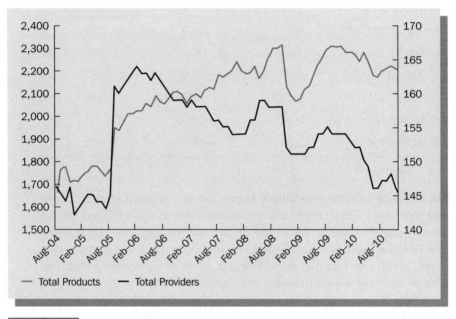

Figure 1.4   **Total savings products and provider numbers**

Source: Moneyfacts

Add it all up and you have a vastly greater pool of savings chasing an ever smaller number of providers willing to offer products, with a consequent collapse in interest rates, made worse by central bankers willing to lend money at close to zero rates.

But this dreadful situation – for savers at least – is made even worse by a series of knock-on developments. Many investors long ago gave up on the thought of deriving a healthy income from high street savings accounts and opted instead for an income through dividends paid by companies. These offer the prospect of both a generous income yield – from those regular dividend cheques – and the possibility of some capital appreciation as the share price rises over the long term. As we'll see in later chapters, most academic research suggests that investors can expect a long-term rate of return from shares (equities) of around 6–7% per annum with a bit more than half of that derived from those dividend cheques piling up.

But in 2009 even this story started to sour with company after company, blue chip and small, lining up to say that they were stopping or reducing the dividend cheque as the economy plummeted into recession. One analysis from the US stockmarket analysed the popular S&P [Standard & Poor's] 500 index of top stocks and suggested that in 2009 total dividends paid out fell by $52.6 billion, or 21.4%, from 2008. In dollars, that is the largest decline ever, and in percentage terms it's the biggest drop since 1938, when dividends fell 38.6%. From September 2008 to March 2009, S&P 500 companies stopped paying $65.4 billion in dividends. Of that amount, 68% was due to cuts at financial firms, i.e. banks like CitiGroup. In the UK, dividends also fell off a cliff. Many companies that had kept progressively increasing their dividend payouts year in year out, suddenly stopped. Industrial giant GKN was one such progressive hero, constantly increasing its dividend payout until the dark days of 2009 when it announced that it would stop its payment altogether!

in the UK, dividends also fell off a cliff

Here's Sir Kevin Smith, GKN's chief executive, on the announcement:

> *We haven't withheld a dividend for 29 years and we have a progressive dividend policy, so it's a very big decision for us. But under the circumstances it's better to preserve cash. Our automotive revenues have fallen by about 40 per cent since the middle of last year.*

In 2009 GKN's shares crashed by nearly 70% and following that announcement they fell another 2.5%. But GKN is far from being alone in its decision to abandon the ranks of progressive dividend increasers – only a few days before its decision, Anglo American, the mining giant confirmed that it too would be stopping its dividend; National Express also did so for a short time. Figure 1.5 is from researchers at investment banking group Numis and shows dividend growth in the all important FTSE All Share index – a measure of nearly 98% of the entire UK listed market.

The researchers at Numis then carefully listed all the companies in 2009 that stopped or cut their dividend payouts (see Table 1.4). For income investors this read like a long list of the great and good, once reliable companies that many had depended on for an income, companies such as BT, M&S and Lloyds.

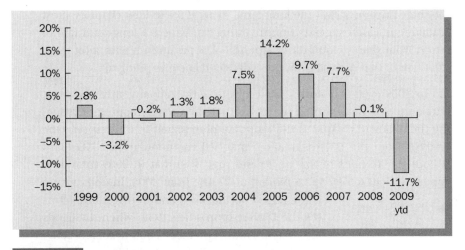

Figure 1.5   **FTSE All Share dividend growth**

Source: Numis Securities Investment Companies Research, Datastream

Table 1.4 Key contributors to dividend growth by FTSE market in 2009

Sector	Change (%)	Negative
Basic Materials	−58	Anglo American, Rio Tinto, Xstrata, Kazakhmys
Financials	−33.5	Barclays, RBS, Lloyds, Old Mutal, Liberty, 3i
Technology	−26	Logica
Consumer Services	−16	BA, M&S, Kingfisher, Carnival
Industrials	−13	Wolseley, Rexam
Telecoms	−11	BT

Source: Numis Research

By 2010 the dividend story had brightened somewhat although only one of the big banks – Barclays – had resumed its dividend payments. Some companies then started increasing their dividend payouts as the economy slowly pulled out of its nosedive but income investors had become terrifically reliant on just a few big payers. Table 1.5 from 2010 shows the companies in the FTSE 350 index (the biggest 350 companies by market capitalisation) and how much of their dividends comprise the total payout.

Table 1.5 FTSE 350 dividend contribution by stock

Company	Percentage of dividend comprising total payout
BP	13
Royal Dutch Shell	12
HSBC	9
Vodafone	8
Glaxo	6
BAT	4
BHP Billiton	2
AstraZeneca	2
Tesco	2
Diageo	2
The Rest (the other 340)	40

Source: Numis Research

One name should stand out at the top of this analysis – BP. This work from Numis was released in the first part of 2010 and predated BP's catastrophic oil spill disaster in the Gulf of Mexico after which they cancelled their dividend payouts for the foreseeable future. So not only was over 60% of the total dividends paid out by FTSE 350 companies accounted for by just ten big blue chips but a stunning 13% was paid out by one very big company that decided to stop paying because of massive operational issues.

What can you do?

It was very easy to become completely depressed by these big headline numbers and broad trends. Investors could decide to just throw in the towel and play to the slothful-like characteristics of capital, sit tight and put up with the low rates of return on offer via cash savings accounts, safe in the knowledge that their capital was safe!

The central bankers of course desired a very different result. They had deliberately cut base rates and crushed income yields to encourage investors to spend their money or at worst invest their money in more risky things like shares issued by companies looking to raise capital to expand. In fact the last thing the governments and central bankers cared about was whether risk assets were being over-bought – to combat a great global depression they need investors to start taking risks. And as sure as night follows day, investors piled out at the first hint of a recovery and pumped up share prices, as well as gobbling up riskier bonds such as those issued by big corporations. Asset prices shot up and some investors made an absolute fortune by investing in what was nicknamed 'The Dash for Trash' – massive profits from buying beaten-up assets and shares at bargain prices in fundamentally terrible companies that would just about survive the recession. And then, just as any fool could predict, those risky assets came crashing down in price, as investors found themselves spooked by talk of a double dip recession in 2011 and massive tax rises. This mad dance with risk embraced every form of income producing asset imaginable, with bonds, dividend paying stocks and other myriad hybrids discussed later in this book, shooting up and down in value.

The smart investor – one who has hopefully read this book – might have taken up the central bankers' invitation to spend their low interest cash on slightly riskier assets but they might have done so with more care. They might have embraced a variety of simple but sensible ideas including the need to *diversify* their range of investments, to understand the premium attached to riskier assets that produce an income (*the risk spread*), and appreciate that the risk of *default* (total loss of capital) is ever present and carries a price. They'd also understand why the *duration* of an investment matters and why the more liquid an asset is, the less risky it is compared to a more illiquid peer. We'll discuss these terms – and a few more – in more detail later on. But these smarter investors might also understand that markets don't really change over history, nor do the structures used for investment purposes. Markets career up and down, as do interest rates and the rate of inflation. Risk is always present as is the potential for reward. To understand this, one needs to understand why humans have been making the most basic of mistakes for hundreds of years.

The history of investing for an income

Investing in order to produce an income hasn't always been popular, or even allowed by past (and present) cultures. Here's the Greek scholar Aristotle on the subject, with emphasis added in bold:

There are two sorts of wealth-getting, as I have said; one is a part of household management, the other is retail trade: the former necessary and honorable, while that which consists in exchange is justly censured; for it is unnatural, and a mode by which men gain from one another. The **most hated sort,** *and with the greatest reason,* **is usury, which makes a gain out of money itself,** *and not from the natural object of it.* **For money was intended to be used in exchange, but not to increase at interest. And this term interest, which means the birth of money from money, is applied to the breeding of money because the offspring resembles the parent. Wherefore of all modes of getting wealth this is the most unnatural.**

Modern Islamic Finance is also built around similar prohibitions, with usury or the object of making a gain out of money itself explicitly banned. Here's one excerpt from the Koran used by many modern scholars to ban all forms of interest:

Those who eat Riba (usury) will not stand (on the Day of Resurrection) except like the standing of a person beaten by Shaitan (Satan) leading him to insanity. That is because they say: 'Trading is only like Riba (usury),' whereas Allah has permitted trading and forbidden Riba (usury). So whosoever receives an admonition from his Lord and stops eating Riba (usury) shall not be punished for the past; his case is for Allah (to judge); but whoever returns [to Riba (usury)], such are the dwellers of the Fire – they will abide therein.

(فرقبلاقروس), Al-Baqara, Chapter #2, Verse #275)

Readers might, having read these two fairly forceful passages, have concluded that the concept of interest and receiving an income from your investments is a fairly modern innovation. Sadly, for the moralistic amongst us, the authors of the Koran and Aristotle are very much in a minority on the subject of interest and investment income. Anyone wanting evidence of this contention – and proof of the enormous complexity of investing for an income over time – should make sure they read a wonderfully erudite academic text (beautifully annotated) called the *The Origins of Value: Financial Innovations that Created Capital Markets*, edited by William N. Goetzmann and K. Geert Rouwenhorst and published (2005) by Oxford University Press. This sets out in detailed chapter after detailed chapter (by some of the world's leading professional economists and historians including Robert Shiller from Yale and Niall Ferguson) the origins of both modern investing in bonds and equities and the development of interest and investment income.

For instance in the chapter entitled 'The Invention of Interest – Sumerian Loans' by Marc Van De Mieroop (Professor of Ancient Near East History at Columbia University), we begin to see the emergence of what we might term loans as early as the fourth millennium BC or year 3200. Based on the archaeological records it would seem that the royal palace controlled rations of food and materials, aided in part by people donating a part of their production to this central institution. As Professor Van De Mieroop notes 'contributions became mandatory and credit became a necessity. When farmers, fishermen or others were unable to pay they had two options: they could either remain in arrears to the institution or borrow from someone who had sufficient capital at hand.' These loans were given various titles over time but the word 'ur' seemed to settle and we have copious evidence of the terms applied to these contracts. One such contract stipulated a silver loan to be repaid as follows: 'One and one sixth shekels silver (i.e. 9.3 grams) to which the standard interest is to be added, Ilshu-bani, the son of Nabi-ilishu received from (the god) Shamash and from Sin-tajjar. At harvest time he will repay the silver and the interest. Before five witnesses (their names listed).'

Already we can see some simple-to-understand concepts emerging – a rate of interest, the concept of repaying the principal amount, and a duration over which the loan is made. It's also clear that the issuing of these loans could frequently get out of hand with royal decrees annulling debts, with reference to 'establishing order in the land'. The government also involved itself in the regulation of interest: 'From the early second millennium a number of royal decrees exist that always proclaim a 20% interest rate for silver loans and a 33.3% interest rate for barley loans,' notes Professor Van De Mieroop.

This short passage demonstrates again that nothing much changes over the millennia – this attempt to control interest rates is yet another government attempt to regulate the cost of debt in order to stimulate or control the economy with varying interest rates for different forms of capital.

As we move from the Sumerians, new concepts, now familiar to us, start to emerge, concepts like shares and formal bonds. In 'Roman Shares' Ulrike Malmendier looks at the emergence of companies which issue shares called Societas Publicanorum. These companies boasted shares that clearly had a market value or price: 'Cicero speaks of partes illo tempore carissimae of "shares that had a very high price at the time".' We don't have any evidence examining whether these companies formally issued dividends as such but it's safe to assume that investors in these companies almost certainly derived some form of income from their shares. In a later chapter we move on to the medieval era, still in Italy, to the City states, in 'Bonds and Government Debt in Italian City States 1250–1650', penned by Luciano Pezzolo. This analysis starts with the decision of the Venetian government to issue a decree in 1262 which establishes the basic principles of government debt:

> *The decree permitted the government to spend for its ordinary needs up to 3,000 lire a month; spending beyond that had to be used to pay 5% interest to those from whom the government had borrowed money. The interest had to be paid twice a year and once paid if additional money was available it would be used first to finance the current war [with the Byzantines] and wars to come and second to pay off the loans. No one was allowed to revoke the statute.*

This government debt soon turned into one series called a Monte which could in turn be traded in a secondary market and traded around the city, Italy and potentially the world. Pezzolo shows how this market did indeed develop with different values ascribed to the price of these debts in different years – and other city states soon followed the lead of Venice, each assigning its own rate of interest, which in turn changed its interest rates or yields over time, as can be seen from Table 1.6.

Table 1.6 Nominal interest rate on government loans 1250–1525

Period	Venice	Genoa	Florence
1251–1275	5	8	
1276–1300	5		10
1301–1325	5		8
1326–1350	5		12
1351–1375	5	10	5
1376–1400	4	8	5
1401–1425	4	7	3.75
1426–1450	4	4	3.37
1451–1475	4	3.5	3.25
1476–1500	5	2.8	2.5
1501–1525	5	4	

Source: *The Origins of Value: Financial Innovations that Created Capital Markets* by W.N. Goetzmann and K.G. Rouwenhorst

The medieval era also saw the growth of another financial instrument we will encounter later in this book, the annuity. In one form or another these had actually been around since the Roman era but the attempt by the Roman Catholic Church to ban usury in the 1300s and 1400s greatly increased the attractiveness of a financial structure that allowed the regular payment of income for an initial upfront investment, all over the lifetime of the 'borrower'. James Poterba in his chapter 'Annuities in Early Modern Europe' notes how 'when borrowers were not allowed to pay more than a legally established interest rate on loans but credit market equilibrium dictated a higher rate, annuities provided one way to circumvent the usury laws ... Ray D. Murphy reports that monasteries and churches were among the institutions that sold annuities.' We also know that by the 1600s Dutch companies such as the VOC – the Dutch East Indies Company – were issuing dividends to their shareholders and that an options market was beginning to develop that would attempt to estimate future returns from an investment. During this same era in Holland we also see the emergence of what are called perpetuity loans – loans issued by a government or organisation that would pay out interest for ever unless they were called (bought back). The UK government still has a small body of perpetuities in existence within its debt portfolio called Consuls, which can be traded through any stockbroker.

By the 1700s we witness an even more startling innovation, namely the issuance of inflation-linked government bonds by the Commonwealth of Massachusetts to help fund the Revolutionary War. In a chapter by US economist Robert Shiller in the Goetzmann and Rouwenhorst volume, we see that the new government on the American continent had realised that inflation – the measure of rising household prices over time – would have an impact on ordinary investors and so decided to compensate for this 'loss of purchasing power' by incorporating some measurement of inflation into the value of what were called depreciation notes issued to its soldiers as part payment for fighting in the Revolutionary wars. Shiller notes:

> already by 1780 the state of Massachusetts had long longstanding problems with an unstable price level due to the state government's excessive printing of paper money. These problems had persisted for the better part of a century when the depreciation notes were issued. Inflation had been a deep set prob-

*lem that accounted for a lot of problems of the state and that had occupied a
great deal of public attention over these years.*

In the modern era we witnessed a rapid succession of new structures and
models emerged including the first mutual or collective funds that bought
bonds or equities for their investors – and derived an income. These
emerged first in Holland in the 1700s but spread over the British Channel,
resulting in the formation of the Foreign and Colonial Government Trust
in 1868 in London, a fund that still exists today and pays out a generous
and reliable dividend yield.

Interest and Inflation rates through history

As we move into the 19th and 20th century a wealth of new data becomes
available to us, especially around some of the economic measures we've
already noted in Goetzmann and Rouwenhorst's book. By the Victorian
era economists were diligently noting down both inflation and interest
rates, and detailed records exist of everything from stock market prices
through to government bond yields.

One of the most comprehensive source's of this historical data is the
excellent Equity Gilt Study run every year by analysts and economists at
British investment bank BarCap. This is an exhaustive look not only at
current market trends but also past data stretching back into the 1800s
and beyond. It compares a whole series of investment products over time,
ranging from high street savings accounts through to gilts and equities,
looking at both capital price returns and income yields.

Figure 1.6 for instance looks at UK interest rates since 1694 and shows
that interest rates have varied between 6% and just over 2% for nearly
200 hundred years, though it's worth noting in passing that interest rates
never dipped below 2% and certainly never reached the levels of less than
1% seen today.

Those ultra-long-term trends in interest rates didn't really change much
as we move through time. Table 1.7 shows interest rates from the modern
period between 1950 and 1972 – again rates moved in a broad sweep
between 2% and 7.5%.

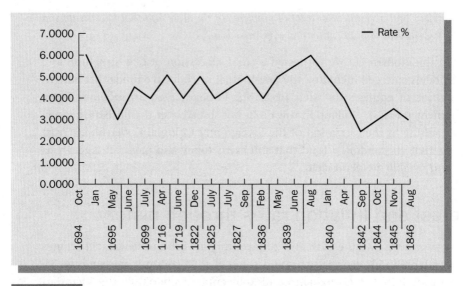

Figure 1.6   UK interest rates (1694–1846) as a percentage

Source: BarCap

Table 1.7 Interest rates 1950–72

Year	Interest rate (%)	Year	Interest rate (%)	Year	Interest rate (%)	Year	Interest rate (%)
1950	2.0	1956	5.5	1962	5.5	1968	7.5
1951	2.5	1957	5.0	1963	4.0	1969	8.0
1952	4.0	1958	6.0	1964	5.0	1970	7.5
1953	3.5	1959	6.0	1965	6.0	1971	6.0
1954	3.0	1960	5.0	1966	7.0	1972	6.0
1955	3.5	1961	7.0	1967	6.5		

Everything changes by the 1970s! Figure 1.7 – sourced from the Bank of England – shows how interest rates started rising inexorably as the great post World War 2 boom came to an abrupt end. By the mid 1970s and 1980s effective interest rates had shot up into double figures hitting over 16% in the mid 1970s.

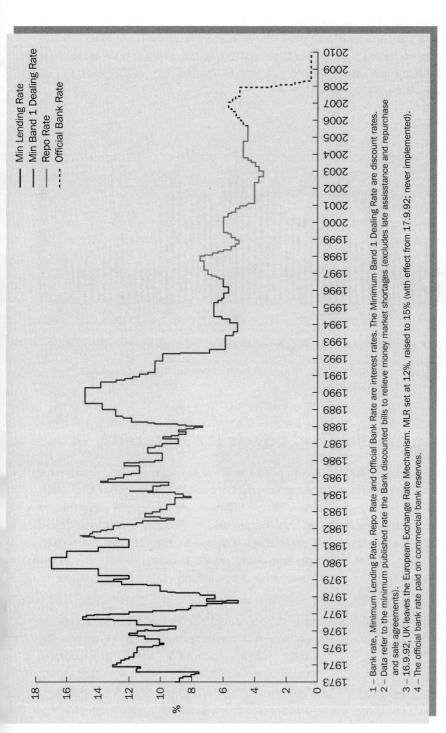

Legend:
— Min Lending Rate
— Min Band 1 Dealing Rate
| Repo Rate
⋯ Official Bank Rate

1 – Bank rate, Minimum Lending Rate, Repo Rate and Official Bank Rate are interest rates. The Minimum Band 1 Dealing Rate are discount rates.
2 – Data refer to the minimum published rate the Bank discounted bills to relieve money market shortages (excludes late assisstance and repurchase and sale agreements).
3 – 16.9.92, UK leaves the European Exchange Rate Mechanism. MLR set at 12%, raised to 15% (with effect from 17.9.92; never implemented).
4 – The official bank rate paid on commercial bank reserves.

Figure 1.7   Changes in bank rate, minimum lending rate, minimum band 1 dealing rate, repo rate and official rate

Source: http://www.bankofengland.co.uk/mfsd/iadb/notesiadb/wholesalebaserate.htm

That sudden spike can be seen in the Figure 1.8 – it's from the research-ers at BarCap again and shows how interest rates on high street savings accounts varied hugely over time, starting at just over 6% after World War 2, hitting just under 16% in the mid 1970s and then falling back to just over 4% by 2008.

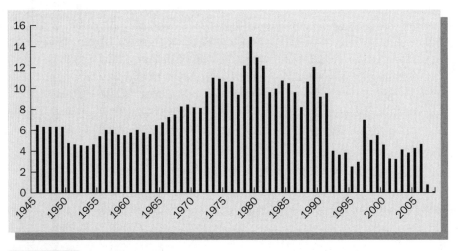

Figure 1.8   Annual savings return on high street savings accounts as a percentage

What is inflation and how is it measured?

One of the major reasons behind the constant increase in interest rates – and thus interest earned on savings accounts – throughout the 1960s and 1970s is the remorseless rise of inflation. We've already encountered this crucial idea earlier in this chapter and in Chapter 3 on index-linked government bonds we'll explore modern bond structures that attempt to reward investors for rising household prices. However, before we do it's worth reminding ourselves of what we're actually talking about when we refer to inflation.

Simply defined, inflation is the sustained rise in overall price levels. As an economy grows, businesses and consumers spend more money on
simply defined, inflation is the sustained rise in overall price levels   goods and services and in some circumstances this increase in demand far outstrips the supply of goods, in turn allowing producers to raise their

prices. As a result, the rate of inflation increases until it hits a runaway level also sometimes called hyperinflation, experienced recently in Zimbabwe and most famously in Weimar Germany after World War 1 when wheelbarrow loads of money were required to pay for just one loaf of bread!

Hyperinflation is the stuff of modern legend but investors also need to be careful about other forms of inflation. Stagflation is an especially nasty beast as it inflicts on its sufferers both higher prices for basic goods and services, and low growth rates. An equally nasty menace is something called deflation or disinflation, where the rate of inflation dips into negative territory, i.e. prices fall. It's worth noting that the longest and most severe period of deflation over the past century occurred in the 1920s and in the 1930s during the Great Depression. Most economists regard deflation as almost as deadly a phenomenon as hyperinflation, as it slowly destroys the incentive to invest in new capacity to increase production.

Investors also need to understand that the very measures used to define exactly what kind of inflation we're experiencing are also the subject of much debate and statistical jiggery pokery. Most major measures of inflation – or deflation for that matter – look at something called 'headline' or reported inflation, which is also known as core inflation. In the USA for instance there are two main measures – the Producer Price Index (PPI) and the Consumer Price Index (CPI) while in the UK you'll also see something called the Retail Price Index (RPI) bandied about. In simple words these terms mean the following:

■ The PPI, previously called the wholesale price index, measures prices paid to producers, usually by retailers.

■ The more widely followed CPI reflects retail prices of goods and services, including housing costs, transportation and healthcare. In the UK this measure is used by the government to target inflation levels and covers the full range of consumer purchases made by households in the UK (excluding most owner-occupier housing costs)

■ In the UK you'll also see the RPI mentioned frequently. The RPI is also used by the government for the indexation of pensions, state benefits and housing costs. It measures the average change from month to month in the prices of goods and services purchased in the UK. You might also see two commonly used RPI measures: RPIX – all items excluding mortgage interest payments; and RPIY – all items excluding mortgage interest payments and indirect taxes.

■ Finally investors may also encounter something called the Gross Domestic Product deflator (GDP deflator) which is a broad measure of inflation reflecting price changes for goods and services produced by the overall economy

Regardless of which measure was used for much of the 20th century investors didn't seem too menaced by the reality of inflation. Figure 1.9 is from BarCap's Equity Gilt Study and shows the annual inflation rate since the early 1900s. For much of the 1920s and the 1930s the UK experienced either low inflation or deflation, with inflation levels rarely rising much above 5% until the early 1970s. The stagflationary 1970s put paid to that complacency and rates shot up, hitting over 20% before tumbling back down to low single figures in the 1990s and first decade of this century.

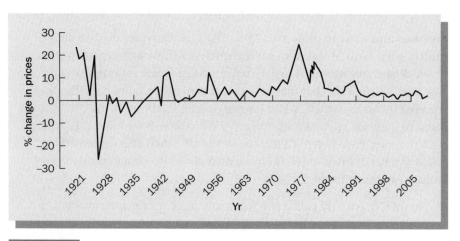

Figure 1.9   **Annual inflation rate as a percentage**

Source: BarCap

But that sudden bout of inflation in the 1970s and 1980s had a huge impact on overall pricing levels. Figure 1.10 shows the cumulative level of the Retail Prices Index over the very long term. By the 1970s this index had started an inexorable climb upwards, destroying the value of a fixed price asset or security – bonds tend to suffer in inflationary eras as we'll discover later in this book.

There's one last long trend series worth examining in detail before we take stock and examine some core ideas in income investing. Figure 1.11 shows the average dividend yield of the UK stockmarket since the 1870s.

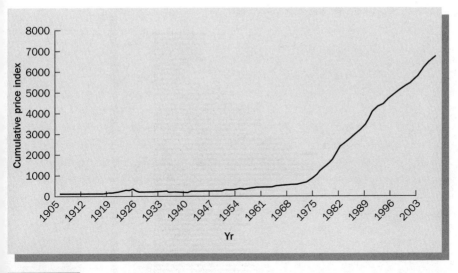

Figure 1.10   UK inflation

Source: BarCap

It's a fascinating time series and shows that in key periods of UK history, a basket of diversified dividend stocks could have paid out over 7% per annum, well above both bond and high street savings rates. Even as late as the 1970s dividend rates were on average still above 5% but by the 1980s the rot had set in – equity prices kept on rising and by the end of the 1990s the overall dividend yield of the UK market had fallen below 2%, before rising (marginally) in the first decade of the new century.

Some basics

It's worth recapping some of the insights gained from this quick historical detour, courtesy of both BarCap and the academic pairing of Goetzmann and Rouwenhorst: that interest rates from time immemorial have been set by the powers that be and can change over time; that inflation is a problem if it gets out of control; that some of the biggest borrowers of money from investors are the governments through their issuance of bonds or gilts; that debts can be vulnerable to non-payment and government decisions; that interest and inflation rates can vary enormously over time as can dividend yields; that the basics of investing for an income have been pretty constant over time; and that most really important innovations started many centuries before.

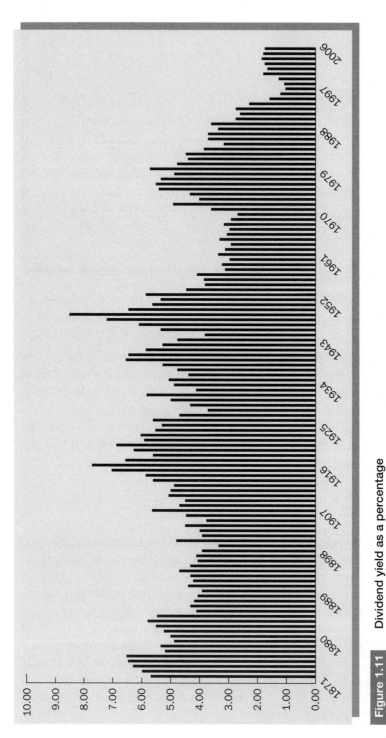

Figure 1.11   Dividend yield as a percentage

Source: BarCap

Over the next few chapters we'll pick up these ideas as we look at everything from investing in government bonds through to equity investing to sourcing a dividend. Before we do, its worth establishing some simple ideas that have held true for many, many centuries:

■ **Yields vary over time and between assets.** Governments have always tried to vary their interest rates and that variance in rates also prompted investors to constantly alter their perceptions of future value. That meant the price of key instruments such as government bonds changed over time and between states based on interest rates and perceptions of risk. We can extend this notion of volatility out to the income received and not just the price paid to buy the asset. Income rates – dividend yields, bond yields and savings account yields – change over time, between countries and within asset groups. The idea that yield or interest rates are stable over extended periods of time is laughable and not proven by any historical data.

■ **Time is money – duration matters.** It's worth looking back at Table 1.3 that we considered when we looked at the sorry state of income investing in the second decade of the 21st century. It's sourced from the research team at stockbrokers Killik and Co. and looks at the yield – income paid relative to the purchase price – of a range of international government bonds (also known as gilts). In each country you might notice a clear trend – the yield or income received grows over the duration of the gilt. The concept here is simple – the longer you borrow, the higher the income return or yield. This higher rate of return is to compensate you for the possible long-term risk of inflation, war, chaos or even default. The future is unknown, and that means you could encounter risk – and the more potential for risk, the greater the potential reward. So currently the cost to Her Majesty's government of borrowing for two years is just 77 basis points (0.77%) but that rises to 4.12% for borrowing over 30 years. Critics might wonder whether an extra 3% or more is worth that extra potential risk but the idea of 'duration' or 'term' carrying a cost is clear. As we'll see in Chapter 3 on bonds this rule of paying extra for longer durations isn't always valid (there are exceptional circumstances where long-dated durations actually pay a little less) but for the vast majority of history a 20–30-year bond generally commands a higher yield (reward) than a very short dated bond.

■ **The greater the risk, the greater the potential for reward... most of the time!** By this point in the discussion it's patently clear that there's a trade off between risk and reward, i.e. the more risk you take the greater the potential for reward. There are times though when this relationship breaks down – there are for instance many opportunities where a realistic assessment of risk would suggest one sensible price yet the wider market is pricing in near default levels and thus a ridiculously low price. These 'good value' opportunities happen in all markets, and at many times over long periods of time – the markets don't always price risk efficiently. Equally, income producing investments that to most observers appear to be high risk can sometimes produce a low yield. Mortgage-backed securities in the USA were carved up into endless 'tranches' or layers of debt in the first part of this century and then sold on to other institutional investors. Layers of debt repackaged into exotic structures found themselves with very credible credit ratings awarded by specialist agencies charged with looking at risk – these diversified baskets of homeowner loans were judged to be of superior quality and lower risk and were awarded a coveted AAA rating. We'll encounter this ratings system in Chapter 3 on bonds, but investors took this as a seal of approval and plunged into a reckless buying frenzy. As they bought more and more of this (toxic) product the yield payable collapsed. Any sensible observer looking on would have been confused by the display – how could baskets full of mortgages given to low income US households be viewed as low risk, especially if the US housing market suddenly fell in value? The yield was low but the risk was high, an inversion of normal prudent policy. The crash did come, house prices fell, mortgages defaulted at an alarming rate, and those supposedly safe mortgage backed securities were found to be almost worthless as defaults mounted. Sanity was restored but the lesson was learnt – markets don't always price correctly given the appropriate level of risk and therein lies both opportunity and risk.

■ **The risk of default is ever present.** One of the more quaint ideas prevalent amongst investors is that defaults are rare, especially amongst governments. Table 1.8 is from Moody's, one of the major ratings and research services used by financial institutions to assess the risk of their income producing assets. The Moody's research looks at the instances of default by governments between 1998 and 2006. In those 8 years the analysts spell out 12 defaults by governments, largely in the developing world. To be fair, very few developed world governments have defaulted on their national debt but as this is written speculation is rife that Greece – a member of the European union – will eventually have to enforce some form of repudiation of its debts, as may Ireland.

Table 1.8 Moody's rated sovereign bond defaults since 1998

Default date	Country	Total defaulted debt ($ millions)	Comments
Jul-98	Venezuela	$270	Defaulted on domestic currency bonds in 1998, although the default was cured within a short period of time.
Aug-98	Russia	$72,709	Missed payments first on local currency Treasury obligations. Later a debt service moratorium was extended to foreign currency obligations issued in Russia but mostly held by foreign investors. Subsequently, failed to pay principal on MINFIN III foreign currency bonds. Debts were restructured in Aug 1999 and Feb 2000.
Sep-98	Ukraine	$1,271	Moratorium on debt service for bearer bonds owned by anonymous entities. Only those entities willing to identify themselves and convert to local currency accounts were eligible for debt repayments, which amounted to a distressed exchange.
Jul-99	Pakistan	$1,627	Pakistan missed an interest payment in Nov 1998 but cured the default subsequently within the grace period (within 4 days). Shortly thereafter, it defaulted again and resolved that default via a distressed exchange which was completed in 1999.
Aug-99	Ecuador	$6,604	Missed payment was followed by a distressed exchange; over 90% of bonds were restructured.
Jan-00	Ukraine	$1,064	Defaulted on DM-denominated Eurobonds in Feb 2000 and defaulted on USD-denominated bonds in Jan 2000. Offered to exchange bonds with longer term and lower coupon. The conversion was accepted by a majority of bondholders.
Sep-00	Peru	$4,870	Peru missed payment on its Brady Bonds but subsequently paid approximately $80 million in interest payments to cure the default, within a 30-day period.

▶

Table 1.8 Continued

Default date	Country	Total defaulted debt ($ millions)	Comments
Nov-01	Argentina	$82,268	Declared it would miss payment on foreign debt in November 2001. Actual payment missed on Jan 3, 2002. Debt was restructured through a distressed exchange offering where the bondholders received haircuts of approximately 70%.
Jun-02	Moldova	$145	Missed payment on the bond in June 2001 but cured default shortly thereafter. Afterwards, it began gradually buying back its bonds, but in June 2002, after having bought back about 50% of its bonds, it defaulted again on remaining $70 million of its outstanding issue.
May-03	Uruguay	$5,744	Contagion from Argentina debt crisis in 2001 led to a currency crisis in Uruguay. To restore debt-sustainability, Uruguay completed a distressed exchange with bondholders that led to extension of maturity by five years.
Apr-05	Dominican Republic	$1,622	After several grace period defaults (missed payments cured within the grace period), the country executed an exchange offer in which old bonds were swapped for new bonds with a five-year maturity extension, but the same coupon and principal.
Dec-06	Belize	$242	Belize announced a distressed exchange of its external bonds for new bonds due in 2029 with a face value of U.S.$ 546.8. The new bonds are denominated in U.S. dollars and provide for step-up coupons that have been set at 4.25% per annum for the first three years after issuance. When the collective action clause in one of Belize's existing bonds is taken into account, the total amount covered by this financial restructuring represents 98.1% of the eligible claims.

Source: From *Sovereign Default and Recovery Rates, 1983–2007* by R. Kantor, K. Emery and E. Duggar, www.moodys.com

Once we move away from supposedly ultra-safe government bonds, the threat of default rises inexorably. Figure 1.12 is also from Moody's and looks at another form of income-producing asset, this time the bonds sold by corporations, large and small, in the USA. The Moody's analysis spans just under 80 years between 1920 and 1999 and compares the corporate debt default rate – the left-hand scale and the lower line in black – with changes in a key US industrial output index. This latter index is a reasonable gauge for a slowdown in output and thus a recession: investors should expect a slowdown in output to eventually produce a slowdown in profits which will result in companies going bust and repudiating their debts.

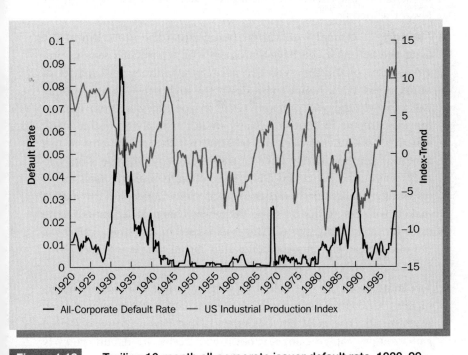

Figure 1.12   **Trailing 12-month all-corporate issuer default rate, 1920–99**

Source: Soverign Default and Recovery Rates, 1983–2007 by R. Kantor, K. Emery and E. Duggar, www.moodys.com

As Figure 1.12 clearly demonstrates, default rates have on occasion shot up in the USA hitting just over 9% in the early 1930s alongside over 2% in 1970 and 4% in the 1990s. The moral of this data is that the corporations that issue bonds frequently go bust. They also repudiate their debts and if you'd had a basket of these bonds in the 1930s you'd have experienced some massive losses from defaults.

Here are some more ideas:

- **Frequency of payment matters.** One of the great attractions of many high street savings accounts is that they pay interest on a monthly basis which is a great deal more useful than those income producing investments that only pay a dividend, for example every six months or annually – many bonds also pay out their coupons or interest annually. But that frequency of payment comes with an obvious cost – the sheer bother of organising a monthly payment tends to incur a cost, a cost that the investor ends up paying in terms of lower interest rates or yields. As a general rule of thumb, the more often the payment, the lower the income.

- **Liquidity is crucial – all things being equal the more liquid the asset the better!** If you have a problem with a particular savings provider, most of the time you can access your money in a matter of hours, if not days. A quick visit down the high street, or a telephone call to a helpline, will probably result in you accessing your money. But investments in bonds or shares are not as easily accessible – you can ring up a stock broker and buy and sell the investments in real time but you'll probably have to wait many days for the money to arrive in your account. Also many more obscure or exotic investments (especially smaller bonds and shares) are thinly traded and the market makers who determine the price frequently charge an enormous extra price for establishing a price. This is expressed in something called the bid offer spread and in some bonds that spread can be as high as 10%, i.e. you instantly lose 10% on the trade.

- **Tax matters.** In the box below we've summarised the main elements of the UK taxation regime as it applies to the income produced from investments. The most obvious point is that if you receive a capital gain, you pay capital gains tax, but if you receive an income, you pay income tax. As you'll see from the box there are some crucial distinctions between income received from dividends (usually paid out by shares but they can also be paid out by income producing preference shares) and income received from savings accounts and gilts. This all makes the decision of which investment to choose immensely complicated, and frankly very personal.

HMRC GUIDANCE ON TAX RATES ON INCOME-PRODUCING ASSETS

Tax on UK dividends – dividend tax rates 2010–11

There are three different income tax rates on UK dividends. The rate you pay depends on whether your overall taxable income (after allowances) falls within or above the basic or higher rate income tax limits. The basic rate income tax limit is £37,400 and the higher rate income tax limit is £150,000 for the 2010–11 tax year.

Dividend tax rates 2010–11

Dividend income in relation to the basic rate or higher rate tax bands	Tax rate applied after deduction of personal allowance and any blind person's allowance
Dividend income at or below the £37,400 basic rate tax limit	10%
Dividend income at or below the £150,000 higher rate tax limit	32.5%
Dividend income above the higher rate tax limit	42.5%

Tax on savings income

There are four different income tax rates on savings income: 10%, 20%, 40% or 50%. The rate you pay depends on your overall taxable income.

How you pay tax on savings income

Savings income is added to your other income and taxed after your tax-free allowances – for example personal allowance – have been taken into account, as follows:

■ taxable savings income that falls within the £2,440 starting rate for savings income tax band is taxed at 10% – but only if the rate band has not been used up by other income as savings income is taxed last

■ taxable savings income (included with any other income) that rises above the £2,440 starting rate for savings income tax band, but falls within the £37,400 basic rate band, is taxed at 20%

■ taxable savings income (included with any other income) that rises above the £37,400 income tax band, but falls within the £150,000 higher rate band, is taxed at 40%

■ taxable savings income (included with any other income) that rises above the £150,000 income tax band is taxed at 50%

■ if it falls on both sides of a tax band, the relevant amounts are taxed at the rates for each tax band.

Savings income normally has 20% tax taken off before you receive it. This is confirmed by the entry 'net interest' on your bank or building society statement.

The interest on gilts, corporate bonds and PIBs is subject to income tax although it is usually paid out without any income tax being deducted, unlike other income investments such as a savings account for example. You can put gilts, corporate bonds and PIBS into an ISA and thereby avoid paying any income tax on them. Any capital gains you make are free from all CGT.

Source: HMRC

Next steps

Armed with these basic ideas we're going to start our journey through the investment landscape with perhaps the simplest income producing products on offer – savings accounts offered by large high street banks and building societies (see Chapter 2). In Chapter 3 we'll also look at another form of savings product called the guaranteed income bond, effectively a structured long-term savings bond. We'll also examine the market leading products offered by National Savings and Investments and finally, in Chapter 3, we'll examine the complex but important world of annuities.

After these annuities we move away from the high street and enter the more complex world of bonds issued by large corporations and the government. In Chapter 3 we'll run into some of the basic ideas mentioned in this chapter concerning duration, risk and differing levels of risk dictating different levels of income, and see how these concepts are incorporated into the structure of the fixed income security.

After examining bonds in great detail we encounter the all-important world of equities or shares (see Chapter 4). For many investors this is a largely unexplored world consisting of scary companies that pay out a dividend, but hopefully by the end of Chapter 4 the reader will begin to realise that there is a huge opportunity to construct a diversified portfolio of stocks and funds that pay out a relatively high level of income, as well as the chance to grow your capital over time.

That idea is taken up in more detail in Chapter 5 where we look at the various equity based funds that seek to explore particular themes within this huge investment universe. We'll look at investment trusts and unit trusts, at infrastructure funds as well as hybrid structures such as preference shares that share characteristics of both equities and fixed income securities.

We close our gallop through the world of equities by focusing on another very specialist equity based product – structured products – in Chapter 6. This sometimes controversial investment niche can, with the right provider and the right structure, provide a very high level of secure income with relatively low levels of risk. But as Chapter 6's author Chris Taylor of InCapital Europe (a specialist structured products provider) points out, you absolutely need to understand the product you are investing in!

Chapters 7 and 8 attempt to tie up all these ideas into simple themes around which you can build a portfolio. In particular financial adviser James Norton from Evolve Financial Planning looks at some radical ideas centred on building a portfolio that produces a decent and sustainable income over the long term. In Chapter 8 we pick up on these ideas and attempt to construct three model portfolios based on different levels of risk and differing requirements for income. Many of the funds, bonds and structures mentioned in Chapter 8 will be slightly more complex than normal but they should all offer some useful ideas for the enterprising and diligent investor willing to do their own research.

Our very last chapter (Chapter 9) is aimed at the more sophisticated equity investor – it echoes some ideas from earlier in the book about the importance of equities as a source of income. In particular it explores how equities can help produce a diversified income by using an innovative idea called dividend weighted indices. These ideas build on a revolution in investing that is sweeping the USA at the moment – instead of trusting managers to look after your money and take risks, why not just track an index? But that index is very different from its normal siblings – it's comprised totally of stocks that pay out a high and sustainable level of dividends. Jeremy Schwartz from specialist fund management firm WisdomTree looks at why these dividend weighted indices are so important.

2

Savings accounts and annuities

The basics

Investors usually approach the task of building a sensibly diversified portfolio – producing a decent income perhaps – with a bucketful of behavioural biases, quirks and idiosyncrasies. Perhaps the most deadly of these vices are those of over confidence and persistent optimism. Over confidence usually involves the investor taking shortcuts which generally result in permanent capital loss, yet oddly enough persistent optimism is perhaps the more deadly of the two. Although it must be right that we approach life with an Epicurean sense of 'what could be' – the Greek Epicureans had no time for the permanent cynics and the half-empty glass brigade – it may be more sensible to approach the task of investing in high street savings products with more than a healthy dose of cynicism, if not outright suspicion.

Why this bearish countenance, this mawkish suspicion of reality? In simple terms the grounds for suspicion rests on the rock solid foundations of modern marketing theory. As you will discover later in this chapter, many of the different structures and product types are based not on complex financial engineering but on marketing concepts. In fact if you were to have the misfortune of spending anything more than a few minutes in the company of a modern financial marketer you'd soon realise that the savings business is almost entirely based on the following ten marketing principles:

1 The more profitable a sector, the more choice there is as new providers flood in to provide consumers with alternatives.

2 As choice grows, consumers become confused by the sheer surfeit of offers.

3 To help differentiate their product, the product provider ideally creates a brilliant product with the right range of features (some of them hopefully original) at the right price, i.e. a great innovative, market leading proposition.

4 Back in the real world not everyone can produce a genuinely innovative, market leading proposition, so they produce a product that is a bit different from the rest by tweaking a feature, such as the rate offered.

5 This product differentiation comes at a cost to the consumer – new and clever features usually come with either an overt or hidden cost, i.e. it costs more or it has special conditions or clauses which harm the consumer's interests.

6 As choice and confusion intensify, the temptation is to produce sham innovation, i.e. a product or feature that looks new but is in fact a shameless rip-off or the same product with some new but useless features. Alternatively the product provider tries to use special, time-based features such as *sales* or *special offers – for one week/month/day only*.

7 Eventually the consumer is overpowered by all this innovation and reacts by adopting complacency, i.e. trusting in what they know, even if it is inferior but nevertheless comes from a trusted brand.

8 Some smarter consumers decide to conduct their own research and spend inordinate hours scouring the full universe of products or they hire experts who help them research the market, at a cost!

9 State sponsored regulation in hugely diversified markets consisting of popular products eventually produces confusion and allows complex terms to emerge that make the regulator feel good but confuses everyone else.

10 The massive universe of product differentiation and choice eventually produces an inferior product for most consumers.

These slightly depressing principles can be found every day in the world of savings products. The sheer choice of products, structures and providers is absolutely bewildering – the cynic might be forgiven for thinking that this profusion of choice is deliberate and designed to confuse the consumer so that they are befuddled into inertia or making poor choices.

One small example should suffice. In Table 2.1 we've reproduced the current full range (as at January 2011) of Nationwide's savings products. As you can see the list is in fact very long and we've made no attempt to include any sense of the various specific clauses and conditions applied to each and every account. To be fair to Nationwide, it is generally regarded as a fine organisation with an outstanding reputation for providing its customers and investors – remember it is one of the last remaining independent mutual's operating at the national level – with decent products at good rates. It's not always *the* most competitive provider of savings and mortgage products but it is certainly top quartile most of the time. Yet even Nationwide engages in endless product launch, innovation and re-engineering – change that could have the effect of confusing its customers, assuming that these existing customers are always told of all the latest new products, rates and ideas.

Table 2.1 Nationwide Building Society's full range of products

Notice period	Account name	Rate (%)	Interest paid	Minimum investment (£)
Instant	InvestDirect	0.2	Yly	100
Instant	CashBuilder Book	0.1	Yly	100
No Notice	e-Savings	0.45	Yly	1
30 Day	Bonus 30 (1 + withdrawals)	0.2	Yly	100
30 Day	Bonus 30 (No withdrawals)	0.7	Yly	100
Instant	Monthly Income 60+	0.55	Mly	100
Instant	CashBuilder Card	0.1	Yly	100
No Notice	e-Savings Plus (0 – 5 withdrawals pa)	2	Ann'sry	1
No Notice	e-Savings Plus (6+ withdrawals)	0.1	Ann'sry	1
60 Day	Champion Saver	2.5	Yly	1K
No Notice	MySave Online Plus	2.75	Mly	1K
1 Year Bond	1 Year Tracker e-Bond	2.75	Ann'sry	100
1 Year Bond	1 Year Tracker e-Bond	2.7	Mly	100
1 Year Bond	1 Year Tracker Bond	2.6	Mly	100
1 Year Bond	1 Year Tracker Bond	2.65	Yly	100
1 Year Bond	1 Year Combination Savings Bond	3.2	Mly	3K
1 Year Bond	1 Year Combination Savings Bond	3.25	Yly	3K
3 Year Bond	3 Year Combination Savings Bond	4	Mly	3K

Table 2.1 Continued

Notice period	Account name	Rate (%)	Interest paid	Minimum investment (£)
3 Year Bond	3 Year Combination Savings Bond	4.1	Yly	3K
5 Year Bond	5 Year Fixed Rate Bond	3.65	Mly	1
5 Year Bond	5 Year Fixed Rate Bond	3.75	Yly	1
2 Year Bond	2 Year Fixed Rate e-Bond	3.3	Ann'sry	1
2 Year Bond	2 Year Fixed Rate e-Bond	3.25	Mly	1
3 Year Bond	3 Year Fixed Rate e-Bond	3.5	Ann'sry	1
3 Year Bond	3 Year Fixed Rate e-Bond	3.4	Mly	1
1 Year Bond	1 Year Fixed Rate e-Bond	2.75	Ann'sry	1
1 Year Bond	1 Year Fixed Rate e-Bond	2.7	Mly	1
1 Year Bond	1 Year Fixed Rate Bond	2.6	Mly	1
1 Year Bond	1 Year Fixed Rate Bond	2.65	Yly	1
3 Year Bond	3 Year Fixed Rate Bond	3.4	Mly	1
3 Year Bond	3 Year Fixed Rate Bond	3.5	Yly	1
5 Year Bond	5 Year Fixed Rate e-Bond	3.8	Ann'sry	1
5 Year Bond	5 Year Fixed Rate e-Bond	3.7	Mly	1
Instant	Smart	0.75	½ Yly	1
Instant	Regular Savings	0.1	Yly	1
Instant	Instant Access ISA	0.25	Yly	100
30 Day	Members ISA Bond	0.5	Yly	100
60 Day	Champion ISA	2.5	Yly	1K
No Notice	e-ISA	2.8	Yly	1
5 Year Bond	5 Year Fixed Rate ISA	3.65	Mly	1
5 Year Bond	5 Year Fixed Rate ISA	3.75	Yly	1
3 Year Bond	3 Year Fixed Rate ISA	3.4	Mly	1
3 Year Bond	3 Year Fixed Rate ISA	3.5	Yly	1
1 Year Bond	1 Year Fixed Rate ISA	2.7	Mly	1
1 Year Bond	1 Year Fixed Rate ISA	2.75	Yly	1

Source: Moneyfacts

Luckily there are research houses such as Moneyfacts that attempt to make sense of this vast market – its team of researchers are constantly tracking new products issued by outfits such as Nationwide. This chapter features much of their analysis and data alongside some specific market analysis by one of their leading commentators, Darren Cook. Most of Darren's research is aimed at professional advisers and institutions but the website at www.moneyfacts.co.uk does provide a hugely useful summary of the current best buy savings products.

Table 2.2 shows Moneyfacts Best Buys. What's striking about this list is the sheer range of different providers, the terms used to describe the products and, of course, the *low* rates of interest on offer (compared to the 1980s and 1990s).

Table 2.2 Moneyfacts Best Buys

	Account	Notice or Term	Deposit	% AER	Interest Paid
NO NOTICE ACCOUNTS WITHOUT BONUS					
West Brom BS	Branch Easy Access 2	Instant	£1,000	2.40	Yly
West Brom BS	No Notice Saver Direct 2	None (B)	£1,000	2.40	Yly
Skipton BS	Telephone Saver	None (T)	£25,000	2.25	Yly
State Bank of India	Instant Access Savings	Instant	£500	2.00	Mly
Leeds BS	Postal Max	None (P)	£25,000	2.00	Yly
Chorley & District BS	Chorley Postal	None (P)	£25,000	2.00	Yly
INTERNET ACCOUNTS WITHOUT BONUS					
West Brom BS	WeBSave Plus	None	£1,000	2.61	Yly
Halifax	Web Saver Extra	None	£1	2.50	Yly
Northern Rock	E-Saver Issue 3	None	£1	2.50	Yly
Barnsley BS	Online Saver Issue 2	None	£1	2.50	Yly
Skipton BS	My Savings	None	£1	2.50	Yly
Intelligent Finance	isaver	None	£1	2.49	Yly

Table 2.2 Continued

	Account	*Notice or Term*	*Deposit*	*% AER*	*Interest Paid*
NOTICE ACCOUNTS WITHOUT BONUS					
Hinckley & Rugby BS	90 Day Notice Postal	90 Day (P)	£2,500	2.65	Yly
Aldermore	45 Day Notice	45 Day	£1,000	2.54	Yly
Monmouthshire BS	Income Generator	120 Day	£5,000	2.53	Mly
Northern Rock	Branch Saver 90 Iss 1	90 Day	£1	2.50	Yly
FirstSave	90 Day Notice	90 Day	£100	2.50	Yly
Progressive BS	Postal 7 Day Notice 8	7 Day (P)	£500	2.46	Yly
MONTHLY INTEREST WITHOUT BONUS					
West Brom BS	WeBSave Plus	None	£1,000	2.61	Mly
Aldermore	45 Day Notice	45 Day	£1,000	2.54	Mly
Monmouthshire BS	Income Generator	120 Day	£5,000	2.53	Mly
Northern Rock	E-Saver Issue 3	None	£1	2.51	Mly
Northern Rock	Branch Saver 90 Iss 1	90 Day	£1	2.51	Mly
Barnsley BS	Online Saver Issue 2	None	£1	2.50	Mly
ACCOUNTS WITH INTRODUCTORY BONUS					
Dunfermline BS	60 Day Notice	60 Day (B)	£1,000	3.00*	Yly
Cheshire BS	30 Day Postal Saver	30 Day (P)	£1,000	2.95*	Yly
Post Office®	Online Saver	None	£1	2.90*	Yly
Stroud & Swindon BS	90 Day Notice	90 Day	£1,000	2.90*	Yly
Northern Rock	Rainy Day Saver	120 Day (P)	£5,000	2.90*	Yly
Kent Reliance BS	2012 Bonus Account	60 Day	£500	2.87*	Yly

▶

Table 2.2 Continued

	Account	Notice or Term	Deposit	% AER	Interest Paid
ACCOUNTS FOR OVER 50'S					
West Brom BS	High Income Over 50	90 Day (S)	£5,000	2.63	Mly
SAGA	Saga Telephone Saver 2	None (T)	£1	2.55*	Yly
SAGA	Saga Internet Saver 2	None	£1	2.55*	Yly
Saffron BS	e-saver 55-plus Issue 2	None	£1,000	2.30	Yly
Coventry BS	Sixty-Plus PostSave 3	None (P)	£500	2.25*	Yly
Stroud & Swindon BS	Sixty-Plus PostSave (4)	None	£500	2.25*	Yly
REGULAR SAVINGS ACCOUNTS					
Norwich & Peterborough BS	Regular Saver	Instant	£1pm	4.00*	Yly
Principality BS	Regular Saver Bond 10	1 Yr Bnd	£20pm	4.00 F	OM
Saffron BS	12 Month Regular Saver	12 Month Bnd	£10pm	4.00 F	Yly
Teachers BS	Regular Saver (Issue 2)	None (T)	£10pm	4.00*	Yly
Santander	Fixed Monthly Saver 12	13 Month Bnd	£20pm	3.99 F	OM
Buckinghamshire BS	Chiltern Gold Builder 2	Instant	£25pm	3.50	Yly
CASH ISAS					
Santander	Flexible ISA Issue 3	Instant	£1	2.85*	Yly
Halifax	Cash ISA Direct Reward	None (H)	£1	2.80*	Yly
Principality BS	e-ISA Issue 2	None	£1	2.80*	Yly
Northern Rock	ISA Saver	120 Day	£1,000	2.80*	Yly
Nationwide BS	e-ISA	None	£1	2.79*	Yly
Newcastle BS	Reward Saver ISA	120 Day	£500	2.75*	Yly

Table 2.2 Continued

	Account	Notice or Term	Deposit	% AER	Interest Paid
FIXED RATE BONDS					
Coventry BS	Fixed Bond (128)	30.04.16	£1	4.75 F	Yly
Kent Reliance BS	Fixed end date bond	31.05.16 (P)	£500	4.51 F	Yly
AA	Fixed Rate Savings	5 Yr Bnd (P)	£1	4.50 F	Yly
SAGA	Fixed Rate Savings	5 Yr Bnd	£1	4.50 F	Yly
State Bank of India	Hi Return Fixed Deposit	5 Yr Bnd	£1,000	4.50 F	Yly
Birmingham Midshires	Fixed Rate Bond	5 Yr Bnd (P)	£1	4.40 F	Yly

* = Introductory rate for a limited period.
B = Operated by Post or Telephone.
F = Fixed Rate.
H = Operated by Internet or Telephone.
K = Operated by Internet, Telephone or Post.

OM = Interest paid on maturity.
P = Operated by Post.
S = Available to those aged 50 and over.
T = Operated by Telephone.
All rates are shown as AER.

All rates and terms subject to change without notice and should be checked before finalising any arrangement. No liability can be accepted for any direct or consequential loss arising from the use of, or reliance upon, this information. Readers who are not financial professionals should seek expert advice. Figures compiled on: 6 January 2011.
Source: Moneyfacts

This list in Table 2.2 is of course just a summary and does not purport to be a detailed reference featuring all product features and conditions. Dig beneath this table of best buys and you'll soon discover that there's a lot more to choosing the right savings product than just the headline rate on offer. *Do you trust the institution making the offer? Is it available to all customers, even those with just £1? Are there any specific conditions over accessing the money? Is it only available online?* Later in this chapter we'll run through our own checklist of key issues ... but most investors would be forgiven for burying their heads in their hands and despairing!

As predicted by models of financial marketing innovation, a few, wealthier investors react by bringing in expert help – back in the spring of 2010 for instance the *Sunday Times* newspaper ran a story featuring a new service from

wealthier investors need to box clever

financial advisers Jonathan Fry.[1] The key observation of this article was that wealthier investors need to box clever when it comes to not only getting the right rate but also protecting their money in case of bank failure.

As we discuss below, the all-important Financial Services Compensation Scheme (FSCS) only covers investors for up to £85,000 for each major provider – anything above that level and you're effectively without protection if the bank or building society collapses. Working out which financial institutions to trust as well as what's covered by the FSCS is probably more than most private investors – wealthy or not – can cope with, which is presumably why Jonathan Fry have launched their Dynamic Cash Management product.

According to the *Sunday Times* this expert service:

> *identifies and monitors homes for clients' cash in return for an annual fee of 0.3% ... [and] uses more than 50 accounts from more than 125 banks and building societies. Interest rates and institutional strength are regularly monitored, and cash is switched when rates or financial strength assessments change ... David Carr, chief executive of Jonathan Fry, said: 'Our view is that for many investment managers cash is regarded as a sideshow and that they would prefer clients to invest in higher risk investments where higher charges can be levied.' Weigh the risk you want to take, how long you can tie up your money, the interest rate you can earn, and the regulatory protection you will get for each holding.[2]*

These are exactly the sort of questions that every investor should be asking of their current and future savings accounts, questions which we'll look at in the next section. But before we leap into the heady world of high street savings accounts it's worth noting one last comment from the *Sunday Times* article on the Jonathan Fry service. The writer helpfully finishes with a concrete example:

> *Jonathan Fry recently advised a married 52-year-old entrepreneur from London, who had received £2.65m from the sale of a business in October 2009. It used a mixture of easy-access accounts, three-month bonds, one-year bonds and two-year bonds. In all, his holdings were spread across six accounts in joint names with his wife to double up on FSCS protection. The six accounts are: Ulster Bank Pathway, paying 3.1% a year; Alliance & Leicester's Online Saver, 2.75%; Cheshire Building Society's 30-day Postal account, 3.25%; Investec High 5 account, 3.19%; Post Office one-*

[1] Nina Montagu-Smith (2010) 'Where to park a windfall: A new service helps take the pain out of finding the best home for a lump sum' *Sunday Times*, 14 March, http://www.timesonline.co.uk/tol/money/investment/article7060789.ece.

[2] Ibid.

year Growth Bond, 3.30%; and ICICI's HiSave two-year fixed-rate bond, 4.25% ... 'We increased the interest rate earned from virtually zero to more than 3.2% a year on average before charges. We also moved money to joint accounts which produced considerable tax savings as his wife was not a higher-rate taxpayer,' Carr said.

Most readers probably won't have anywhere near this amount of money to invest in savings accounts but the sheer variety of accounts chosen by advisers at Fry is fascinating. The advisers identified a mainstream bank savings account, a Post Office savings bond, an internet-based account and an innovative private bank savings account (from Investec) which looks at the top rates offered in the Moneyfacts Best Buy table and then pays out the average. This huge range of accounts and structures speaks to the vast choice on the market and the absolute need to understand exactly what it is that you are investing your hard-earned money in.

Different types of high street and internet-based savings accounts

Instant access accounts

These savings accounts are also known as no notice accounts and they allow immediate access to your savings without any penalty. Usually investors can start these accounts with as little as £1 but interest rates are frequently very low and will fluctuate. Access to the account is usually via a passbook or a savings card although if you choose to run the account online you'll usually get a better interest rate. These accounts are perfect for investors looking for a home for their emergency cash but beware – interest rates are usually dreadful! Recent figures from the Bank of England show the average interest rate paid on a branch-based instant access account has slumped to just 0.17% in summer 2010, so you absolutely need to shop around for the best rate. Most of the time you'll get a better rate from an internet-based provider, if only because they don't have the extra cost of providing a branch network!

Notice accounts

With notice accounts you engage in a simple trade-off – you receive a higher rate of interest by locking up your money in an account which requires that you give some notice of withdrawal. But be aware, as with easy access accounts, rates can change at short notice. The 'notice periods' vary enormously but most tend to be in the range of from a week to 120 days or more. Some notice accounts are also postal-based, and require a form to be filled in and sent to a savings provider.

The minimum deposit is usually above £100 (£500 is not uncommon as is £1000) and if you do make a withdrawal before the term is complete a penalty will usually be calculated on the amount.

Monthly interest accounts

Like notice accounts you enter into a trade-off with these accounts – these savings accounts tend to be notice accounts where the interest is paid monthly rather than annually but the rates paid on the accounts are usually slightly lower than for notice accounts.

Fixed-term savings accounts and bonds

The marketing concept here is incredibly simple – agree to lock your money away for a fixed period of time and the financial provider will agree to pay a fixed rate above the market for the duration, with more interest paid for longer durations. The obvious benefit of this fixed-term, fixed-rate savings accounts is that you can be certain the interest rate on your cash will not fall over the term of the product.

The obvious drawback is that you don't have access to your money for the term of the account. Savings bonds, the most common fixed-rate product, are available for as little as three months, or as long as five years, or more. You may also run into **escalator bonds** which operate between three and five years and feature progressively increasing rates each and every year. Interest on these bonds can be paid monthly (most providers) or annually and once you've invested your fixed amount you're usually not allowed to add any more money to the account.

Regular savings

Many investors prefer to put aside money each and every month, making the regular savings account the perfect product for the diligent investor. As long as you can guarantee to deposit a certain amount monthly (usually via standing order), you will be rewarded with higher rates of interest, frequently in the form of a special bonus at the end of the term.

Savings providers usually set limits on the minimum and maximum amount you can deposit – typically a minimum of £20 and a maximum of £2,000 (The Chelsea Building Society). Under the terms of the accounts, you agree to pay in a set amount of money every month for a year, although it's sometimes possible to vary the sum. Also you usually can't withdraw any of the money until the end of the year, when the interest is added to it and the total is usually transferred to a lower interest account. It's also worth noting that if you fail to make a payment your account will revert to an ordinary saving account and you'll lose interest (i.e. you will lose the special rate) although a few providers do allow for a maximum of one missed payment a year. The other key feature to note about these accounts is that they're frequently used by big banks as a perk to customers who already have a current account with them, as an incentive to build loyalty.

STATS AND DAMNED LIES – WHAT DOES AER MEAN?

AER stands for annual equivalent rate and allows you to compare interest rates across accounts, reflecting not just the amount of interest but also how often it is paid: the higher the AER, the greater the return.

For example, take two accounts that advertise a 10% a year rate. One pays out all the interest (10%) at the end of the year while the other pays you 5% every six months. If you invested £10,000 then by the end of the year the first account has grown to £11,000 but there should be more than £11,012 in the second account as the interest credited after six months in the latter account has itself earned interest during the second six months, increasing the return. The AERs for the two accounts are 10% and 10.12% respectively.

Cash ISAs

These are simply savings accounts using a tax wrapper so that you don't have to pay any interest on the income earned in the account, although there is a limit to the amount of money you can hold in an ISA (see the box below). Cash ISA accounts can take many forms and although cash ISAs don't always offer the highest rates of interest, once you've taken into account that there is no tax to pay on the interest you'll find that the best accounts easily beat the higher-paying ordinary savings accounts. In structural terms most cash ISAs are easy or instant-access accounts but occasionally the rate is fixed.

Because these are government regulated tax schemes, investors need to be especially careful about how they operate an ISA:

- Once money is withdrawn from an ISA it *cannot* be re-deposited into your existing cash ISA, i.e.. if you have £5,100 deposited, and you withdraw £600 in one tax year, then you cannot at a later date add that £600 back into your cash ISA in the same tax year. (The maximum that can be deposited in a cash ISA is currently £5,100.)
- You can move money between different ISA providers but beware of bonuses that encourage you to apply for the product.
- Many ISA providers give an added bonus for a short period of time, say for the first six months, before the rate drops to an uncompetitive rate.

■ You also need to watch out for any transfer out fees levied – usually about £25 charged to transfer to another provider once the rate drops. Check the Terms and Conditions to ensure that there is *no* transfer fee attached to the cash ISA account.

■ Last but by no means least remember that if you are switching ISAs do not just withdraw the cash – you will lose your tax-free element! Make sure the new bank or building society can effect the transfer for you so that the money switches between banks without coming to you.

HOW MUCH CAN I INVEST IN AN ISA ? THE RULES...

You can invest in up to two separate ISAs each tax year – a cash ISA and a stocks and shares ISA.

■ **Cash ISA:** you only need to be 16 years old to open one of these savings accounts. Cash ISA savers can also transfer money saved in their cash ISA to a stocks and shares ISA but only when they are 18. Remember that when you compare rates between ordinary savings accounts and cash ISAs, look for the gross rate paid on a cash ISA and then compare it with the net rate you will receive on a standard savings account.

■ **Stocks and shares ISA:** these may involve investment funds, unit trusts, shares and bonds, as well as life insurance policies, and are usually opened via an investment company. You must be over 18 to invest in this type of ISA.

The annual ISA allowance is currently £10,200, with up to £5,100 allowed in a cash ISA with any one provider, while the other £5,100 can be invested in stocks and shares with either the same provider or a different one (see Figure 2.1). Note – if you have an old style mini cash ISA, TESSA only ISA or have cash components of a maxi ISA, your account will have automatically been switched to a cash ISA while all mini stocks and shares ISAs and the stocks and shares components of maxi ISAs will have automatically become stocks and shares ISAs. Finally, if you have a Personal Equity Plan (PEP) it will have automatically become a stocks and shares ISA.

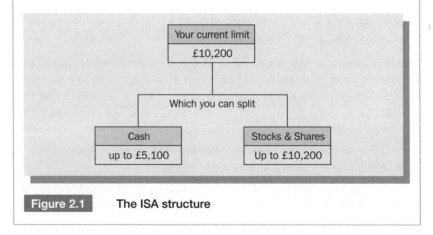

| Figure 2.1 | The ISA structure |

Children's accounts

These savings accounts are obviously aimed at children, primarily as a way of encouraging the savings habit! They take on many different forms including regular saver, fixed rate or instant access accounts and frequently pay excellent interest rates. You may also be offered free gifts, but there could be a number of restrictions in force, such as notice periods, limited withdrawals and size of investments – and remember that the parents will have to operate the account. It's also worth noting that interest rates on these accounts will usually be quoted as a gross rate as no tax is payable by minors. The Labour Government also introduced the Child Trust Fund – an innovative savings scheme that was shut down in 2010. The Labour initiative offered tax-free savings and investments for children born after September 2002 who were eligible for child benefit. The government gave a £250 voucher to help start them off with their savings, and then another £250 when they were 7 years old. After this, friends and relatives could invest up to £1200 per year and the child is not able to access the money until they are 18 years old.

Over-50s savings

It's not only children who get their own special account – there are a handful of accounts available rewarding older savers with competitive rates of interest. However, make sure you check the whole market before opting for an over-50s account. There might be better deals available on accounts open to everyone. Like other accounts, interest may be fixed or variable, and the account may be on a notice or no notice basis and come with specific terms and conditions.

make sure you check the whole market before opting for an over-50s account

---

GOVERNMENT PROTECTION – WHAT'S THE PROTECTION ON OFFER?

If a bank or building society can no longer afford to pay out to its investors or savers and becomes bankrupt, the government is usually forced to ride to the rescue, either through a savings guarantee or a bail out of the bank. That usually means an encounter with the savings protection scheme which comes in the form of a special guarantee to compensate savers who have lost deposits up to the value of £85,000, through the Financial Services Compensation Scheme (FSCS).

The key point to remember here is that each saver can only get a maximum of £85,000 per single institution – so don't go opening ten different £85,000 savings accounts with one bank thinking you're protected, as only the first £85,000 account is actually protected. (Joint account holders are each protected for £85,000 so a husband and wife, for example, are covered for £170,000.) Compensation limits are per person, per firm, and per claim category.

▶

The FSCS scheme was supposed to be a scheme of last resort but the events of 2008 and 2009 have sadly reminded investors just how seriously they should take the prospect of a bank becoming insolvent. Icelandic savings banks Icesave and Kaupthing Edge both went belly up and savers had to wait many weeks and months before they could get their money back (and as of summer 2010 the UK government is still waiting to get its money back from the Icelandic government).

Note: as of 2010 the FSA has announced that it will introduce faster payout rules for the Financial Services Compensation Scheme and deposits will be ring fenced where a depositor has savings and loans with the same firm. The fast payment rules will see compensation paid within a target of seven days and all payments will be made within 20 days. Payouts will also be made on a gross basis. The new rules will apply to banks, building societies and credit unions from 31 December 2010.

Countries covered (source Moneyfacts)

This list below from research provider Moneyfacts shows which countries are covered by the FSCS. The scheme covers the main UK banks and some of their subsidiaries operating abroad as well as banks from the rest of the European Union. If in doubt contact the FSCS direct on (telephone) 020 7892 7300.

- **Cyprus:** Maximum level of compensation per depositor per bank is €100,000.
- **European Union deposit takers** (including deposits with UK branches of those institutions): minimum level of protection €100,000 per eligible depositor.
- **Gibraltar Deposit Guarantee Scheme:** 100% of the total of all qualifying deposits up to a maximum of €50,000.
- **Guernsey:** The first £50,000 per individual claimant per licensed bank.
- **Ireland:** For institutions regulated in Ireland, the deposit guarantee scheme covers 100% of the first €100,000 per depositor per institution. Additionally 100% of all deposits are covered until 28 September 2010 under the Irish government's guaranteed arrangement scheme with the following institutions: Allied Irish Bank, Anglo Irish Bank Corporation Ltd, Bank of Ireland, Educational BS, Irish Life & Permanent and Irish Nationwide BS.
- **Isle of Man:** Compensation of Depositors Regulations 2008 as amended by the Compensation of Depositors (Amendment) Regulations 2008 – up to £50,000 of net deposits per individual depositor.
- **Jersey:** Jersey's States Assembly has approved legislation to set up a Depositors Compensation Scheme (DCS) in the Island. The scheme provides protection of up to £50,000 per individual, per Jersey banking group, for local and international depositors in line with international standards.
- **Netherlands:** All Dutch banks that operate under licence from De Nederlandsche Bank are covered by the Dutch deposit guarantee scheme. The limit is €100,000 per person per institution until 31 December 2010.

National Savings accounts

No canter through the range of savings accounts offered on the high street would be complete without an examination of those products offered by National Savings and Investments, the government-owned savings institution. NSI as it is known offers almost exactly the same range of savings accounts offered by its peers on the high street including regular savings accounts, notice accounts and fixed term savings bonds. But NSI offers two sets of unique products that have attracted huge consumer interest over the years – index-linked savings certificates and premium bonds.

The index-linked savings accounts offered by NSI sits within a family of products known as savings certificates. Many investors love the certainty of the Fixed Interest Savings Certificates which are designed to offer a guaranteed rate of interest to investors for the term of the investment. They are made available in issues, meaning that new series of certificates are released at regular intervals, each of which has a different interest rate. You can invest in as many issues as you like, but each investor is only permitted to buy a maximum of £15,000 worth of bonds per issue.

In recent years enthusiasm has grown for the index-linked variants of these certificates – in fact demand for these inflation-linked products (once known as Grannybonds) has been so intense that as of summer 2010, NSI stopped selling new certificates. A cursory look at the product features easily explains why so many investors have opted for this product. These certificates offer tax-free returns *and* a hedge against inflation by offering a guaranteed rate of interest above the Retail Prices Index (the RPI, a measure of inflation) over three (called the 20th series) or five (the 47th series) years. Here's how they work: if the guaranteed rate is 1% and the rate of increase in the RPI was 4% over five years, the certificate would return 5%. And remember that these rates are net of any tax – so the equivalent gross rate for a 50% highest rate taxpayer would then be 10% pa.

Interest rates in the future could be considerably lower, especially if inflation rates slump back (although RPI rates have historically been higher than CPI rates used by the government to measure core inflation). You also need to remember that you'll lose out on interest if you cash the certificates in early, although it's worth remembering that the certificates will not fall below the value you paid initially. The minimum you can invest – when offered to the public – is £100 while the maximum is £15,000 although you can reinvest any other fixed or index-linked issues of savings certificates you hold when they reach their original maturity date after two, three or five years and you may also hold more if you inherit them. Interest rates are variable with a minimum guaranteed rate and interest is only paid out when the certificates are cashed in.

> you'll lose out on interest if you cash the certificates in early

Premium bonds

An astonishing 23 million people currently invest in premium bonds offered by NSI. Many investors are tempted by the promise of big wins from this hugely innovative scheme which successfully combines elements of gambling and saving in one simple to understand product. The gamble? Every month more than a million prize winning numbers are chosen at random and one lucky bond-holder pockets £1 million (down from two winners early in 2009). Other prizes include a million prizes at £25, through to three payouts at £50,000 and two at £100,000. The odds of winning a very large amount of money? Very low indeed! In 2009 the number of prizes fell by approximately 20,000 to 1.07 million, and according to NSI the chances of winning *any* prize with a single £1 bond are around 36,000:1, up from the odds of 23,000:1 in 2006. The sheer enormity of these odds inevitably lends comparison to the National Lottery but with Premium Bonds you don't lose your principal (your initial investment) and you do earn an interest rate that could be the equivalent to 1.5% per annum, tax free. And there's always the chance that if you buy more premium bonds, your chance of winning might increase. NSI claims that with the maximum £30,000 investment, with average luck you should win 15 prizes a year courtesy of Ernie, the Electronic Random Number Indicator Equipment.

But premium bonds are nevertheless absolutely a play on luck and the power of random numbers – and some fairly articulate critics have recently lambasted the scheme. In particular Martin Lewis at www.moneysaving expert.com has conducted detailed research into the actual odds of winning money on the premium bonds. Every month Lewis's team of researchers and number crunchers updates the raw data at http://www. moneysavingexpert.com/savings/premium-bonds but the overall title of his online article 'Are they worth it?' rather gives the game away with the question mark. Lewis believes the bonds are over-hyped and under-analysed.

According to MoneySavingExpert:

> In a typical draw, each bond's chance of winning a million is over 40 billion to 1. Of 40 billion pounds in Premium Bonds, each month, there's nearly 1.7 million prizes given out of between £25 and £1 million each. Over 1.6 million of these are £25, 30,000 are £50 and £100 and the remaining 5,000 or so are between £500 and a million (only one is £1 million though)... Yet because of the way the prizes are allocated, the majority of people will win much less than the interest rate anyway.

According to Lewis, the challenge is to look beyond these headline num-bers and examine your actual likely chances of winning (see Table 2.3). 'Your chance of winning the jackpot per £1 spent on the lottery is one in 14 million, far out-stripping the one in 40 billion chance of becoming a millionaire through the Premium Bond draw,' says Lewis.

Table 2.3 Premium bond prize distribution (last updated 1 May 2009)

Prize level	Amount per month	Odds of winning per £1 bond
£1 million	1	1 in 40,453,000,000
£100,000	4	1 in 10,113,000,000
£50,000	8	1 in 5,057,000,000
£25,000	17	1 in 2,379,000,000
£10,000	40	1 in 1,011,000,000
£5,000	82	1 in 493,000,000
£1,000	1,010	1 in 40,052,000
£500	3,030	1 in 13,350,000
£100	29,725	1 in 1,361,000
£50	29,725	1 in 1,361,000
£25	1,621,892	1 in 24,941
£0	40,451,146, 838	1.00004

To be fair to NSI most investors don't actually expect to win the jackpot but they do expect to win lesser sums – in fact they expect to earn the equiva-lent of about 1.5% per annum in winnings. But the MoneySavingExpert team decided to test this out – using 'very advanced multinomial probability equation[s] devised by a post-doctoral cosmology statistician', Lewis looked in detail at the odds of winning a decent return.The results of this detailed analysis are shown in Table 2.4 – only a higher rate taxpayer would stand less than a 4 in 1 chance of beating a savings account by using premium bonds. For the average basic rate taxpayer with say £100 the chances of pre-mium bonds beating a savings rate were estimated to be 1 in 20.

Table 2.4 How do premium bonds stack up?

| Amount of bonds | Odds of winning £0 | Chance of beating inflation (RPI)[1] | | Chance of beating a savings account | | | |
| | | | | Basic rate | | Higher rate | |
		Amount needed to beat inflation	Odds of earning this or more with premium bonds	Interest in savings account[2]	Odds of earning this or more with premium bonds	Interest in savings account[2]	Odds of earning this or more with premium bonds
Over one year							
£100	95% chance	N/A	N/A	£2.64	1 in 20	£1.98	1 in 20
£1,000	61% chance	N/A	N/A	£26.40	1 in 10	£19.80	1 in 2.5
£5,000	1 in 12	N/A	N/A	£132	1 in 13	£99	1 in 3.5
£30,000	1 in 3,270,019	N/A	N/A	£792	1 in 29	£594	1 in 11
Over five years							
£100	78% chance	N/A	N/A	£13.20	1 in 4.5	£9.90	1 in 4.5
£1,000	1 in 12	N/A	N/A	£132	1 in 12	£99	1 in 3.5
£5,000	1 in 268,406	N/A	N/A	£660	1 in 30	£495	1 in 10
£30,000	Negligible	N/A	N/A	£3,960	1 in 125	£2,970	1 in 24

[1] The RPI rate of inflation is currently negative, making any comparisons with premium bonds slightly irrelevant. Of course technically it means you have a 100% chance of beating RPI inflation as the worse that can happen is you win nothing, but your capital is safe.

[2] Top saving account paying 3.3% interest, it assumes the interest is withdrawn not compounded, as this is how most people use premium bonds. Note where the odds are better than 1 in 2, they are expressed as a percentage.

Armed with this analysis Lewis suggests that premium bonds are in fact much worse than most top savings products. Table 2.5 is based on the assumption that 'you *would* win the £1 a year for every £100 saved' yet clearly shows other savings accounts out on top.

Table 2.5 How premium bonds compare (October 2009)

		Returns based on £1,000 over a year		
	Interest rate	Non-taxpayer	Basic tax	Higher tax
Premium bonds[1]	1.5%	£15	£15	£15
Top savings account	3.3%	£33	£26	£20
Top cash ISA	3%	£30	£30	£30

[1] **Someone with average luck is actually likely to win less than this.**

Money market accounts

Many wealthier investors make use of an institutional savings structure known as money market accounts. These offer depositors access to something called the wholesale money market – this is the internal market run between the big banks and building societies where they lend and borrow money from each other using either cash or what's called 'near cash' (short-term commercial paper that is deemed to be very safe). Wealthy private investors are usually able to access these accounts through the treasury department of their clearing high street or investment/merchant bank.

The rates paid should reflect wholesale money market rates represented by the London Interbank Offered Rate (LIBOR), established daily as a summary of actual rates offered in the money market between banks.

It all seems very complex to the lay observer but many investors use these accounts because the rates on offer change almost instantly as base rates move up and down. Crucially these accounts come in a massive range of terms – from one day to one year, all usually boasting interest rates above those on offer on the high street from no notice easy access accounts.

Last but no means least investors also seem to like the ability to 'roll over' their money market deposit: this means that the deposit can be automatically renewed each time it matures and this can include the interest accrued. This is particularly useful if you expect to need the savings at short notice, but don't know when. There are needless to say some major drawbacks to accessing these very flexible, institutional accounts – some accounts charge commission, and most providers don't publicise their rates on the web. Also minimum amounts usually tend to be above £25,000 or even £100,000.

Smaller investors can access these specialist accounts through unit trusts offered by the big investment houses. In Figure 2.2 we've outlined the key holdings of one such account, run by assurer LV=. Their money market account, called LV= UK Money Market Retail Account currently offers a standard interest rate of below 1%, through a range of investments that are in effect 'near-cash', i.e. securities that can be turned into cash overnight if need be! These unit trust based money market accounts are especially popular with investors when markets are in turmoil, and investors often shift part of their pension fund into a money market as they near retirement.

Top 10 Holdings	% Part.	Maturity Range	%
Bbva 0.65% Cd 10/08/10 2010–10–08	5.79	1 to 3	0.00
Nordea Cd 0.66% 09/10	5.59	3 to 5	0.00
Barclays 1.4% Cd 11/10 2010–08–11	5.00	5 to 7	0.00
Lloyds Cd 0.84% 08/10 2010–10–08	4.99	7 to 10	0.00
Ing Bk 0.85% Cd 19/10/10 2010–10–19	4.99	10 to 15	0.00
Nationwide Cd 0.81% 09/10 2010–09–22	4.69	15 to 20	0.00
Royal Bank of Cananda 4.625% 2010–12–07	4.55	20 to 30	0.00
Aust & Nz Bk Grp 4.5% 2010–12–15	3.74	Over 30	0.00
Bank Of Nova Scotia 4.625% 2011–01–25	3.05		
Nationwide Cd 0.78% 07/10 2010–07–21	2.50		

Figure 2.2   **LV= UK Money Martket Retail Acc – July 2010**

Source: LV=

GUARANTEED INCOME BONDS

Traditionally it's not only been the banks and building societies that are keen to 'tap' savers and investors for fixed term money. Insurance companies have also wanted to borrow money for anything between one and five years through a structure known as a guaranteed income bond. Guaranteed income bonds (GIBs) are a life assurance-based investment offered by insurance companies and pay a fixed rate of interest over a fixed term – typically one to five years – promising you your capital back at the end. You can take your income annually or monthly.

These bonds differ from bank and building society savings bonds in that the income is automatically paid out after 20% savings tax. (Note that you can't claim that tax back from the Inland Revenue so these bonds are not suitable for non-taxpayers.) Higher rate taxpayers may be subject to additional income tax liability on the interest payments although offshore GIBs are paid gross, and deferment of tax is permitted.

Back in the first half of 2010 market leaders Pinnacle and AIG (Alico) pulled out of the market for GIBs. To date no new GIBs have been offered.

Savings accounts caveats: a checklist

What should investors be looking out for when they open any one of the myriad different savings accounts available through high street financial institutions? Below we've detailed a checklist of key issues, followed by a dozen tips from Darren Cooke from Moneyfacts.

■ **Opening restrictions.** Check you can actually open the account with your initial capital – many of the best accounts operate high minimum deposits, starting at £1,000 or more. The account might also only be open to existing customers or in certain areas (a big problem with regional building societies) and you may have to take out other products with the provider at the same time to qualify for the account you want.

■ **Look for providers with consistently competitive interest rates.** Banks and building societies nearly always use headline rates to attract in customers and then dump those rates shortly afterwards. Look for providers with a consistently good record of topping the best buy tables.

■ **Interest rate bonuses.** Many advertised interest rates include an element of bonus. Some will be unconditional bonuses which apply for a certain period of time. Others will be conditional, for example on how long you hold the money with the provider, or on the number of withdrawals made.

■ **Withdrawal penalties.** What's it going to cost you to withdraw your money? Normally you'll lose some interest although some accounts will allow a certain number of withdrawals per year before you have to pay a penalty. Some savings accounts include conditional bonuses in their rates of interest. These often relate to the number of withdrawals that are made over a certain time period. If these are exceeded, interest can be lost.

■ **Don't be loyal.** Banks and to a lesser extent building societies don't tend to reward their most loyal customers. If you think you're receiving sub-standard rates shop around. There are no rewards for customer loyalty!

■ **Be careful with products offering a rate guarantee.** Some banks and building societies offer a rate that is guaranteed to be a certain level above or below the Bank of England Base Rate – beware as many are for a limited period only so act essentially as a bonus as well.

Darren Cooke is also very cautious about the huge amount of product innovation in the savings space. Here are his tips for surviving:

1 **Bonuses.** 18% of all variable rate accounts include a bonus as part of the rate. For many of the best deals in the market, the temporary bonus makes up the larger portion of the rate. When the bonus ends and you don't move to a better paying account, you are likely to remain on a very uncompetitive rate.

2 **Withdrawal penalties.** Many of the best easy access accounts allow you to withdraw your money immediately if needed, but there may be restrictions on the number of withdrawals that can be made, or made penalty free.

3 **Bigger doesn't mean best.** Building societies are restricted to how much funding for mortgages they can raise through the money markets. As a result, most of their funding is raised through their savings books, so they have to offer competitive rates to attract new money. Around two-thirds of the Moneyfacts best buys are made up of products offered by building societies.

4 **Perceived foreign banks.** After the Icesave debacle many savers refused to invest with 'foreign banks'. However, today banks in the UK market with a parent company overseas are fully registered in the UK and therefore eligible for the same protection under the Financial Services Compensation Scheme (FSCS) as the majority of other banks, or are registered under schemes that offer better protection than the UK scheme (e.g. ING Direct is covered by the Dutch scheme). Plus, because their brand names are less well known, they tend to offer better rates to get their name out there.

5 **Fixed Rates.** Fixed rate bonds offer some of the highest rates on the cash savings market, but most don't allow access to your money during the term of the deal (up to five years). In the current environment, with rates likely to increase in the not too distant future, what may be a competitive rate now may not be a competitive rate in a couple

of years' time. However, in a time of base rate falls, locking for longer periods if you don't need access to the money can be a real benefit.

6 Regular savers. Regular savings accounts can offer what appear to be high rates, but you are restricted on how much you can invest each month. As a result, the level of interest you actually receive is much lower than what you would have received had you invested the same amount as a lump sum at the start of the term.

7 Opening other accounts. Some accounts offer market leading rates, but to qualify you need to open a fee paying current account with the provider, or a more risky longer-term investment product. If you weren't in the market to go for these other products then it's best to stay clear.

8 Earning an income. Some savings products offer you the option of monthly interest, so that you can earn an income from your nest egg. If you opt for this the effective interest rate earned is likely to be lower as you won't benefit from compound interest.

9 Prepare for the worst. Until 2007, nobody ever thought a bank would fail but, as we now know, it is possible. The FSCS covers £85,000 per person per deposit taking provider. As long as you invest no more than this with each provider your money will be 100% protected. However, some providers are covered under the same banking licence (e.g. Bank of Scotland and Halifax). If both banks under one licence fail you will only be protected once up to £85,000. Check before investing your money that the new provider isn't covered under the same licence as any other you are already invested with.

10 Regularly check the rate of interest you are receiving. Rates are regularly reviewed by banks, particularly when base rates change. What may be a good rate now may be less so in a few months' time. If you keep an eye on the rate of interest, either online or in branch, you can make sure you are making the most out of your money.

11 Cash ISAs. As interest earned is tax free, ISAs are most savers' first port of call. However, many of the best deals will only accept the current year's allowance and won't allow you to transfer existing ISA limits to the higher interest rate. Don't forget about previous years' allowances, regularly review the rate being paid and transfer to a new account.

12 Don't withdraw ISA money. Unless absolutely necessary, don't withdraw money invested in an ISA. If you do, the money will lose its tax free status and you will only be able to re-invest up to that year's ISA allowance limit (assuming you haven't used it already). If you need to move the money from one ISA to another, make sure you use the ISA transfer process.

ANNUITIES

For many investors the reality of investing for an income boils down to one very simple product, first encountered in our tour through the history of financial innovation – the humble annuity. At its simplest the annuity is a brilliantly conceived idea – a stream of income payments is paid out over the lifetime of the recipient, for which the recipient makes an initial up-front contribution. The risk for the investor is obvious – they make a large contribution up front, expecting a long line of payments but then proceed to drop dead the next day! That's clearly terrible news for the annuity investor's family but fabulous news for the annuity issuer! But the annuity issuer – in many cases an insurance company – must also cope with the opposite scenario, namely the recipient who lives for what seems like an eternity. That capital paid out up front will soon look meagre compared to the long stream of annuity payments.

Back in the real world annuities are, obviously, a great deal more complicated than our simple example. In recent years many new types of annuity have appeared, especially for those approaching or already in retirement. The annuity market is an increasingly complex market full of structures and providers – which is why this next section on the ins and outs of annuities is written by Gemma Goodman, head of research at specialist advisers Annuity Bureau Alexander Forbes.

THE INS AND OUTS OF ANNUITIES (BY GEMMA GOODMAN, HEAD OF RESEARCH AT THE ANNUITY BUREAU)

A brief history

Famously, in annuity circles anyway, Jane Austen wrote in *Sense and Sensibility* in 1811. 'An annuity is a very serious business; it comes over and over every year, and there is no getting rid of it.'

The earliest recorded annuities can be traced back to Roman times, when citizens could purchase contracts called 'annua' (or annual stipends). These provided an income for a fixed period, or life, in exchange for an up-front payment.

In the medieval period, some monasteries offered 'corrodies', which entitled the purchaser to accommodation, clothing, food and drink for the remainder of their life. Since all income payments from a corrody were made in the form of the real goods, this may be the earliest example of a truly inflation-proofed annuity product.

During the 17th century, a number of annuity and annuity-like products were used by European governments to fund the near constant warfare of the period. These ranged from the lottery-style 'tontine', where an individual would make an initial payment in to a communal fund and receive a regular dividend that increased with the death of each member, to straightforward annuities that offered a fixed income for life.

The first modern-day annuities, priced using actuarial methods, were offered by the Equitable Assurance Society (later to become Equitable Life) in 1762.

Since these early days, annuities have evolved a great deal and expanded into a wide range of investment and retirement products. Consequently, there are a number of options and products to consider when purchasing an annuity

Annuity income products

There are two fundamentally different types of annuities: purchased life annuities, where an individual invests their own capital with a view to obtaining a secure income, and pension annuities, where the capital used to purchase the income comes directly from an approved pension arrangement.

Purchased Life Annuities

A Purchased Life Annuity (PLA) can be an attractive option for those who have a lump sum to invest and require a secure and tax-efficient income.

A PLA works in much the same way as a traditional annuity – the investor pays the insurance company a lump sum in exchange for a guaranteed income, either for a fixed period, or for the rest of their life. Unlike a traditional annuity, which is purchased with the proceeds of a pension arrangement, the lump sum payment for a PLA can come from any number of sources – a tax-free cash payment from a pension plan, an inheritance or the proceeds from the sale of a house, to name but a few.

The attraction of PLAs lies not only in the secure income that they can provide, but also in the unique and tax-efficient way in which that income is paid.

Unfortunately, the purchased life annuity product is not as advanced as other retirement products. Typically, the annuity rates offered are lower than conventional annuities as there is a belief that only the healthy would be interested in purchased life annuities and therefore this reduces the mortality profit. Recently, enhanced annuity providers have begun offering impairment increases in their purchased life annuities.

The income received is divided into two parts – capital and interest – with each part being subject to a different tax-treatment:

■ Capital – as the investment made into the annuity is usually from a large lump sum, it is assumed that tax has already been paid. The majority of the income is therefore treated as a return of capital and is untaxed.

■ Interest – the only taxable part of the income is the interest element, which is treated as savings income and is taxed at the savings rate applicable at the date that it is paid. The insurance company will generally deduct basic rate tax from the interest element before it is paid, but if the recipient is a higher rate taxpayer, they will be responsible for any additional tax liability.

Pension annuities

When an individual decides to draw benefits from the pension arrangements in which they have been accruing capital through contributions, there is a requirement that they are provided with a regular income. Whilst in final salary or defined benefit schemes, this income will be provided by the scheme trustees (typically from the scheme assets, rather than via an annuity), the proceeds from money purchase or defined contribution arrangements, such as personal pensions or stakeholder pensions will need to be converted into an income by purchasing an annuity.

Some restrictions may apply on the type of annuity that is purchased by pension arrangements, but aside from taxation (see below) these purchased life annuities and pension annuities share the same fundamental structure and options.

Conventional annuities

Conventional annuities provide a guaranteed income for life in exchange for an initial payment. The income is subject to neither investment risk nor mortality risk. This means that it doesn't matter what happens to stock markets, house prices or any other investments, the income will continue to be paid out even if the annuitant breaks the longevity record. Once purchased, these annuities can pay either a fixed level of income or an income that will increase each year. These increases can be at a fixed rate, or in line with an index, such as the RPI.

▶

This security and the fixed nature of conventional annuities are provided at the expense of flexibility. Once bought, they cannot be changed, transferred or cashed in.

Investment-linked annuities

The annuitant can exercise a degree of control over the level of income they receive via an investment-linked annuity. This involves setting an assumption for the future rate of growth of an underlying investment fund. The higher the assumed rate of growth, the higher the initial income will be, but it is important to note that if the fund grows at a slower rate than was assumed, the income will be reduced to reflect this.

The initial income from an investment-linked annuity will be relatively low compared to a conventional, non-increasing annuity, but this **income levels under** is offset by the potential for income increases to **an investment-linked** combat the effects of inflation and the opportunity **annuity will fluctuate** for 'real' growth. It is worth noting, however, that income levels under an investment-linked annuity will fluctuate and, while there will generally be a guaranteed minimum income level, the investment risk involved means that they will not be suitable for everyone.

Another type of investment annuity is a with-profits annuity, which pays a retirement income, primarily based on the investment performance of the annuity provider's with-profits fund. The investment returns received by the with-profits fund are then passed back through bonuses; hence the income is linked to the performance of this fund.

With-profits annuities are considered to be a lower risk than other investment-linked annuities. As well as investing in shares, property and other assets offering potential growth, part of the with-profits fund is held in the same type of secure fixed interest securities that a guaranteed pension annuity uses. Some providers invest a greater proportion of assets in lower risk investments. This limits the investment risk and means returns should not fluctuate to the same highs and lows as unit-linked funds. However, it also limits the potential investment.

Fixed term annuities

A number of unique products have been developed by annuity providers. Although they are all different in design each aims to provide flexibility and growth potential.

Fixed term annuities combine the features of both the traditional options by allowing you to draw an income for a set period of time, usually up until your 75th birthday, as well as giving you the option of a guaranteed maturity value. Once your plan comes to an end, you can then use your maturity value to buy a conventional annuity, or transfer to an unsecured pension.

The annuity options

There are a number of optional benefits to be considered when setting up an annuity. Some benefits will considerably reduce the initial pension income available, whilst others will have a negligible effect. More importantly, the benefits selected need to be appropriate to the annuitant's personal needs as well as their financial dependants'/family's needs. The most common options that can be added to an annuity are detailed below, though not all of the options are available for every annuity product:

Frequency of income

The annuitant can choose the frequency of their pension payments at the outset. Most people choose to receive monthly payments, but income can be paid quarterly, half yearly or annually.

Income paid in advance or in arrears

Payments can be made either in advance or in arrears. Opting for monthly income and purchasing an annuity on 1 July and receiving a payment on that day means the payments are in advance. If the first payment is not made until 1 August, the payments are in arrears.

Generally people opt for monthly in arrears because the slight increase in lifetime income is favoured over the slight increase in speed of payment, which in practice is less than one month, as the annuity provider must take receipt of the pension fund monies before they can make payment.

The longer in arrears income is paid, the higher the income.

Increases in payment

An escalating annuity is one that increases each year. Choosing this option will result in a lower starting income than would be available under a level (non-escalating) annuity. The greater the escalation, the lower the initial income will be. It is therefore important to balance carefully what is needed now against what is likely to be needed in the future. Consideration should be given to the likely life expectancy of the annuitant, based on health and the family's history of longevity. Generally, a fixed rate of increase of 1% to 8% is available.

An annuity can also be linked to the RPI. This means that the pension payments will increase each year in line with inflation as measured by the RPI. It should be noted that, in times of deflation, the annuity income may also fall.

Partner's income

This option is not usually relevant to single people but most couples choose to have an annuity that includes benefits for their surviving spouse or partner. This option means that, when the main annuitant dies, an income is paid to the surviving partner for the rest of his or her life.

The partner need not be a wife or a husband; any person of either sex may be eligible for a partner's pension, although some companies will insist on proof that the partner is financially dependent on the main annuitant. Financial dependency may also need to be proven if and when the dependant's annuity comes into payment. The partner's pension is sometimes called a spouse's pension or a reversionary pension because the income reverts to the surviving partner.

Partner's pensions are usually only payable to the person named at the outset. However, if married, it is possible for this benefit to be payable to any spouse. This means that providing the annuitant is married at death, the benefit will be paid to the then spouse, i.e. this takes remarriage into account.

Under this option a dependent's income can be set as high as 100% of the named annuitant's pension. Most couples, however, opt for an income of between one-third and two-thirds of the annuitant's pension. The more that is payable to the partner, the lower the starting income under the annuity will be. Furthermore, the

▶

age of the partner will affect the income payable. The younger he or she is, the lower the starting income will be. If the fund being used to purchase the annuity contains protected rights from contracting out of the State Second Pension (S2P), a spouse's benefit must be provided from the protected rights portion.

Guarantee period

Including a guarantee period means that pension payments will continue for a fixed number of years, even if the annuitant dies within that period. The most common guarantee period is five years, but it is possible to guarantee payments for up to ten years. A guarantee period is a cost-effective way of providing a level of security as it does not greatly reduce the yearly income. The shorter the guarantee period, the greater the initial income will be.

With or without proportion

Another choice, but only for those paid in arrears, is to have an annuity with or without proportion. An annuity with proportion will pay a prorated amount for the period from the last payment until the date of death. This option is not expensive to provide, but if an income is needed for the protection of others, consideration should be given to including a partner's or dependant's pension.

With or without overlap

Usually only available to retirees from company pension schemes where a five-year guarantee period and a spouse's pension are required. Otherwise, all annuities are paid without overlap. If the annuitant dies within the guarantee period, 'with overlap' means that the spouse's provision starts immediately and is paid in addition to the remaining guarantee period pension. Without overlap means that the spouse's pension does not start until the end of the guaranteed period.

Annuity protection lump sum

This option means that if the annuitant dies before their 75th birthday and they have not received income payments that equal (usually) the original purchase price, the balance can be paid as a lump sum on the member's death. This is called an annuity protection lump sum death benefit and is taxable at 35%.

The decision as to whether or not to include this protection must be made at the outset. Although allowed by current legislation this option is not yet widely available from annuity providers.

Pension Commencement Lump Sum

The Pension Commencement Lump Sum (PCLS) is more commonly known as tax-free cash. Broadly speaking, the maximum cash sum that is available is limited to of 25% of the underlying fund value from a pension. If the policy is an occupational pension scheme with benefits built up before 6 April 2006, the tax-free cash entitlement may be in excess of 25% of the fund value.

Even if the aim is purely to generate income it is often a good idea to take the tax-free cash entitlement as it is sometimes possible to generate income in a more effective and tax-efficient way.

How annuity rates are calculated

The components of an annuity calculation are based on the personal details of the annuitant (traditionally the health, age and gender of the annuitant), the terms of the annuity (escalation, frequency, spouse's benefit), amount invested and the rate of return that the insurance company can expect to receive on the funds.

Smoking habits and medical conditions, both past and present, can all affect normal life expectancy. Some annuity providers now take this information into account when setting their annuity rates. In some cases, this can mean substantially higher income levels than those payable from standard conventional annuities.

Annuity calculations are becoming increasingly personalised – they often now even take into account the postcode area that the annuitant resides in. Life expectancy is steadily increasing and this means that your annuity is likely to have to pay out for longer. The insurance company needs to factor this in to the annuity purchase.

annuity calculations are becoming increasingly personalised

The insurance company providing the annuity will generally invest the funds in government securities (gilts). This is a very safe investment as it is backed by the government, but building on the maxim that low risk investments do not need to demonstrate high yields in order to attract investors, the yield on gilts is typically not significantly higher than cash-based investments. Recent years have seen falling interest rates in the UK and against this backdrop, even discounting central government intervention in the economy through the sale of gilts, gilt yields and annuity rates have dropped too.

The open market option

The open market option gives those close to retirement the right to purchase an annuity or other pension benefits with a different provider from the one with whom their pension has built up. This is important, as regardless of how well a pension provider has performed before the benefits are taken, they may not offer the best annuity rate when it comes to retirement.

Even for conventional annuities, providing the same benefits, the difference in lifetime income can be 20% or even more in some cases. Unfortunately, recent research by the Association of British Insurers (ABI) has indicated that only 32% make use of the open market option (even though 67% investigate it). The government is considering making the open market option compulsory.

There are three wrongly perceived myths about the open market option, these being:

■ the perceived complexity and effort involved

■ assumptions that pension providers will reward loyalty

■ the belief that smaller funds are just 'not worth it'.

End to compulsory annuitisation at 75

Under current legislation there is a requirement to either purchase an annuity before age 75 or enter an Alternatively Secured Pension (ASP) on reaching this age.

As part of the emergency budget on 22 June 2010, the government announced that the effective requirement to buy an annuity before the age of 75 is to be removed and, as an interim measure, anyone reaching 75 on or after the date of the budget is able to defer the purchase of an annuity until their 77th birthday.

▶

Further details of the changes, which are due to take effect from 6 April 2011, were published on 9 December 2010. They include:

■ The removal of the restriction on taking tax-free cash after the age of 75.

■ The ability for individuals using Unsecured Pension (USP) – also known as income drawdown) – to take withdrawals from their fund without any cap, provided they have a secured pension income of at least £20,000 per annum (this can include the state pension, annuity income and income from occupational pension schemes).

3

Bonds – government and corporate

The basics

The wide and wonderful world of bonds represents a kind of *terra incognita* for most private investors. In popular lore bond investing is the preserve of the rich and wealthy investment banker, sitting in his gilt-edged tower lording it over the rest of the planet. When bond investors start asking awkward questions of governments and their credit worthiness, the term 'bond vigilante' is usually invoked and it's instructive that nearly every 'bond vigilante' this author has ever interviewed is a professional, institutional fund manager or banker.

By contrast over in the world of shares – otherwise known as equities, and explored in the next chapter – it's automatically assumed that private investors have a big role to play. Yet this perception of equities as being easy for the layperson to understand in contrast to bonds is almost certainly false. In many respects bonds are a simpler idea to grasp than equities or other complex financial instruments and can provide a steady, long-term secure income.

In fact building a portfolio of diversified bonds – be they issued by governments or corporations – as well as equities is an eminently sensible and practical idea for both cautious and adventurous investors. In this chapter we'll look at how a bond is structured and also analyse the various types of bonds issued, with issuers as diverse as global superpowers and small companies. Later on in this chapter we'll also look at how to trade bonds, before concluding with some simple trading strategies.

Let's start this adventure into the world of bonds with a simple definition of what constitutes a bond. In essence a bond is a very simple creation. A bond is nothing more than a loan structured as an IOU and issued by a borrower.

Imagine if you lent say £10,000 to the government or a company and they make a payment comprised of interest which works out at 5% per annum. That means as the investor who makes the loan you receive a yield (or coupon) that's equivalent to £500 per annum. The crucial twist is the structure of the loan – that IOU. That IOU is structured as a note or bond, with various terms written on the piece of paper or via the electronic record, i.e. the name of the borrower, the interest rate expressed as a coupon, the face value of the note or bond and, crucially, the duration of the loan (this represents the bond's maturity).

Later on in this chapter we'll explore these simple concepts in much greater depth but in summary a bond is just a piece of paper that constitutes an IOU issued to the investor who made the loan to the borrower. Crucially that piece of paper, electronic record or note – the bond itself – can be held until the end of its 'life' (called redemption) or traded to another party on a market of some form, at a given price well before the bond is due to redeem or mature.

This simplicity of construction – easily tradeable paper with clear features, understood by all as part of a contract between a lender and borrower – has allowed a massive global market to emerge incorporating a diverse range of buyers ranging from pension fund managers through to a much smaller number of private investors. This market has also enabled investors to construct diversified portfolios of different types of bonds, issued by different borrowers, over different time frames and with different interest rates or yields.

Before we go any further, it's worth noting a couple of key features from our simplistic IOU-based description. The most immediately obvious one is the price attached to that piece of paper which constitutes the bond. The principal – let us say you lent out £10,000 – might be split up into lots of smaller units each with their own initial, par value: for example, if you lent £10,000 and that's been broken down into 10,000 £1 notes or bonds, each bond will be issued at par or valued at £1 per bond.

Crucially you should receive back the principal per unit – that par of £1 – when the bond matures at the end of the period agreed between the lender and the borrower. There is of course an obvious risk that your borrower defaults, in which case you might get back nothing. This potential for default is crucial – many investors assume that all bonds are somehow risk free, unlike supposedly riskier equities, and there

many bonds issued by corporations can and do default

are indeed some bonds issued by the likes of the UK and the US governments that are (almost) risk free. But note the use of that weasel word 'almost' because there is a tiny chance that in the future a government might have to default on that payment. That risk of potential default is tiny with the UK or US governments but many bonds issued by corporations can and do default – bonds can be a risky investment.

To summarise, in this simple example we've already encountered some key terms:

■ **Bonds** are in effect IOUs – loans – structured as a form of note.

■ The **issuers** of these bonds can vary enormously. If you buy a corporate bond, you're lending a private business or even a large corporation your money. If you buy a government bond (also known as a **gilt**), you're lending to the government.

■ A bond pays interest periodically (usually either annually or every six months) and repays the principal in the future (the **redemption date**).

■ There's an issue price, called the **par** (or the **face value**).

■ Each bond also has an annual interest rate expressed as a percentage, and known as the **coupon**.

■ The bond's issuer will also announce a timeframe or **duration** for the loan – this will include an end date when they will repay (hopefully) the principal at **par value**.

One last point – as we've already noted there's always some element of risk. The biggest risk is that our borrower defaults, i.e. doesn't pay back the principal. And all things being equal, it's obvious that that risk (chance of default) grows over time, i.e. a loan over five years is likely to be less risky than a loan over 50 years, unless of course it's the UK or US government, neither of which have ever defaulted on any payments! This concept of risk increasing over time needs to be reflected somehow in the interest rate charged or income: in the vast majority of cases an issuer will pay a higher interest rate for a long-term bond. An investor therefore will potentially earn greater returns on longer-term bonds, but in exchange for that return, the investor incurs additional risk.

In detail: price and duration

Now that we've surmised some basics about bonds it's time to dig a little deeper and try to establish some of the internal mechanics of the bond industry. We'll start with perhaps the most important feature of a bond for a purchaser, namely how we arrive at the **price** of a bond. This involves understanding how the forces of supply and demand work together to help establish a price for a bond in the wider marketplace. Three factors stand out:

- the interest or the coupon rate
- the date in the future when the bond matures, also known as the term to maturity
- the interest rate or yield to maturity.

The first two factors have already been explained in some detail but the last – the interest rate or yield to maturity – needs some explaining. Lurking behind this term is a simple idea – that the price of a bond may change as it reacts to different external influences, such as the prevailing interest rate set by the government.

Imagine that a company issues a bond valued at £100 paying the prevailing interest rate at the time (5%) plus an additional 2% for the extra risk of investing in this private enterprise. Thus our interest rate or yield at issue is 7% (£7 per annum per £100 bond issued), in this case paid as an annual coupon until the bond matures in ten years' time. Let's imagine that one year later interest rates suddenly collapse to just 1%. The attractions of our bond paying 7% are now obvious to all and sundry – a 6% spread between the prevailing interest rate and our bond. That massive spread lures many usually risk averse investors to take a punt on our riskier private company, which in turn helps push the price per bond up beyond its initial £100.

Given the higher level of risk – already reflected by the higher initial yield – investors decide that they'd be willing to buy the bonds for as much as £200 per bond. At this £200 purchase price level our £7 annual coupon translates to an annual yield of 3.5% if the investor bought the bond for £200 . But there's a problem: investors aren't stupid and they know perfectly well that in nine years they'll only get back £100 for each bond which actually cost them £200 to buy on the secondary market. Suddenly there's a discrepancy between the yield at issuance (7%), the yield at the current market price (3.5%), and yield based on what they'll get back when the bond is redeemed in nine years' time, called the yield to maturity. Each yield will be different.

From this very simple example one can begin to see that there are in fact a great many variables that combine together to affect both the pricing of a bond and the various different yields, with prevailing interest rates being one, alongside both the risk of the issuer and the duration of the bond. Crucially we can see that a bond's yield *declines* as the price paid to buy the bond *increases*.

But how do we know how much a bond's price will change as wider interest rates change? To work out how much a bond's price will move when interest rates change, bond investors uses a measure called **duration**. This widely used measure is actually defined as the weighted average of the present value of a bond's cash flows, a rather technical term to describe a series of regular coupon/interest payments followed by the final redemption payment at maturity when the bond matures and the nominal or par value is repaid. Crucially this duration measure will also be affected by the size of the regular coupon payments and the bond's face value.

The actual equation used to work out this duration value is:

$$D = \sum_{i=1}^{n} \frac{P(i)t(i)}{V}$$

where:

■ i indexes the cash flows

■ $P(i)$ is the present value of the ith cash payment from an asset

■ $t(i)$ is the time in years until the ith payment will be received

■ V is the present value of all cash payments from the asset until maturity.

Each 'duration' measure – one number, expressed in years – is unique to that bond and it is, in effect, a risk measure that lets us compare bonds with different terms, coupons and par values. In effect this duration measure tells us the approximate change in price that any given bond will experience in the event of a 1% change in interest rates by the central bank or government. To understand how this works imagine that interest rates fall by 1%, causing yields on every bond in the market to fall by the same amount. In that event, the price of a bond with duration of two years will rise 2% and the price of a five-year duration bond will rise 5%. Because interest rates directly affect bond yields, the longer a bond's duration, the more sensitive its price is to changes in interest rates.

In detail: the yield

In our previous example of a simple £100 corporate bond we can see how the price paid on the open market after issue has varied enormously (influenced in our example by prevailing interest rates) as did the different yields on offer (the initial yield of 7% versus the current or running yield of 3.5% as the bond hits £200 in value). Many investors will buy a bond when it's issued and hold it through to maturity. Hopefully if the bond pays off in full, their issue price and redemption price will not differ, nor will the net effective yield (the income stream) over the term of the investment. In this case they paid £100 for each bond and received £100 per bond at maturity and all the way through the investment term they received their £7 per annum coupon, or £70 in total.

But some investors buy bonds on the open market – the secondary market – *after* issue and that price may vary enormously (in our example hitting £200 per bond). The cause of these price movements – and yield variations – is dictated by a bundle of factors (prevailing interest rates, duration, risk) summed up in the concept of supply and demand.

To understand these myriad interactions let's assume a decline in interest rates – in this situation a bond paying a high and safe fixed rate of interest every year will become increasingly in demand from investors which will in turn have the effect of pushing up the share price.

Equally, as interest rates rise, investors – all other things being equal – will find this fixed income stream less attractive and as a consequence the market price of that bond will fall. This relationship between price and yield is key to understanding what powers the market for fixed income securities or bonds.

this relationship between price and yield is key

The other key insight is to look on a bond as a promise which is in turn based around cash payments – you pay out cash up front to buy this bond and then over the course of the bond's life the investor will receive several cash payments plus a final cash payment at maturity. Those payments are all fixed and known in advance unlike the dividends received from holding shares, which are unpredictable and liable to termination in a sudden economic downturn. In this respect, bonds differ fundamentally from equities, in that the future cashflows are known. Combine this knowledge of those future cashflows alongside the duration and the current market price and we can identify a number of different yields on offer:

■ **The simple yield**. This is probably the best 'back of an envelope' guide to the returns available on a single bond and is calculated using the following formula:

Annual coupon/market price + (par-market price)/Market price/life × 100

■ In our example, if we move through time and find ourselves in the ninth year, we might find that the bond has fallen in price to £80 per bond yet is still paying out the £7 per annum coupon. If an investor bought this bond for £80 and held it until maturity (now in just a year's time) they'd receive the final £7 annual coupon but in addition they'd also benefit from an extra £20 in profit as the bond matures at par value at the end of the ten-year term, i.e. a total profit of £27 against a purchase price of £80 or a simple yield of 33% in total for the final year.

■ **The income or running yield**. In our example from above, remember how the £100 bond that pays out £7 per year shot up to £200 in value at the end of year one as interest rates fell to 1%. What's the yield at the end of the first year for the investor who paid £200 to buy the bond? The equation for working out what's called the income or running yield is:

$$\frac{\text{issue price or par}}{\text{purchase price}} \times \text{coupon} = \text{running yield}$$

■ So in our example this looks like 100/200 × 7 = 3.5%. This running yield doesn't take into account any profit (or loss) through holding the bond to redemption, and simply assumes that the investor will be able to sell the bond at the same price that they purchased it for on the open market.

■ Finally we come to perhaps the most important and widely used measure of yield namely the **Yield to Maturity (YTM).** This is effectively the internal 'rate of return' on the investment, allowing for each and every cash flow paid and reflects all of the interest payments from the time of purchase until maturity, including interest on interest. Equally important, it also includes any appreciation or depreciation in the capital price of the bond. This yield will change as the purchase price changes although the cash flows from the gilt are fixed: i.e. as prices rise you are effectively paying more for a series of fixed cash flows so the yield falls, and if prices fall the yield rises. In summary the redemption yield reflects the net present value of the future flow of interest and includes the effect of the capital gain or loss from holding the gilt until maturity, at a given price. The formula here is:

$$c(1 + r)^{-1} + c(1 + r)^{-2} + \ldots + c(1 + r)^{-Y} + B(1 + r)^{-Y} = P$$

where c = annual coupon payment (in pounds, not a per cent); Y = number of years to maturity; B = par value; P = purchase price. (It's worth noting that YTMs can be worked out using the YIELDMAT function on Microsoft Excel.) By examining yields to maturity, investors can compare bonds with varying characteristics, such as different maturities, coupon rates or credit quality.

Trade that bond!

The global market for bonds is enormous and growing all the time, with every permutation and variable closely analysed by an army of bonds analysts. When listed on the open, secondary market, a bond's **price** and **yield** determine its value. The most obvious relationship here is that a bond's price always moves in the opposite direction to its yield. Also the previously remarked upon relationship with wider interest rates is crucial, i.e. when central bank determined interest rates fall, 'older' bonds of all types become more valuable because they are sold in a higher interest rate environment and therefore have higher income coupons. In effect investors who own these older coupons can charge a 'premium' to sell them in the open market.

These relationships are easily expressed in the price and yield – both of which are reported in all coverage of the bond markets. Take a newspaper and look at its bonds section and you'll see a range of numbers quoted including the price to buy the bond, its yield and probably some mention of its duration. But these market quotes might also contain some slightly more curious items of information – you may notice for instance that prices include fractions like $\frac{1}{32}$ as the last digits, not decimals.

To understand how these bonds are 'quoted' let's assume you see a government bond or gilt quoted at '97' in the market – this means the price is £970 for every £1,000 (or £100 or £1 depending on the par) of face value and the bond is said to be trading at a 'discount'. If the bond is trading at '110', it costs £1,100 for every £1,000 of face value and the bond is said to be trading at a 'premium'. If the bond is trading at 100, it costs £1,000 for every £1,000 of face value and is said to be trading at 'par'. You'll also see columns in a newspaper and on the internet featuring YTM which, as we have seen, means the yield to maturity, plus there'll be a bunch of abbreviations including 'm' which means matured bonds or 'cld' means called (i.e. redeemed and bought back by the issuer). There's also some specific data which relates to government bonds or gilts as they are also called

– remember that interest on gilts accrues on a daily basis between one coupon (or dividend) date and the next. You'll also see something mentioned called ex-dividend dates – interest payments are usually made to the person who is the registered holder of a gilt seven business days before the coupon payment date (ten business days for 31/2% War Loan) unless alternative instructions have been given to the Registrar. These periods are known as the ex-dividend periods.

Probably the best source for information on bonds is online, on the internet at a British-based website called www.bondscape.net. This is actually the public facing part of a bonds trading network run by investment bank Barclays Capital and Winterflood Securities, a market making firm. Underneath this platform sits a trading engine that's used by many of the UK's leading stockbrokers to buy bonds on the open markets but this website isn't only a trading site – it also features excellent information on the structure of bonds by an analyst called Mark Glowrey, as well as a button that calls up all the closing market prices for major bond issues on the platform (see Figure 3.1).

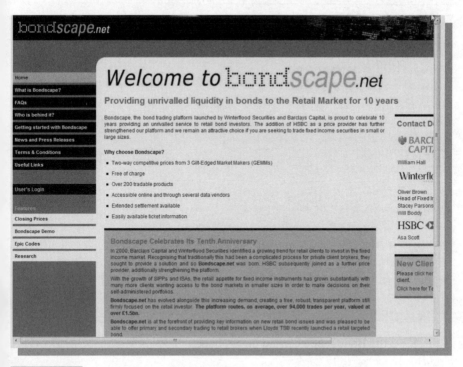

Figure 3.1   The Bondscape homepage

Source: www.bondscape.net

In Figure 3.2 we've shown this closing prices page – on the Bondscape platform there are literally hundreds of different bonds and government gilts. You'll also see from the graphic that a range of information is featured, including:

■ epic – this is the ticker or identification initials given to the bond by market makes

■ description – the name of the bond generally including the issuer

■ coupon – this tells you the initial interest rate or coupon paid at issue

■ maturity – how many years the bond has left, based on the maturity date

■ bid/ask – the purchase/sale price

■ change – change on the previous day

■ income yield – the running yield

■ gross redemption yield – the yield to maturity.

epic	description	coupon	maturity	bid	ask	change	income yield	gross redemption yield
CN4	Uk Gilt Consols	4.0	Perpetual	80.95	83.75	-0.10	4.86	4.86 *
WAR	Uk Gilt War Loan Stk	3.5	Perpetual	74.69	77.64	-0.07	4.60	4.60 *
CV3H	Uk Gilt Conversion Stk	3.5	Perpetual	74.40	77.38	-0.09	4.61	4.61 *
T3U0	Uk Gilt Treasury Stk	3.0	Perpetual	62.50	85.24	-0.05	4.70	4.70 *
CN2H	Uk Gilt Consols	2.5	Perpetual	53.40	55.24	0.01	4.60	4.63 *
T2H	Uk Gilt Treasury Stk	2.5	Perpetual	54.20	56.30	-0.01	4.52	4.52 *
T6Q	Uk Gilt Treasury Stk	6.25	25-Nov-2010	101.55	101.71	-0.02	6.15	0.52
TR11	Uk Gilt Treasury Stk	4.25	07-Mar-2011	102.06	102.15	-0.01	4.16	0.55
CV11	Uk Gilt Conversion Stk	9.0	12-Jul-2011	107.56	107.66	-0.00	8.36	0.65
T11	Uk Gilt Treasury Stk	3.25	07-Dec-2011	103.35	103.45	0.02	3.14	0.66
T512	Uk Gilt Treasury Stk	5.0	07-Mar-2012	106.62	106.71	0.03	4.69	0.72
TR12	Uk Gilt Treasury Stk	5.25	07-Jun-2012	107.92	108.01	0.04	4.86	0.83
TY12	Uk Gilt Treasury Stk	9.0	06-Aug-2012	114.50	116.90	-0.33	7.78	0.99
TR13	Uk Gilt Treasury Stk	4.5	07-Mar-2013	108.63	108.70	0.18	4.14	1.07
T813	Uk Gilt Treasury Stk	8.0	27-Sep-2013	120.64	120.77	0.27	6.63	1.23
TR14	Uk Gilt Treasury Stk	2.25	07-Mar-2014	102.74	102.84	0.38	2.19	1.45
T514	Uk Gilt Treasury Stk	5.0	07-Sep-2014	112.87	113.15	0.46	4.42	1.68
T15	Uk Gilt Treasury Stk	7.75	26-Jan-2015	109.35	110.65	0.02	7.05	0.82
T4T	Uk Gilt Treasury Stk	4.75	07-Sep-2015	113.28	113.37	0.62	4.19	1.96
TY8	Uk Gilt Treasury Stk	8.0	07-Dec-2015	129.91	130.00	0.70	6.16	2.03
T16	Uk Gilt Treasury Stk	4.0	07-Sep-2016	109.34	109.45	0.71	3.66	2.33
TR17	Uk Gilt Treasury Stk	8.75	25-Aug-2017	139.99	140.12	0.88	6.25	2.50
T18	Uk Gilt Treasury Stk	5.0	07-Mar-2018	115.33	115.40	0.78	4.33	2.74
T19	Uk Gilt Treasury Stk	4.5	07-Mar-2019	111.28	111.35	0.82	4.04	2.99
TR19	Uk Gilt Treasury Stk	3.75	07-Sep-2019	105.11	105.21	0.83	3.57	3.09
T520	Uk Gilt Treasury Stk	4.75	07-Mar-2020	113.13	113.21	0.94	4.20	3.15
TR21	Uk Gilt Treasury Stk	8.0	07-Jun-2021	143.76	143.81	1.15	5.56	3.18
TR22	Uk Gilt Treasury Stk	4.0	07-Mar-2022	104.99	105.05	0.77	3.81	3.47
TR25	Uk Gilt Treasury Stk	5.0	07-Mar-2025	113.75	113.87	0.71	4.39	3.78

Figure 3.2   The Bondscape closing prices page

Sources: www.bondscape.net

HOW DO BONDS REACT TO CHANGES IN INTEREST RATES?

In our earlier example of a £100 bond shooting up in value to £200 as interest rates fall, we established that the price of a bond is hugely affected by the change in interest rates. This impact is based around three key variables:

■ the maturity of the bond

■ the coupon rate

■ the prevailing interest rates at the time of an interest rate change.

Unsurprisingly economists have got to work on the analysis of these variables and five principles have emerged:

1 Bond prices move in the opposite direction to interest rates.

2 Bonds with longer dates to maturity suffer greater percentage price changes for a given change in interest rates.

3 The price sensitivity of bonds increases with maturity, but it increases at a decreasing rate.

4 Bonds with lower coupon rates experience greater percentage price changes for a given change in interest rates.

5 For a given bond, the absolute price increase caused by a fall in bond yields will exceed the price decrease caused by an increase in bond yields of the same magnitude.

The yield curve

In the next section we'll look in detail at the huge variety of issuers and bond structures available to the private investor, but before we move away from the basics of bonds let's explore one last, crucial, concept namely the **yield curve**. Later in this chapter we'll look closely at government bonds or securities (also known as gilts) and discover that there's a massive range of 'maturities' on offer, ranging from short-dated three-month government bills, through to 30–50 year bonds, plus a rare breed of bonds called undated or 'perpetual' bonds with no final maturity.

It's important to understand that bonds of different maturities will boast different yields, produced in part by the markets take on current and future interest rates. Generally speaking investors will want higher yields – greater

> bonds of different
> maturities will boast
> different yields

income payments or coupons expressed as an interest yield – for longer-dated debts. If we show this relationship in a graph it'll probably look a little like Figure 3.3 which shows the 'curve' for gilts in the middle of 2010 – the line in this graph from www.bloomberg.com begins with the *spot interest rate*, which is the rate for the shortest maturity, and extends out in time, typically to 30 years or even more. A yield curve can be plotted for any bond – be it government or corporate – and simply demonstrates the link between bond interest rates and bond maturities.

Figure 3.3 shows that as the term or maturity of the loan increases, the yield paid increases, although this starts to flatten out as we approach bonds with maturities of more than 20 years. Very long-dated bonds, and especially government bonds, are hugely popular with big pension funds who snap them up to match against their long-term liabilities to pensioners. Crucially if investors expect interest rates to rise in the future, the price of longer-dated bonds will fall, pushing up yields at the long end of the curve. This is known as a 'steepening' of the yield curve.

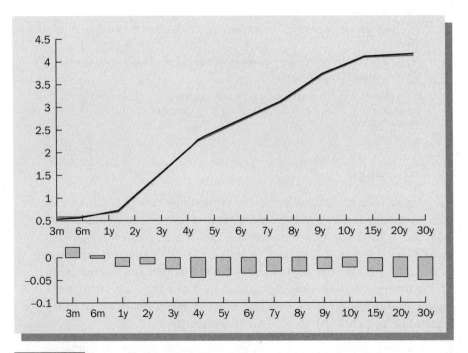

Figure 3.3   **UK yield curve Summer 2010**

Source: Bloomberg Finance LP

Sometimes though the belief that interest rates are going to fall, sharply, can produce another less common phenomena expressed in Figure 3.4 which is called an 'inverse' yield curve – in this situation bond investors race to buy fixed rates at the long end of the curve pushing yields down below current money market rates.

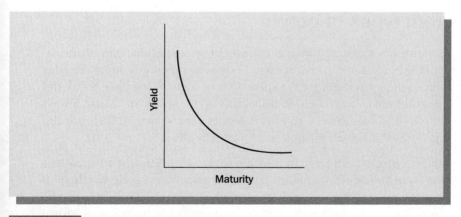

Figure 3.4   Yield curve inversion

In most markets the yield curve for government securities is normal – as in Figure 3.3 – but an inverse yield curve is eagerly seized upon by bears and macro-economists as a sign of impending recession. According to a report on the curve by the massive US bond investor PIMCO:

> *Historically, the slope of the yield curve has been a good leading indicator of economic activity. Because the curve can summarize where investors think interest rates are headed in the future, it can indicate their expectations for the economy. A sharply upward sloping, or steep yield curve, has often preceded an economic upturn. The assumption behind a steep yield curve is interest rates will begin to rise significantly in the future. Investors demand more yield as maturity extends if they expect rapid economic growth because of the associated risks of higher inflation and higher interest rates, which can both hurt bond returns.*
>
> (http://canada.pimco.com/LeftNav/Bond+Basics/2007/Yield+Curve+Basics.htm)

Unsurprisingly the yield curve has become an important tool of analysis for bond market analysts. Again according to PIMCO, the yield curve is useful as an:

> *impressive record as a leading indicator of economic conditions, alerting investors to an imminent recession or signaling an economic upturn, as noted above. Second, the yield curve can be used as a benchmark for pricing many other fixed income securities. Because U.S. Treasury bonds have no perceived credit risk, most fixed-income securities, which do entail credit risk, are priced to yield more than Treasury bonds. For example, a three-year, high-quality corporate bond could be priced to yield 0.50%, or 50 basis points, more than the three-year Treasury bond. A three-year, high-yield bond could be valued 3% more than the comparable Treasury bond, or 300 basis points 'over the curve'.*
>
> (http://canada.pimco.com/LeftNav/Bond+Basics/2007/Yield+Curve+Basics.htm)

Different types of bonds

As we've already noted above, one of the great peculiarities of investing is that so many investors regard bonds as inherently more complex than equities – hopefully our explanation of some of the basic terms and structures used should help to dispel this myth. Bonds are almost always uniform in construction – and the measures used to analyse them are also standardised across all the different types of bonds.

Where confusion can creep in is with regards to the different organisations that issue bonds. An enormous variety of institutions issue bonds (plus a tiny number of famous individuals such as rock star David Bowie who boasts his own Bowie bonds, with interest paid from the royalties earned from his songs!). Most investors in bonds will probably end up investing in one or all of the following issuers.

Gilts or government bonds

These are issued by HM Treasury and are rated as AAA in risk terms (more on these ratings below) by all the major credit ratings agencies and can be viewed as effectively risk-free from the point of view of default – as noted above neither the UK nor US government has ever defaulted or missed a payment on their bonds.

Crucially the notes or bonds issued by the government to fund its public services will fluctuate from day to day in the market, depending on the outlook for interest rates. And it's not just the UK government that issues bonds – nearly every major government in the developed world currently runs a deficit and needs to borrow via bonds on the global markets although it's worth noting that the US, Japan and Europe (primarily the UK, Germany, France, Italy and Spain) dominate the government bond market, accounting for more than 84% of all government bonds outstanding!

Within this broad category of government bonds you may also encounter two different types of bond. The most popular bonds consist of **conventional gilts** – these represent the largest part of the gilt portfolio (78% by 2010) and are in effect a guarantee by the government to pay the holder a fixed cash interest payment (half of the coupon) every six months until the bond matures. On maturity the holder receives the final coupon payment and the nominal capital amount invested. The prices of conventional gilts are quoted in terms of £100 nominal or par. A 'conventional' gilt is denoted by its annual coupon rate and maturity (e.g. 5% Treasury Stock 2014) – with that duration varying between a few months and as much as 50 years! The range of maturities is usually broken down into three main groups:

■ shorts: 1–7 years

■ mediums: 7–15 years

■ longs: over 15 years.

The most popular gilts for private investors are maturities between two and ten years although in recent years the government has concentrated its issuance programme around the 5-, 10-, 30-, 40- and 50-year maturity areas. Investors in gilts may also run into a variety of names including Treasury Stock, Exchequer Stock, Conversion Stock, War Loan and Consolidated Stock. According to the organisation that manages these gilts, the Debt Management Office: 'The names have no significance as far as the underlying obligation to repay is concerned. All new gilts issues in recent years have been named "Treasury Stock"' (www.dmo.gov.uk/docs/publications/investorsguides/mb070605.pdf). You may also run into some oddities called *double-dated conventional gilts* – these are gilts which have two repayment dates, e.g. '7³/4% Treasury Stock 2012–2015'. This complex sounding structure actually means that the government can choose to repay the gilt at any time from 2012 onwards with three months' notice, but must repay the gilt by 2015.

FACTS ABOUT GILTS

■ 2009–10 saw a record volume of gilt issuance. Planned gilt sales increased from £220.0 billion at Budget 2009 to £225.1 billion at the Pre-Budget Report (PBR) in December 2009. The gilt sales outturn was £227.6 billion.

■ Gilt sales at auctions (£187.0 billion) accounted for the bulk (82%) of the issuance.

■ At the end of March 2010 there were 28 conventional gilts with over £15.0 billion in issue and 9 with £25.0 billion or more in issue. The average size of the largest 20 conventional gilts was £24.7 billion.

■ The value of gilts held by overseas investors continued to rise in 2009–10, by £27.7 billion to £243.6 billion, or 29% of the overall portfolio at end-March 2010. According to the DMO, 'In absolute terms, overseas holdings have more than doubled in four years.'

■ At the end of March 2010 nominal value of all gilts in issue was £913.5 billion with a market value of £986.9 billion.

■ This massive bulk of gilt issuance is also tracked by a number of key indices including one managed by Barclays Capital. Figures 3.5–3.7 show the composition of their index of conventional gilts over time, as well as by total market cap (bonds issued).

▶

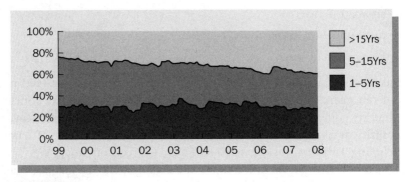

Figure 3.5   Barclays UK Gilt Index historical weights

Source: Barclays Capital

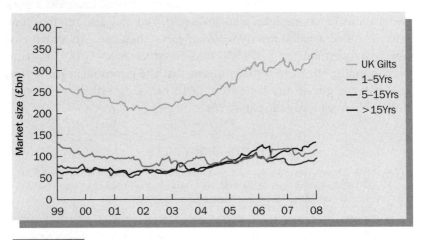

Figure 3.6   Market size growth since 1999 to end August 2008

Source: Barclays Capital

31 August 2008	Market cap £bn	Weight % of overall	No of issues	Average yield (semi)	Average life	Average mod duration
Barclays UK Gilt Index	371.8	100.0	27	4.48	15.37	9.20
1–5 yrs	93.5	25.1	8	4.46	2.69	2.46
5–15 yrs	125.0	33.6	9	4.54	8.82	6.84
>15 yrs	153.3	41.2	10	4.45	27.93	15.24
>5 yrs	278.3	74.9	19	4.48	19.97	11.46

Figure 3.7   Barclays UK Gilt Index characteristics

Source: Barclays Capital

Source: From the government's Debt Management Office report in 2010 (www.dmo.gov.uk/docs/publications/investorsguides/mb070605.pdf)

You may also encounter another form of government bond namely **index-linked gilts**. In the UK, these bonds were first issued back in 1981 and these 'linkers', as they're popularly called now, account for 20.9% of the government's gilt portfolio (based on figures from the DMO at the end of March 2010). In total the government has issued 29 different index-linked gilts of which 12 have since matured.

Index-linked gilts are still bonds issued by the government to pay for spending but their structure of payouts is very different from that of conventional gilts – with linkers the semi-annual coupon payments and the principal (the final payout) are adjusted in line with a measure of inflation called the General Index of Retail Prices (also known as the RPI). This means that both the coupons (the cash flows paid out) and the principal paid on redemption are adjusted to take account of *accrued* inflation since the gilt was first issued. (Note though that the redemption price may be many years away, so prices may fluctuate on a day-to-day basis, reflecting investor's changing yield expectations.)

The idea behind these innovative instruments is to protect the real value of investors' savings against the menace of inflation which is especially dangerous for investor in securities with a fixed income. Many investors buy conventional bonds for the stable and predictable income stream, which comes in the form of interest, or coupon, payments. However, because the rate of interest, or coupon, on the vast majority of fixed income securities remains the same until maturity, the purchasing power of those interest payments falls as inflation rises. Economists even have a measure for this called the *real interest rate* which is the normal or nominal rate minus that of inflation. So, if a bond has a nominal interest rate of 5% and inflation is 2%, the real interest rate is 3%.

> the purchasing power of those interest payments falls as inflation rises

Index-linked bonds or gilts – linkers – help to address this (largely hidden) inflation menace. Rather than pay a fixed interest rate (or coupon) and principal/par on redemption, index-linked gilts set the coupon and the principal repayment based around an index which measures inflation (either the CPI or the RPI, depending on the government). In essence with an inflation-linked bond, the interest and/or principal is adjusted on a regular basis to reflect changes in the rate of inflation, thus providing a 'real', or inflation adjusted, return. But that inflation adjusted return needs to be put into some perspective – in reality there's always a lag between the relevant time period for which an index value is worked out and the date on which that number is published. Here in the UK all new index-linked gilts are issued with a three-month indexation lag (as opposed to the eight-month lag used for earlier issues).

Over the past decade the UK government has started issuing more and more index-linked gilts, especially as inflation rates have hit ever lower levels. But by far the most enthusiastic issuer of index-linked government bonds is the US Treasury. Between 1997 and 2004, the issuance of Treasury Inflation Protected Securities (TIPS) soared almost tenfold from $25 billion to $200 billion – in fact by the end of this decade, the US Treasury expects it will be issuing almost as much in TIPS as in conventional bonds.

HOW TO WORK OUT WHETHER AN INDEX-LINKED GILT IS A GOOD INVESTMENT

Index-linked gilts are a complex and relatively difficult to understand beast. These are all issued at a nominal par price of 100p and then pay a coupon that is determined in part by the RPI level three or eight months prior. Crucially they pay out a coupon which is taxable and is likely to vary with inflation, plus the redemption at maturity is also dependent on inflation levels, i.e. if the duration is many years, they're highly unlikely to pay out at par of 100p. The final redemption amount will vary based on inflation – this is calculated by looking at what's called an RPI index level.

To understand how this might all work let's take two simple examples – one index linker due to mature in 2017 and another due to mature far in the future, in 2055.

- 1¼% Index-linked Treasury Gilt 2017 is trading – as of writing – at 124.83p based on the dirty price. This dirty price is calculated as the product of the real clean price (no interest accumulated at all) and the relevant index ratio (more on that later), plus the accrued interest. Like all index-linked gilts this pays out twice yearly with the coupon subject to further income tax and any capital gains free of tax. Crucially the RPI index levels used for working out final values are based on a three-month lag.

- 1¼% Index-linked Treasury Gilt 2055 is trading at a dirty price – including accumulated interest – at 144.06p.

The next step is work out what these two linkers might be worth under different inflation scenarios. Luckily the government's debt office – the Debt Management Office – has an excellent website with a range of invaluable tools, all at www.dmo.gov. uk. To access most of the gilts-based tools find the tab titled Gilt Market and then search for the side link to Index-linked Gilts. This page contains a number of tools including one called 'calculating estimates of redemption payments' which allows you to input various inflation scenarios and then estimate the final payout amounts.

You may also encounter a peculiar form of government bond known as a **perpetuity**, i.e. a bond issued by the government many hundreds of years ago, that has never been redeemed and continues to pay out an interest rate into perpetuity. One of the most common perpetuity-based securities in the UK is called the 3.5% War Loan which is a gilt first issued by the government in 1917 when it sought to raise finance for World War 1. In its

the War Loan no longer has a maturity date

early life the War Loan paid an income of 5% but this was reduced to 3.5% during the 1930s as a consequence of the economic depression. The War Loan was supposed to reach maturity in 1952 but as yields were above 3.5% at the time the government decided against redeeming the debt. The War Loan no longer has a maturity date.

As we move away from the world of government bonds we also encounter quasi governmental organisations which issue bonds. These bonds might be issued by a variety of 'arm's-length' agencies – on the continent some agencies fund local small businesses through bonds. Alternatively they might be issued by organisations that are not accountable to any one government, such as the European Investment Bank (EIB) or even the IMF. But all these organisations share one common feature – a government or a collection of governments has explicitly stated that they will back these debts, i.e. if all else fails, a government will honour the debt. That 'guarantee' means these are viewed as almost risk free by the market, which allows the issuers to borrow at rates close to gilts.

Last but by no means least investors may also encounter emerging market debt bonds issued by governments in places such as China, Russia and India. These are perceived as being riskier than the equivalent UK or US debt and thus more expensive in terms of the interest rate paid – see the following box.

ALTERNATIVE BOND IDEAS: PART 1

WEALTHY NATION EMERGING MARKET BONDS

Emerging market bonds have been growing in popularity over the past decade – many investors seem to have overcome their worries about third world countries defaulting on their debts and now view the emerging markets as potentially stronger. But that new-found confidence – and enthusiasm for the higher yield on offer - can't hide the fact that many emerging markets do still have weak national balance sheets in that the governments may not owe much but the corporate sector is heavily in debt.

One novel take on this challenge comes from a London-based hedge fund called Stratton Street which has set a Wealthy Nations Bond fund with private bank EFG. This new fund is trying to capitalise on a specific opportunity based on value considerations – it focuses its investment selection criteria solely on bonds from countries where overall levels of indebtedness are low and yields relatively high.

The scoring system that ranks nations is especially interesting and boasts a number of overlays – the fund's managers use a range of debt measures that produce a bias towards oil-rich states for instance. Oil-rich countries such as Qatar and the United Arab Emirates are clearly not going to have problems paying down their debt – their net foreign asset position is incredibly low. Russia is another example of this relative value-based overlay built on macro-economic analysis. Mention

▶

Russian top-tier debt and most investors would reckon you were crazy, but according to Stratton Street, Russia has low overall total levels of debt and the government has explicitly said it will back the debt of its largest state-owned companies. That doesn't necessarily apply all the way down the pecking order to smaller entities but Stratton Street Capital reckon that elevated yields on offer more than compensate for the extra (low in their opinion) risk with investment grade debt.

Add this all up and you end up with an emerging markets debt fund that's paying close to 6% per annum or at least 200 basis points above most UK gilt stock, all achieved with very high credit quality, according to the managers. One of the nearest equivalent funds is an exchange traded fund from iShares which invests in a global index of emerging market government debt – this too has some big Russian debts within its portfolio but there's also plenty of stuff from much riskier (and very indebted) Turkey and Venezuela, and it's paying 200 basis points less in yield for extra risk. The Stratton Street fund managers reckon that this value-based anomaly based on what they regard as investment grade debt will be whittled away over the next few years, generating a handy 20–25% capital uplift.

Corporate bonds

These are issued by companies and corporations, large and small, from almost every sector in the global economy although some of the most popular have been issued by the large private sector banks. In many respects these bonds are almost identical in form and structure to gilts or bonds issued by governments – they feature the full range of structures, with all the same characteristics (coupons, maturities) but with one key difference, namely **risk**. Corporations and companies, banks and industrial companies – all can, and do, go bust from time to time (and especially during recessions), so that extra risk is reflected in the interest rate charged to the borrower.

The issuance of corporate bonds has expanded massively in the last decade as Figure 3.8 from Barclays Capital shows – that growth in the total stock of bonds isn't surprising given the obvious advantages of bonds.

Investors have flooded into funds comprised of corporate bonds for a wide range of reasons including:

■ They're another form of bond with different risk characteristics compared to gilts, thus allowing the investor to build a diversified portfolio of bonds from different issuers.

■ Most corporate bonds provide an income that is both steady and greater than that provided by government bonds.

■ Corporate bonds are also increasingly easy to trade in and out of. In fact corporate bonds are often more liquid than other securities and stocks. In the USA, for example, corporate bond trading averaged about

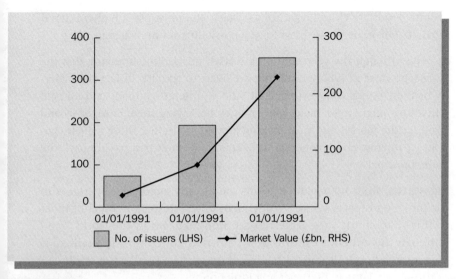

Figure 3.8   Sterling corporate bond market
Source: Barclays Capital

$15 billion per day in 2006, according to the Securities Industry and Financial Markets Association, although it is worth noting that dealing spreads for these bonds are wider than those for gilts with spreads on lower quality bonds typically 0.2% to 0.3%, compared to 0.1% for gilts. Astonishingly the highest quality segment of the corporate market (investment grade – for a description of this market see below) now exceeds the gilt market in size.

■ Risk can be easily measured. In a later section we'll look at the credit scoring system used by the likes of S&P to assess the risk of investing in a particular bond. These measures are now widely used and understood, and investors can sensibly assess the basic risk of a corporate bond within just a few seconds. Other factors being equal, the better a bond's credit quality, the lower the credit spread. Broadly speaking, lower-rated corporate bonds (BBB rated) do, on average, trade on lower prices and higher yields compared to highly-rated, low-risk bonds with a rating of AAA.

Within this vast global universe of corporate bonds you'll encounter two basic distinctions – that between investment grade and speculative grade (also known as high-yield or 'junk') bonds. The first category of bonds (investment grade bonds) itself encompasses a vast range of 'risk levels' (see our discussion of credit ratings later in the chapter) whilst speculative bonds or junk bonds are clearly regarded as riskier, and must pay a higher interest rate to compensate the investor for the possibility of future default.

In reality though the very term junk is itself misleading, implying that the issuers are close to rubbish and thus are likely to go bust. In fact the majority of these bonds will never default, and all interest coupons end up paid – investors might even make some money by buying them cheaply second hand on the market and then waiting around (collecting those regular coupons or interest rate payments) until they redeem at par, paying back the entire principal.

Many large fund management firms are already aggressive operators in the junk bond space. We've already mentioned PIMCO a number of times in this chapter – it's the largest bond fund manager in the world – and although this American firm is best known as an investor in high-grade government bonds, it's also a big fan of investing a small amount of your portfolio in relatively high yielding junk bonds.

The case for investing in junk bonds

The biggest attraction of junk bonds is the relatively chunky yield. According to PIMCO:

> For much of the 1980s and 1990s, high yield bonds typically offered about 300 to 400 basis points of additional yield relative to Treasury securities of comparable maturity... according to [investment bank] Merrill Lynch, high yield bonds offered about 306 basis points of additional yield relative to Treasuries as of Sept. 30, 2005.
>
> (http://canada.pimco.com)

But the attractions of junk bonds don't stop with the yield on offer – investors can also make some big capital gains as these bonds increase in price. This capital uplift can happen after the bonds are upgraded by ratings agencies or because an economic upturn boosts the confidence and underlying profitability of the companies that issue the bonds. According to PIMCO 'high yield bond prices are much more sensitive to the economic outlook and corporate earnings than to day-to-day fluctuations in interest rates. In a rising-rate environment, as would be expected in the recovery phase of the economic cycle, high yield bonds would be expected to outperform many other fixed income classes' (Ibid.). Last but no means least, junk bonds also offer some diversification benefits to investors – the high-yield sector generally has a low correlation to other sectors of the fixed income market.

The risks are also equally obvious. Clearly the chance of default by the issuer is greater compared to investment grade bonds, and very likely to grow as an economy slips into recession. It's also important to realise that if a company's financial health deteriorates credit rating agencies may downgrade the bonds, which can knock prices. Perhaps most importantly PIMCO itself notes that 'companies rated below investment-grade may be more negatively affected by economic downturns and adverse market conditions than those with higher credit ratings' (Ibid.).

> credit rating agencies
> may downgrade
> the bonds

A huge global market for all types of bonds vs equities

Add up all these different structures and issuers and the reader can begin to understand the vast scale of the aggregate bonds space – corporate and government. There are quite literally hundreds of governments and thousands of quasi-governmental organisations (including municipalities in the USA) and tens of thousands of corporations around the world that issue bonds of one form or another. Getting a handle on just how huge this potential market is really isn't actually that easy. For example hundreds of different towns and municipalities in the USA issue their own debts, and some of them are rarely if ever traded on any public exchange, while the European Investment Bank may have several hundred bond issues trading at any one time. One recent stab at putting a total figure on the bond markets was made in a report from Merrill Lynch called 'Size and Structure of the World Bond Market: 2004' which estimated that there was about $45 trillion in global bonds outstanding at the end of 2003 – a year earlier a report by the International Monetary Authority in 2002 estimated the total amount of debt securities as around $43 trillion.

More recently a study by the McKinsey Global Institute, '$118 Trillion and Counting: Taking Stock of the World's Capital Markets', put the size of the global bond market at about $51 trillion in 2003. By comparison the global equity markets – those that trade in stocks and shares – was estimated by this same study to be worth just $32 trillion, around two-thirds the size of the global bond market. There's more detailed analysis available on who issues bonds in Figure 3.9 which is from UK investment bank Barclays Capital and shows the composition of one of their most widely followed bond indices (an index tracks the major issues of a stock or bond), namely the BarCap Global Aggregate Bond index.

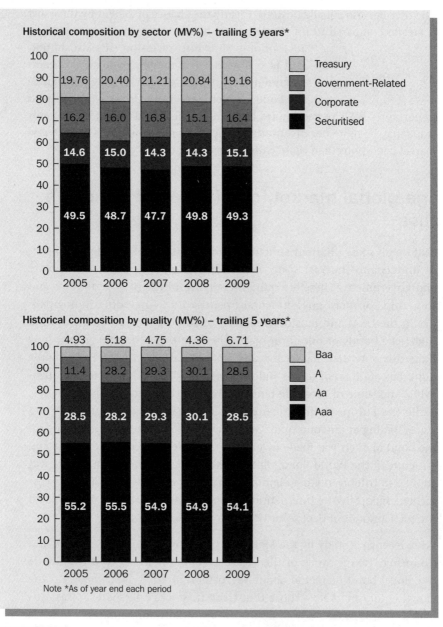

Historical composition by sector (MV%) – trailing 5 years*

Historical composition by quality (MV%) – trailing 5 years*

Note *As of year end each period

Figure 3.9   The size of the global bond market – the BarCap
Global Aggregate Index

Source: Barclays Capital Indices

Measuring risk: credit ratings explained

Bond investors obsess about risk and in particular the chance that an issuer will default on their bonds. The reason for this obsession is obvious – bond investors are reluctant to take on extra risks, unlike most equity investors! Shares go up and down and companies stop paying dividends and then restart them but that large element of risk is compensated for by the potential for extra returns. Bonds by contrast are supposed to be safer and less volatile in terms of price – which also helps explain why returns on bonds have been more modest over the past few decades.

Table 3.1 is from Barclays Capital 'Annual Equity Gilt study' which looks at long-term returns from both shares and equities. Over the 82 years to 2008 equities returned an average of 7.1% per annum while bonds returned 2.3% per annum.

Table 3.1 Real investment returns to 2008

Last	10 years	20 years	50 years	82 years
Equities	4.1	8.9	7	7.1
Bonds	4.4	5.9	2.6	2.3

Source: Barclays Capital

And many analysts expect this underperformance to continue. In the USA the large stockbroker Charles Schwab recently commissioned their researchers to look into likely future returns and they suggested that bonds would continue to underperform (http://www.schwab.com/public/schwab/research_strategies/market_insight/investing_strategies/portfolio_planning/what_are_the_long_term_market_prospects_for_stocks_and_bonds.html).

■ The Schwab study suggested that 'the average return on large-cap stocks are estimated to be about 7.3% per year in the long term (which we define to be 20 years).

■ Mid/small-cap and international stocks are estimated to return about 8.6% and 7.4%, respectively.

■ Bonds are estimated to earn about 3.8% per year in the long term.

Those lower returns are a simple function of risk – the riskier an asset, the greater the chance for potential returns and losses. Chart the annual gains and losses of equities over the past hundred years and an investor in equities would have put up with many, many years where annual losses totalled more than 20% (and a few where they totalled more than 40%). With bonds, by contrast, any charting of annualised returns would show a massive cluster around -15% and +20%. There are *no* years where returns from the Barclays Capital indices show bonds lost more than 20% yet there are a few years where returns exceeded 20%. Even in the last 20 years of returns shown in Figure 3.10, bonds have not lost more than 10% in one year. In essence bonds are less risky and thus less rewarding.

So, risk really matters to investors in bonds and that means they need a reliable way of measuring risk. Luckily this is available through the research of a number of different credit rating agencies – namely S&P, Moody's and Fitch. Each of the agencies has their own specific measures and methodology but they all produce ratings that tend to cluster together and roughly mean the same thing. In Table 3.2 we've compared each of the ratings as they move from the highest grade (safest) which is usually AAA through to lowest grade which is a company in default (usually marked C or D). Investors need to understand that these ratings can change over time. As an example the government of South Korea found itself downgraded from AA- to BBB- in a matter of a few years. The key to this very dynamic process is a regular programme of research.

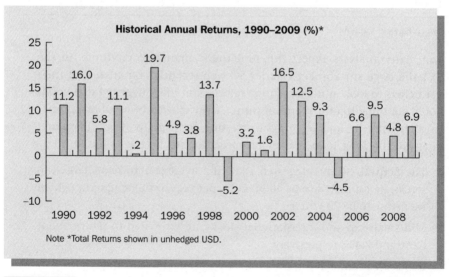

Note *Total Returns shown in unhedged USD.

Figure 3.10   Returns from the BarCap Bonds Index between 1990 and 2009

Source: Barclays Capital Indices

Here's S&P's research (www.standardandpoors.com):

■ Issuer requests a rating prior to sale or registration of a debt issue.

■ S&P analysts conduct basic research including meeting issuer to review in detail the key operating and financial plans, management policies, and other credit factors that have an impact on the rating.

■ Analysts present findings to S&P rating committee of five to seven expert voting members.

■ Rating decided by rating committee.

■ Issuer notified and has the opportunity to appeal prior to the rating publication.

■ Rating is published.

■ Issues are monitored by S&P for at least one year from date of publication. The issuer can elect to pay S&P to continue surveillance thereafter. It is worth noting the relevance of credit ratings in accounting. FRS17 requires the yield on AA rated corporate bonds to be used as the benchmark reference point for assessing liabilities. It is also worth noting that it is the market and not the credit rating that will determine the yield on individual issues. But the credit rating will influence the market yield. A change in rating for an outstanding issue is a discrete event whereas the yield will generally discount such a change over a period.

Table 3.2 Bond credit quality ratings compared: ratings agencies

Investment grade	Moody's[1]	S&P[2]	Fitch IBCA[2]
Highest grade	Aaa	AAA	AAA
High quality (very strong)	Aa	AA	AA
Upper medium grade (strong)	A	A	A
Not investment grade			
Lower medium grade	Ba	BB	BB
Low grade (speculative)	B	B	B
Poor quality and may default	Caa	CCC	CCC
Very speculative	Ca	CC	CC
No interets being paid or bankruptcy	C	D	C
In default	C	D	D

[1] The ratings from Aa to Ca by Moody's can be modified by adding 1,2 or 3 to show relative stature of the company.

[2] The ratings from AA to CC by S&P and Fitch may be modified by adding a plus or minus sign to show the relative strength within the band.

These credit ratings aren't the only measures used to assess the risk of default. Many investors, especially in the institutional space, also use credit risk measures based on swaps which price in the likelihood of default. These financial instruments are known as credit default swap spreads or CDSs. These credit derivatives were first introduced back in 1997 – these swaps are 'essentially an ... agreement/transaction between two parties, in relation to loans, bonds or other debt instruments issued by a company (often called the reference obligation)' (www.incapitaleurope.com/docs/counterparties.pdf).

On a very simplified level swaps are a form of insurance in which one organisation – the seller – offers protection against default to a buyer who wants to insure against the risk of a debtor going bust. That insurance or protection comes with a fee attached to it. When the buyer pays that fee the CDS will then compensate the seller if a credit event (a default for instance) hits the borrower.

Credit default swaps are quoted in the market as an annualised percentage spread, over LIBOR, known as the CDS spread. For example, the CDS spread quoted for a bond issued by XYZ company may be 100bps. If the CDS buyer wants to protect US$10 million investment in an XYZ bond, then the buyer has to pay the CDS seller an annual fee of US$100,000 (typically paid quarterly).

OTHER TERMS YOU MIGHT SEE USED IN THE WORLD OF BONDS

Bond discount: the bond discount is the difference between the par value and the selling price.

The credit spread: the difference between the yield on a lower-rated bond and the LIBOR rate is known as the **credit spread**.

The spread to government: this is the difference between the yield of a fixed-rate corporate bond and a government bond with a similar maturity (in the same currency).

Accrued income: accrued interest is the portion of the next coupon payment that has been earned at the time of purchase.

Accrued interest = current (principal balance) × (interest rate per year) × (amount of time)

$$I_A = F \times P \times I$$

Where:

$$I_A = \text{accrued interest}$$
$$F = \text{fraction of year}$$
$$P = \text{principal}$$
$$I = \text{annual interest rate.}$$

Treasury bills (T-bills): T-bills are obligations of the US Treasury and are equivalent to UK gilts.

Investing in bonds: challenges, opportunities and strategies

Corporate bonds – are they almost as safe as gilts?

Corporate bonds have become hugely popular over the past decade not least because of the sheer choice and range of risk profiles, maturities and, crucially, yields. Corporate bonds tend to offer a higher expected return than gilts. But that risk profile is asymmetric, with the upside limited by the gilt market, i.e. with very few exceptions most corporate bonds will never trade at a lower risk profile than the US and UK government while the downside is potentially a total loss! There are though some very high-grade investment grade corporate bonds that are closely correlated with gilts and may therefore be treated as almost the same asset class as gilts – the average correlation between investment grade corporate bonds and gilts is 90%, with 100% being perfectly correlated.

Table 3.3 Correlation between gilts and corporate bonds

Bond rating category	Average monthly correlation with gilts
AAA	93%
AA	90%
A	83%
BBB	79%
Total investment grade	90%

What about trading in international bonds?

Diversification is always a good idea in any investment portfolio but especially in bonds where the choice is so enormous. That means looking at different risk levels, different issuers and different maturities, but what about international bonds, and especially international government bonds? As we've already discussed earlier, some investors are brimming with enthusiasm for emerging markets bonds but investors don't have to travel quite that far to achieve some international diversification. Table 3.4 is from Standard and Poor's research and it shows the returns – and risks – from investing in international bonds compared to orthodox US Treasury stock. Between 2001 and 2009, for example,

investors don't have to travel far to achieve some international diversification

International Treasuries as an 'asset class' produced an annualised return of 9.1% compared to US Treasuries at 6.41% (UK returns have been close to these US returns). But those higher returns also came with the potential for greater risk– the largest loss in any one year for international treasuries was over 13% compared to just under 5% for US Treasury stock. Perhaps the most obvious portfolio risk is that of **currency risk** – if sterling strengthens against the local currency the return on that bond for a UK-based product will fall! But international bonds, especially those from outside Europe and North America present other challenges including liquidity risk – when markets are deeply uncertain it may become difficult or costly for investors to exit a position – as well as rating and credit risk. Countries can also find their debt downgraded by credit ratings agencies – as has Greece in 2010 – and that can result in falling prices and rising yields.

Table 3.4 Risk and return profile of international and US stocks and Treasury bonds

	International Treasuries	US Treasuries	International stocks	US stocks
Annualised return	9.10%	6.41%	–0.28%	–5.05%
Standard deviation	9.26%	5.28%	17.94%	15.13%
Sharpe ratio	0.664	0.661	–0.064	–0.416
Maximum drawdown	–13.63%	–4.98%	–56.43%	–50.95%

Sources: Standard & Poor's, Citigroup Index LLC and Lehman Brothers. International Treasuries are represented by the S&P Citigroup International Treasury Bond Index Ex–US, US Treasuries are represented by the Lehman US Treasury Index, US Stocks are represented by the S&P 500 and International Stocks are represented by the S&P International 700. Correlations are calculated based on monthly returns from April 2001 to February 2009.

Active or passive?

Most investors choose to invest in bonds through a diversified fund, usually actively run by a fund manager. But in recent years a new form of fund structure has emerged which involves building a diversified range of bonds by tracking a key index that comprises the most popularly traded bonds. These index tracking bond funds span every part of the spectrum of fixed income securities ranging from international index-linked government bonds through to UK corporate bonds.

These index tracking funds are called exchange traded funds or ETFs and this fast growing investment product space is dominated by one key player, iShares, which is in turn owned by Blackrock, a large American fund company that boasts its own actively managed funds. iShares' range of 40 fixed income bond funds now accounts for nearly 50% of total assets in European fixed ETFs, and assets under management have grown at a rate of 44% per year over the past two years. The largest fixed income ETF in Europe is now something called the iShares Markit iBoxx Euro Corporate Bond, which offers exposure to the largest and most liquid Euro denominated corporate bonds and has $4.5 billion in assets.

But investors have also been warming to emerging market bonds according to iShares: 'Corporate and emerging market bonds have offered relatively high yields in a generally low yield environment, and investors have used these sector ETFs to participate from the risk premium over government bonds' (www.ishares.co.uk). Table 3.5 shows the full range of iShares Bond ETFs – all feature low charges, measured as total expense ratios and are easy to trade in through a stockbroker.

Table 3.5 iShares corporate bond fund range

Fund name	Domicile	TICKER/ EPIC	Currency	Total expense	Assets (m in relevant currency)
iShares Barclays Capital $ TIPS	Irish	ITPS	USD	0.25	538
iShares Barclays Capital $ Treasury Bond 1-3	Irish	IBTS	USD	0.20	538
iShares Barclays Capital $ Treasury Bond 7-10	Irish	IBTM	USD	0.20	461
iShares Barclays Capital £ Index-Linked Gilts	Irish	INXG	GBP	0.25	487
iShares Barclays Capital Euro Aggregate Bond	Irish	IEAG	EUR	0.25	202
iShares Barclays Capital Euro Corporate Bond	Irish	IEAC	EUR	0.20	972
iShares Barclays Capital Euro Corporate Bond 1-5	Irish	SE15	EUR	0.20	43

▶

Table 3.5 continued

Fund name	Domicile	TICKER/ EPIC	Currency	Total expense	Assets (m in relevant currency)
iShares Barclays Capital Euro Corporate Bond ex-Financials	Irish	EEXF	EUR	0.20	82
iShares Barclays Capital Euro Corporate Bond ex-Financials 1-5	Irish	EEX5	EUR	0.20	57
iShares Barclays Capital Euro Government Bond 1-3	Irish	IBGS	EUR	0.20	541
iShares Barclays Capital Euro Government Bond 10-15	Irish	IEGZ	EUR	0.20	24
iShares Barclays Capital Euro Government Bond 15-30	Irish	IBGL	EUR	0.20	154
iShares Barclays Capital Euro Government Bond 3-5	Irish	IBGX	EUR	0.20	427
iShares Barclays Capital Euro Government Bond 5-7	Irish	IEGY	EUR	0.20	40
iShares Barclays Capital Euro Government Bond 7-10	Irish	IBGM	EUR	0.20	381
iShares Barclays Capital Euro Inflation-linked Bond	Irish	IBCI	EUR	0.25	685
iShares Barclays Capital Euro Treasury Bond	Irish	SEGA	EUR	0.20	10
iShares Barclays Capital Euro Treasury Bond 0-1	Irish	IEGE	EUR	0.20	21
iShares Barclays Capital Global Inflation-Linked Bond	Irish	IGIL	USD	0.25	140
iShares Citigroup Global Government Bond	Irish	IGLO	USD	0.20	336
iShares FTSE Gilts UK 0-5	Irish	IGLS	GBP	0.20	261

Table 3.5 continued

Fund name	Domicile	TICKER/ EPIC	Currency	Total expense	Assets (m in relevant currency)
iShares FTSE UK All Stocks Gilt	Irish	IGLT	GBP	0.20	377
iShares JPMorgan $ Emerging Markets Bond Fund	Irish	IEMB	USD	0.45	880
iShares Markit iBoxx $ Corporate Bond	Irish	LQDE	USD	0.20	902
iShares Markit iBoxx £ Corporate Bond	Irish	SLXX	GBP	0.20	1244
iShares Markit iBoxx £ Corporate Bond ex-Financials	Irish	ISXF	GBP	0.20	122
iShares Markit iBoxx Euro Corporate Bond	Irish	IBCX	EUR	0.20	3678
iShares Markit iBoxx Euro Covered Bond	Irish	ICOV	EUR	0.20	61

Source: iShare (www.ishares.co.uk)

The idea behind all these ETFs is to simply buy what the market is buying, by tracking the market through a major index. The advantage of this approach is that it cuts out the risks associated with an active fund manager making mistakes. This lack of 'active' management removes a key component of total costs and thus nearly all index-tracking funds are much cheaper in terms of fund management fees. But many big fund groups utilising an active approach such as PIMCO naturally see this index-tracking trend as a threat – PIMCO does issue its own ETFs but in general its suspicious of index tracking with bonds as 'the issuers or sectors with the largest debt are often the least creditworthy and the credit risk tends to increase when their market weighting is rising'. It also notes that 'active managers are free to anticipate rating upgrades and downgrades. By definition the index must follow a downgrade down, and cannot anticipate a new entrant arising from an upgrade. These are low risk opportunities to add value which are denied to the passive manager.' According to PIMCO these arguments are powerful enough to 'favour an active, as opposed to a passive, management approach'. ETF providers would argue strongly against these criticisms, pointing out that cutting costs is absolutely essential in the lower return bonds investment space. Index providers also, rightly, point out that most active fund managers don't actually produce superior performance when compared to the cheaper, dumber, passive index fund. At the end of the day investors need to make up their own minds – bond ETFs are much, much cheaper and take the risk of trusting in an active fund manager whereas active bond managers can help make sensible decisions by limiting risk (investing for instance in the most creditworthy bonds as opposed to the most traded) and can run trading strategies that can make investors money in all markets.

Trading bonds – different strategies

Investors in bonds can run a number of strategies that might make them money if they judge the wider markets correctly. Many bond investors for instance adjust the maturity structure based on anticipated changes in the yield curve, especially as economies move into recession. A slower economic growth rate, all things being equal, tends to result in lower interest rates which makes higher yielding, longer-dated securities more attractive. Another popular idea is to adjust a bond portfolio's duration. If bond

> another popular idea is to adjust a bond portfolio's duration

investors believe interest rates are about to decline, they might lengthen a portfolio's duration by selling short-term bonds and buying longer-term bonds – the longer the duration, the more price appreciation the portfolio will experience if rates decline. On the other hand, a bond manager expecting interest rates to rise would normally shorten the bond portfolio's duration through selling longer-term bonds. Changes in macro-economic growth might also prompt a strategy built around credit quality. As economic growth picks up, bond investors might start investing in lower-grade junk bonds in the hope that greater profits will boost company balance sheets and improve credit ratings.

What about tax?

Corporate bonds and other non-government bonds are treated like all other investments. Income (normally paid gross) is taxed while any capital gains are also taxable on sale. Gilts by contrast have some obvious advantages. Although income (interest) on gilts (both conventional and index-linked) is taxable on the gross amount, UK individual investors are not liable to capital gains tax or income tax on the disposal of gilts. Also no stamp duty or stamp duty reserve tax is payable on purchases or sales of gilts.

ALTERNATIVE BOND IDEAS : PART 2

MORTGAGE-BACKED SECURITIES

Some institutional investors are beginning to champion a relatively contrarian bond investment namely investing in residential mortgage backed securities or RMBS. These may be familiar to students of the 2007–09 financial crises as the 'weapons of mass destruction' that nearly brought down the western capitalist system.

On paper these seemed like a good idea when they were first created back in the 1990s. They are securitised loans in which the cash flows from various types of mortgages loans are bundled together and resold to investors as securities. More particularly RMBS bonds are securities created from the monthly mortgage payments of many residential homeowners. Mortgage lenders sell individual mortgage loans to another entity that bundles those loans into a security which in turn pays an inter-est rate similar to the mortgage rate being paid by the homeowners. In Germany this idea has another name – they're called Pfandbriefe or covered bonds (iShares, the exchange traded fund provider runs a German covered bond index tracking fund).

This securitisation of these mortgage loans into RMBS has now become utterly mainstream and is a key long-term financing tool. Mortgages are initially financed by the lender's balance sheet, but once a sufficiently large pool of mortgages has been issued, the assets are ring fenced, removed from the lender's balance sheet and transferred into a trust which is financed by RMBS investors. The trust holds the mortgages and has first recourse to the properties; however, on a day-to-day basis, the mortgages are administered by the lender as if they had never left.

Crucially the loans are 'structured' into various layers of risk, with different investors taking on different risks. The most senior bonds are typically rated AAA and benefit from several layers of protection against losses – these losses typically only occur when a property is repossessed and then sold for less than the mortgage, thereby wiping out the homeowner's equity. As losses mount, different layers or tranches of investors in these RMBS are hit, with the lowest rated losing their money first. Only when massive losses have been made are the most senior AAA rated bonds wiped out.

On paper RMBS losses should have been minimal during the global financial crisis, especially at the very senior level. Sadly, as we're nearly all aware by now, the massive housing boom in the first decade of this century (in both the US and the UK) encour-aged financial institutions to lend money to home owners who couldn't really afford their mortgages. As more and more 'sub-prime', i.e. less credit worthy and riskier mortgages were issued, house prices increased. But then an eminently predictable dis-aster struck – house prices peaked, and then started falling and many borrowers found themselves unable to pay their mortgages. Losses cascaded through these structured and securitised RMBS products, sinking supposedly safe AAA rated bonds.

Suddenly the massive Wall Street investment banks faced countless tens of billions in losses, and financial meltdown beckoned. The rest is, of course, history as the US and the UK governments stepped into the breach to rescue western capitalism. Understandably many investors now tend to fight shy of any RMBS bonds but a small UK fund management company called 24 reckons there could still be a valid bond investment idea lurking in the carnage of the sub-prime disaster. A few years back this bonds specialist launched something called the Monument Bond fund which invests in a wide range of European (mainly UK) mortgage-backed securi-ties, with well over 60% rated as AAA, i.e. the lowest risk rating possible. Table 3.6 shows the holdings in this fund as of summer 2010.

▶

Table 3.6 Top five RMBS holdings

Security	Issuer (Originator)	%
PERMM (various)	Permanent (Lloyds)	9.1
LAN (various)	Lanark (Clys & Yorks)	8.9
GRANM (various)	Granite (N Rock)	8.9
MFPLC (various)	Mount Fin (BoS)	7.9
KDRE 07-1	Kildare (ICS/BoI)	4.8

According to the fund's managers the financial crisis has exposed an interesting financial opportunity for bond investors – many of the surviving securitised mortgage structures are actually offering better credit quality than equivalent corporate bonds. The managers reckon that this specialist asset class still offers over 1100 different bonds with £1 trillion of issuance in existence. Crucially many of these securitised structures (sold as bonds) offer interest rates that are floating, i.e. they vary with interest rates and inflation. And that yield is anything between 50 and 300 basis points, i.e. 0.5% to nearly 3% higher than equivalent corporate bonds.

4

Investing in shares for a dividend

'A cow for her milk
A hen for her eggs
And a stock by heck
For her dividends'

John Burr Williams[1]

Shares can be a source of income – and a great investment!

For many the world of investing for an income simply implies hunt-ing down bonds and other fixed-income securities – only these financial instruments explicitly provide an income as the stated objective of the underlying structure. In the simple to understand world of bond investing, when a company borrows money from investors and then wraps up that loan into a bond, the entire resulting structure, called a corporate bond, is predicated on that income. Stop paying that income and the security, the bond, will collapse in value.

Equities, by contrast, are regarded by many fixed-income investors as another, almost alien, world. Stocks and shares are regarded primarily as a capital growth opportunity built around growing profits from a core trading

---

[1] 'The Theory of Investment Value', quoted in *Triumph of the Optimists* by E. Dimson, P. Marsh and M. Staunton (Princeton University Press, 2002).

business. And that assumption of great growth potential is not wrong as we shall see shortly. Study after study shows that equities have indeed been a brilliant investment over the long term, consistently beating bonds in capital growth terms.

But equities – stocks and shares – can also provide an income, and in some cases that income can be even bigger than that provided by bonds. Equities can in fact provide the elusive 'double whammy' – they provide the potential to grow your capital sum *and* provide an income. But that double opportunity comes with a fairly obvious cost – your risk increases. Remember that one of the simplest ideas of modern economics is that you can't hope to make super sized returns without taking on super-sized risks, i.e. greater risk equals potential for greater reward.

In this chapter we move away from the world of fixed income securities, of bonds, and enter another investment universe built around equities – stocks and shares. In this parallel universe to bonds the key to providing an income is provided by the humble dividend cheque, paid annually or twice yearly by the company to its shareholders.

Finding companies that pay a generous and regular dividend cheque is a potentially very rewarding exercise in two already stated ways: these generous high-yielding companies can provide a steady source of income *and* help grow your capital. But spotting these companies requires careful analysis, an understanding of different investing strategies and the use of intelligent screens or filters that sift through the massive universe of stocks to find the right companies. In this chapter we'll look at why a focus on equities can work, and we'll examine how you might build strategies that will help you spot the right kinds of company listed on the stockmarket.

In the next chapter we'll take these ideas and extend them into funds that focus on high-yielding stocks, and also look at more exotic structures that combine elements of both bonds and equities, whilst also providing a rich and stable income.

Dividend basics

Before we look in detail at why a focus on shares that produce an income might be a rewarding exercise, it's worth understanding a few basics about companies and equities. To do this we're going to look at a very simple example, popular amongst many income investors – the power company Scottish and Southern Energy, known by its ticker or stockmarket code SSE.

This private utility is hugely successful and is currently valued at over £10 billion by stockmarket investors. One reason for its popularity is that it pays out a generous dividend every six months, a dividend that is in turn backed by an even more generous stream of cash profits (also known as earnings). As this book is being written, SSE's shares are valued by the market at £11.15 each. In the last financial year (2010) SSE paid out to its shareholders a grand total of 70p in dividends. Divide that dividend payout by the share price and you have a **yield** of 6.28% per annum (70/1115 × 100 = 6.28% yield).

The board of SSE could afford to pay this dividend because it also produced profits or earnings that were equivalent to 134p per share. That means that SSE could cover its dividend payout per share more than once. Crucially, by another measure popular with analysts, SSE produced close to 180p in clear cash flow per share from its core businesses. This number basically equates to those profits per share plus the depreciation (an accounting charge) for all the equipment the company has paid out for over many years, plus a few other accounting items. Add up those profits, plus the money 'technically' put aside for that depreciation, and you can see that SSE has its dividend more than twice covered.

But it gets even better when one looks at the core business – it's a regulated utility that is legally allowed to increase its charges year in, year out based on a formula related back to inflation. It faces competition of course but its prices are basically future proofed by agreement with the government appointed regulators. That makes SSE close to a safe-ish bet in a world full of uncertainty. SSE could still get it all horribly wrong, build too many power stations and really annoy its customers but all things being equal, it has a business franchise that is close to a licence to print money!

Unsurprisingly, cautious investors, seeking a safe haven, which pays out a well-backed dividend, have flocked to the shares by their tens of thousands. They like that yield and they also like the fact that its board has a formal policy of trying to increase the dividend payout year in, year out. It's not a guarantee to increase every year but it's clearly one of the management's major objectives. In the investment trade this objective of increasing the dividend is called a **progressive dividend policy**.

Figure 4.1 is from a computer software program called Sharescope which is used by investors to monitor the market and it shows SSE's share price since 2001. As you can see, those shares have risen in value over the nine years since August 2001 from just below £7 a share to just over £11 a share. It's been a rocky ride but ultimately a rewarding one especially

Figure 4.1   Scottish & Southern Energy PLC – share price since 2001

Source: www.sharescope.co.uk

when you consider that this graph only shows the actual share price, not the cumulative total of the change in the share price plus all those dividends paid! In fact if you bought SSE shares for about £6.70 in August 2001, you'd have received over 470p in dividends in total, yet the share price has also gone up from 670p to £11.05, an increase of over 50%.

The crucial point to remember about SSE is that although it's popular and has clearly been a good news story for its long-term investors, it's not unique – far from it in fact! There are, at any time, on the UK and US stockmarket, many, many companies like SSE, with good, sound businesses, paying out well-backed dividends that are increased year in year out. In fact there are on the UK stock market just under 700 companies that pay out a dividend of some sort or another, not all of which pay as much as SSE or have been as successful as SSE as an investment. The moral of the story? There's a huge amount of choice for investors looking to build a portfolio of companies paying an income through dividends. What's even better is that long-term analysis of historical data from the stockmarkets constantly reinforces one observation: equities have been a brilliant investment over the very long term, beating even bonds. Since the Victorian era companies like SSE – which is itself a relatively new business based on mergers and acquisitions over the past few decades post privatisation – have consistently provided investors with successful investments, decade after decade.

> equities have been a brilliant investment over the very long term

Academic studies of equities as a source of long-term profits

Shares have been a great investment for those investors willing to stick with them over the very long term. In virtually every study of extremely long-term data on returns from the global stockmarkets, shares – analysts also use the terms stocks or equities interchangeably – have thumped both bonds and cash.

In the USA, Professor Jeremy Siegel has mined this rich seam of data but probably the most definitive source is a group of British academics based at the London Business School – Professor Elroy Dimson, Professor Paul Marsh and Dr Mike Staunton. In a series of papers and books (namely the seminal *Triumph of the Optimists*) they've delved back into market data all the way through to 1900 and looked at comparative returns – with fairly unequivocal conclusions.

Their most recent publication – the *Credit Suisse Global Investment Returns Sourcebook 2009* – sums it up thus:

> Over the last 109 years, the real value of equities, with income reinvested, grew by a factor of 224 as compared to 4.5 for bonds and 3.1 for bills. Figure [4.2] shows that, since 1900, equities beat bonds by 3.6% and bills by 4.0% per year. Figure [4.3] shows that the long-term real return on UK equities was an annualized 5.1% as compared to bonds and bills, which gave a real return of 1.4% and 1.1% respectively.[2]

Figure 4.2 is fairly typical of this kind of longitudinal data analysis – because it's based on this American data it's able to show data way back into the middle of the 19th century. The message is clear, namely that shares have largely moved upwards with a long-term trend return of just above 6% per annum. Other long-term studies of the US market have put the mean and median return slightly higher at just above 7%, but the message is unambiguous, namely that shares are a great long-term investment idea for those willing to take some risks. That last word is hugely important – **risk** – because you'll notice from Figure 4.2 that the line isn't smooth. Quite the contrary in fact, because in key decades like the 1930s for instance the line looks rather jagged – no prizes for guessing what produced the sharp falls in 1931 and 1936, namely the Great Depression!

---

[2] Elroy Dimson, Paul Marsh and Mike Staunton, *Credit Suisse Global Investment Returns Sourcebook 2009.*

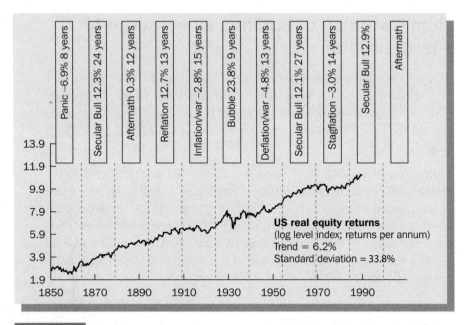

Figure 4.2   US real equity returns

Source: Elroy Dimson, Paul Marsh and Mike Staunton, *Credit Suisse Global Investment Returns Sourcebook 2009* and *Triumph of the Optimists*, Princeton University Press, 2002

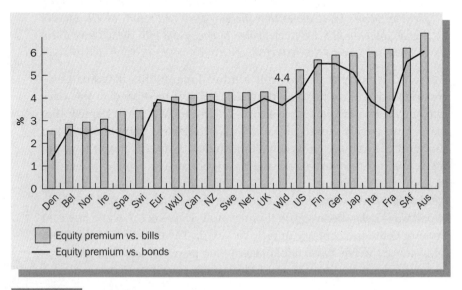

Figure 4.3   Worldwide annualised risk premiums relative to bills and bonds, 1900–2010

Source: Elroy Dimson, Paul Marsh and Mike Staunton, *Credit Suisse Global Investment Returns Sourcebook 2011* and *Triumph of the Optimists*, Princeton University Press, 2002

These 'jagged returns' remind us that shares are risky but on balance they've been worth that risk compared to supposedly safer assets like bonds and cash – in fact in the UK the return from shares has been worth about 4% extra on average since 1900, as shown in Figure 4.3. This graph shows the annualised risk premium received for investing in equities versus Treasury Bills and bonds – add 4% per annum up over 100 or more years, factor in the magic of compounding, and hey presto, shares have been the wunderkind of the investment universe!

Which shares for the long term?

These huge exercises in data mining are of course fraught with danger and difficulty: what is generally true over long periods of time for instance isn't always true during smaller periods of time. A great many analysts, like US fund manager Rob Arnott of Research Associates, have been pointing out that over the 20 years between 1989 and 2009 shares have been a lousy investment compared to bonds. Perhaps the most stunning example of this revisionism is contained within a wonderful study called 'A New Historical Database for the NYSE 1815 to 1925' by William Goetzmann, Liang Peng and Roger Ibbotson.[3] This rather dry sounding historical paper digs out data from as far back as 1815 and looks at returns up to 1925. The authors report that the capital appreciation over this period was a rather less exciting 1.24% per annum, a good 5% below most estimates for long-term equity growth. The message from the revisionists? Equities have largely been a great investment but that's not true for every period under analysis.

There is also a more insurmountable difficulty: how to access this long-term average return. Precisely because this huge mountain of data is as wide and comprehensive as possible you face the not inconsiderable problem of 'buying the long-term positive trend'. The vast majority of investors – both private and institutional – would never have been able to buy all the contents of the S&P 500 or the FTSE All Share 100 or whatever share index is tracked for their portfolio. They'd have to have waited until the very back end of the 20th century before they could buy the entire contents of an index through an index tracking fund, i.e. a period in which equities have been a dreadful performer relative to bonds according to Rob Arnott!

---

[3] Orginally published in the *Journal of Financial Markets*, March 2001; subsequently in W. N. Goetzmann and R. G. Ibbotson (eds), *The Equity Risk Premium: Essays and Explorations* (Oxford University Press, 2006).

But the Dimson, Marsh and Staunton study for Credit Suisse does provide a valuable clue as to how you might have captured this return, using a more focused strategy, but you'd have to have dug around in a companion book to their study called the *Credit Suisse Source Book 2009*. Leafing through the graph- and table-filled pages of this definitive tome you'd eventually stumble upon a chapter called 'Investment Style: Size, Value and Momentum'. In this chapter the academics begin to filter through the 'aggregate market' – in effect screening the vast universe of stocks for particular themes or characteristics – and focus on particular types of company. Their analysis suggests that much of the premium derived from investing in shares can be attributed to companies that pay out a dividend, like our example of SSE.

How might this have worked? You might have for instance picked a bunch of shares that paid out a big dividend cheque relative to the share price (giving you a big yield as a percentage) and then focused on the biggest companies as measured by their market capitalisation. The results are startling: high-yielding stocks amongst the top 100 companies between 1900 and 2008 would have given you an average annual return of 10.8% compared to 9.2% for the market and 7.7% for low-yielding stocks.

Add these numbers up and a number of conclusions emerge: that shares have in the past beaten all other asset classes; that they can be risky; but that the most rewarding have been those that paid out a dividend.

The academic evidence for why dividends matter

Why are these dividends so important? The academic literature – backed up by a mountain of analysis from City strategists like Andrew Lapthorne at SocGen – suggests that dividends benefit investors over the long term in a number of different ways.

The first and perhaps most obvious is the actual regular dividend payment as a contributor to what are called shareholder returns, but the magic of dividends doesn't stop there. There is some evidence that a strategy of buying the right kind of dividend payers (progressive dividend payers with a decent balance sheet) will actually delivers better returns in and of itself, i.e. the market itself tends to prioritise the attractions of certain dividend payers and awards their shares a premium rating. The reason for this market preference is obvious in retrospect: dividends are easy to calculate and involve simple, hard numbers made in regular payments. But dividends also tend to be much more stable over time compared to earn-

> dividends are easy to calculate and involve simple, hard numbers

ings (annual earnings growth has historically been 2.5 times more volatile than dividend growth according to SocGen) while the discipline of making the regular dividend payout encourages a more focused management, determined to conserve the financial resources of the firm. As Lapthorne at French investment bank SocGen reminds us, 'the retention of a too high proportion of earnings can encourage unnecessary mergers and acquisition (and often wasteful) investment in the pursuit of higher earnings growth'.[4] As an example of this discipline and focus it's worth noting that very few companies ever set their management teams a dividend target as a way of calculating their bonuses: the cynic might note how difficult it is too manipulate the dividend stats compared to earnings.

Dividends are boring and steady. Figure 4.4 and Table 4.1 below come from a study by French bank BNP Paribas and looks at both US and European Dividend growth over the very, very long term. The top line figure matters. Using long-term data from the US stock market, this study suggests that US equities have not only risen consistently faster

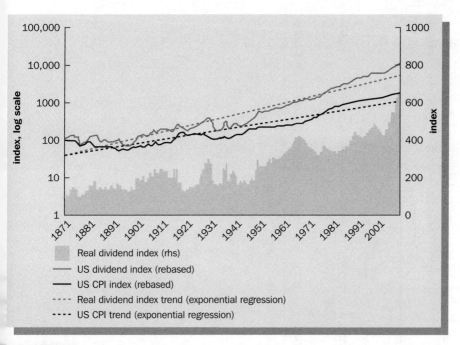

Real dividend index (rhs)
— US dividend index (rebased)
— US CPI index (rebased)
- - - Real dividend index trend (exponential regression)
- - - US CPI trend (exponential regression)

Figure 4.4   US equities real dividend growth 1871–2008: +1.4% CAGR

Source: BNP Paribas, Robert Shiller

---

[4] Quoted in article by David Stevenson in *Investors Chronicle*, 8 April 2009 (www. investerschronicle.co.uk).

Table 4.1 US, UK long-term nominal and real dividend growth

Average:	Dividend growth	Real dividend growth	Inflation rate	Earnings growth	Real earnings growth	Real GDP growth	Payout ratio	Dividend yield	10-year bond yield	Real 10-year bond yield
US:										
1871–2008	3.5%	1.4%	2.1%	2.7%	0.6%	n/a	63%	4.5%	4.7%	2.4%
1945–2007	6.2%	2.1%	4.0%	7.1%	2.9%	3.5%	50%	3.6%	5.9%	1.8%
UK:										
1970–2008	8.4%	1.9%	6.5%	9.7%	3.2%	2.4%	56%	4.4%	8.9%	2.4%

Source: BNP Paribas, Robert Shiller, Datastream

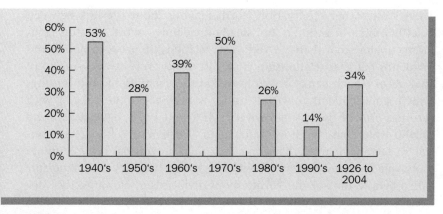

Figure 4.5   Dividend income as a percentage of monthly total return of
the S&P 500

Source: Standard & Poor's

than inflation but have increased by a fairly steady 1.4% per annum in
compound annual terms (CAGR stands for Compound Annual Growth
Rate). An extra 1.4% every year, compounded, makes a huge difference to
returns data as we shall discover.

Sadly most investors don't tend to focus on the boring old dividend
payout – they're much more enthused by the profits or earnings numbers.
But these widely followed numbers based on cash profits are also hugely
volatile. More and more analysts' now reckon that earnings estimates are
in fact so random – and so liable to sudden downwards revision – that
investors should ignore them altogether. One simple example should suffice. In 2009 analysts' estimates for global developed markets suggested
that they might be valued at anything between 8 or 13 times estimates
for earnings in 2009, i.e. they could be cheap or they could be expensive
depending on how optimistic you are!

The one key measure that many analysts keep falling back on is those dividend payouts. These twice-yearly payments are the nearest thing to a sure
thing in equity investing. They are of course to a degree dependent on profits and cashflow but many company managers are aware of their totemic
value to investors and are reluctant to cut dividend payouts even if profits
fall back. In fact a decent number of large UK companies have spent the
past 10–20 years building up a cast iron reputation for being progressive
dividend payers – always maintaining their dividend payout and increasing
it every year without fail. In a world of horrific volatility, that reputation
has a very real value, sometimes allowing the company shares to trade at a
premium as global equity income investors snap them up.

There's one other observation worth making about the link between volatile profits or earnings and steady dividends – most investors commonly assume that there's a very close relationship between profits and dividends but that relationship is not, in reality, very strong. A team of analysts at French bank SocGen looked at the volatility of both earnings growth and dividend growth. Earnings were hugely more volatile, with earnings growth oscillating between –35% and +40%, against dividend growth which has stayed in the range of –7% to +19%. In overall terms the SG team concluded that annual earnings growth has been 2.5 times more volatile than dividend growth. Crucially, when they used a measure called beta to look at the sensitivity of dividends to earnings, they discovered relatively low numbers (0 indicates no sensitivity while 1 implies absolute sensitivity) of between 0.12 and 0.50 for nearly all major equity sectors with the exception of healthcare, building and construction, and travel and leisure. The point here is that dividends don't change as much as earnings, and markets value that consistency.

Turning to the academic research on dividends it's clear that the long-term case for dividends and their importance to private investors rests on a huge range of factors – the dividend payout itself, the rating attached to a high yielder and the stable growth in the dividend payout over time. However it's the reinvestment of these dividend payouts that really makes the huge difference over time. The hard spade work on this analysis comes from the London Business School Professors Dimson, Marsh and Staunton, featured regularly in their *Credit Suisse Global Investment Returns Yearbooks*. Like many analysts they break down the long-term returns from equities into four components:

- the actual yield itself (usually compared to the risk-free rate of return from holding cash or index-linked gilts)
- the growth rate of real dividends (increased dividends above the inflation rate)
- the way that the market rewards a company because of its dividend, i.e. the rating it will give the shares via a measure like the price to dividend ratio
- and last but no means least, the reinvestment of the dividend using schemes like the dividend reinvestment investment plans or DRIPs.

According to Dimson *et al.* 'the dividend yield has been the dominant factor historically' and they add that 'the longer the investment horizon, the more important is dividend income'. Dimson's point is that, in fact, the long-term real dividend growth rate is actually only about 1% per annum and thus can't make that big a difference, while the rerating of stocks based on their multiple to dividends is also very variable over time and doesn't make that much of a difference. As the authors note 'dividends and probably earnings have barely outpaced inflation'.

But the actual payout is dwarfed by the importance of *reinvesting dividends*. Looking at the 109 years since 1900 Dimson *et al.* suggest that the average real capital gain in just stocks plus the dividend payout is about 1.7% per annum (an initial $1000 would have grown six-fold), but over the same period dividends reinvested would have produced a total return of 6% per annum (or a total gain of 582 times the original $1000). Dividend reinvestment *really* matters and luckily most big progressive dividend payers have their own easy-to-use dividend reinvestment plans.

City-based analysis of dividends

This academic research into dividends has been tested over shorter, more recent periods of time, by a number of leading investment bank economists, but particularly Tim Bond, formerly at British bank BarCap, and Andrew Lapthorne at French investment house SocGen.

Tim Bond is the author of the hugely influential annual *Equity Gilts Study*, a definitive work on long-term returns which is used by many analysts as their default reference guide. A large part of that study focuses on the relative returns of equities versus gilts but dividends feature prominently. Tim Bond summarises the conclusions of this study thus:

> *Between 1925 and 2004, dividends provided 27% of total US equity returns. In the UK, from 1899 to 2004, dividends provided 31% of total returns. Both calculations assume the reinvestment of dividends, a practice which provides a very sizeable element of long run equity returns, just as coupon reinvestment provides much of the return from bonds. To illustrate this point, consider that £100 invested in 1899 would be worth just £9,961 today without reinvestment, but a cool £1,103,668 if dividend income had been reinvested. Without reinvestment of dividends, equity returns barely beat inflation. In real terms, the £100 invested in 1899 would now be worth £170 without dividend reinvestment, but £18,875 with reinvestment.*[5]

Bond's long-term comprehensive market data very much backs up the conclusions of the London Business School (LBS) team, although his data suggests that dividends play a less important role over the short term.

---

[5] Quoted in 'Global Speculations: Dividend Delights' by Tim Bond, Barclays Capital Research (www.scribd.com/doc/19586723/Barclays-Capital-Dividend-Delights).

without constant
reinvesting back into
the shares, equities
barely hold their own
against bonds

Crucially though, Bond backs up the central idea of dividend reinvestment – without constant reinvesting back into the shares, equities barely hold their own against bonds. But Bond's analysis also reminds us that dividend importance varies hugely over time – in recent years dividends have mattered much less:

The contribution of dividend income to total UK equity returns fell to an all-time low in 2000 [see Figure 4.6], at the peak of the bubble, as payout ratios drifted down and investors focussed on the rampant price gains delivered by soaring valuations. At the margin, changes in the UK tax treatment of dividends for pension funds in 1997 reduced investors' preference for dividend income, whilst changes in corporate taxation had much the same effect in the late 1980s in the US.[6]

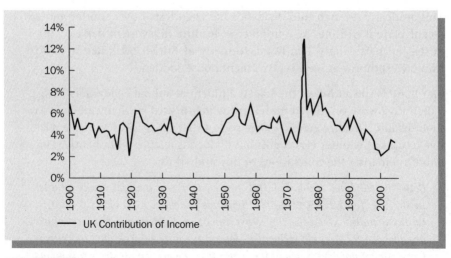

Figure 4.6 Contribution of dividend income to UK equity total returns, 1900–2004

Source: Barclays Capital Equity Gilt Study

The BarCap analysis has one other crucial observation worth noting in passing – dividends are a good hedge against inflation, i.e. they tend to increase with inflation. The BarCap study observes that:

Annual changes in dividends display a moderately positive correlation with inflation, averaging 38% over the 1950–2004 period in the UK and 26% in the US. When changes in dividends and inflation are considered over longer

---

[6] Ibid.

periods of time, the correlation improves, as would be expected from a volatile series. Over 5 year periods, the correlation is 54% in the UK and 52% in the US, whilst over 10 years the correlation is 56% in the UK and 70% in the US.[7]

Andrew Lapthorne at French bank SocGen has echoed many if not all the conclusions of both Tim Bond and the LBS team. His key observation over the post-war period is that most real returns have not been from share price appreciation but almost exclusively dividends and their subsequent growth and reinvestment. He summarises his case for what he calls **income investing** through dividends, thus:

1 *The bulk of historical real returns have come from re-invested dividends. Using data back to the 1970s, this ranges from 56% of total returns in Japan to 96% in the UK.*

2 *A strategy of buying above average yielding stocks has strongly outperformed buying those with below average yields.*

3 *With bank deposits currently earning very little interest, many will be pushing equities (with their higher yields) as a more attractive (albeit far riskier) proposition.*

4 *Dividend yields are easy to calculate. Dividends are also far more stable than earnings during downturns – annual earnings growth has historically been 2.5 times more volatile than dividend growth.*

5 *Dividend payments should encourage management discipline. The retention of a too-high proportion of earnings can encourage unnecessary M&A [Mergers & Aquisitions] (and often wasteful) investment in the pursuit of higher earnings growth.*[8]

Lapthorne and his quantitative team at SocGen (SG) have focused their analysis on data from global markets since 1970. Their analysis has some different twists and turns compared to both BarCap and the LBS study. The SG team reckons that the actual dividend yield represented just 30% of the nominal returns versus 70% for dividend growth, with their analysis suggesting that real dividend growth has been closer to 1.2% over the period. Looking at the UK, the SG team reckon that of total annualised equity returns since 1970 of 11.4%, the actual dividend yield accounted for 4.3% per annum, dividend growth 8% per annum, and multiple expansion (a higher or lower share price to dividend yield) –1.1%, i.e. high-yielding shares were actually rated lower by the market.

* Barclays Capital Equity Gilt Study 2010, www.barcap.com.
‡ 'Rock steady income? Seeking an Optimal income investing strategy', *The Global Income Investor*, SG Quantitative Research, 3 February 2009.

Citi on dividends

It's worth noting the analysis of one last team of investment bank strategists working on dividends, and why they matter – those at American bank Citi led by Rob Buckland. Yet again Buckland and his team declare that '**dividends matter**' observing that:

> They have been an important contributor to historical equity market returns. Since 1970 they have made up 30% of the annualised total return from global equities [see Figures 4.7 and 4.8]. Contribution to individual markets has been greater. In the UK it was 37% of the return. But their importance increases dramatically during periods of equity market weakness. In the 2000s they contributed 144% of global equity return (i.e. the capital return has been negative). While in the 1970s it was nearly 60%.[9]

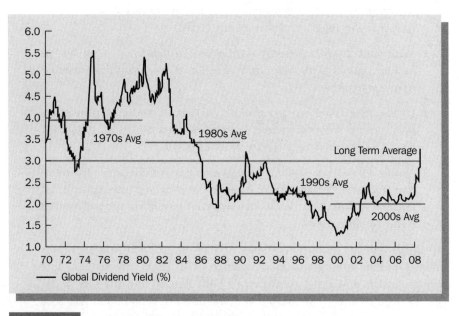

Figure 4.7   **MSCI world trailing dividend yield and averages (%)**
Source: MSCI, Citi Investment Research

The Citi team make one crucial additional point – that stock selection built around high yielding stocks has also been a very profitable strategy:

> From an investment perspective dividend yield strategies have also proved profitable for investors. For example, since inception the MSCI World High

---

[9] 'Global Equity Strategist, Dividend Resilience' by Robert Buckland, Citibank, 30 September 2008 (http://icg.citi.com).

Dividend Yield Index has fairly consistently outperformed the MSCI World, both through good and bad times [see Figure 4.9].[10]

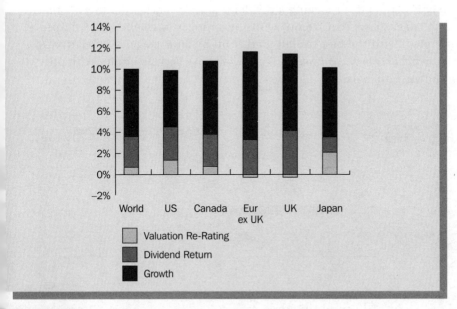

Figure 4.8   **Contribution to equity market returns**
Source: MSCI, Citi Investment Research

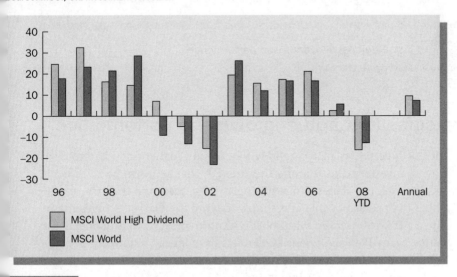

Figure 4.9   **MSCI high dividend yield index performance (%)**
Source: MSCI, Citi Investment Research

[10] Ibid.

This point is rammed home in the next graph from the Citi team (see Figure 4.10) which looks at different regions around the world and their relative strength in making a dividend payout. Buckland observes that the table 'shows that regions with the strongest dividends have outperformed, with the best overall market up by an average 18% relative. *It hasn't paid to own the dividend laggards.* All have been associated with price underperformance.'[11]

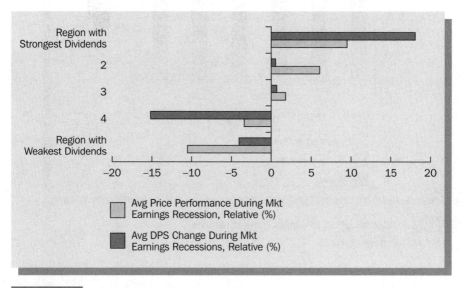

Figure 4.10   Regional dividends and performance

Source: MSCI, Citi Investment Research

Strategies for capturing dividend performance

All this investment analysis and wisdom won't matter one iota though if private investors can't capture the strength that seems to be so inherent in high-yielding shares. Unsurprisingly, most academic theorists suggest doing as little as possible and simply 'buying the market' – investing in, say, a FTSE 100 tracker will probably capture most of that dividend premium. Many IFAs and financial planners have indeed followed this advice and invested a large amount of clients' money into equity-based funds that track simple, dividend-weighted indices like the FTSE UK Dividend Plus,

[11] Ibid.

tracked by an iShares ETF (Exchange-Traded Fund), with disastrous results as can be seen from Figure 4.11 which tracks this very popular index.

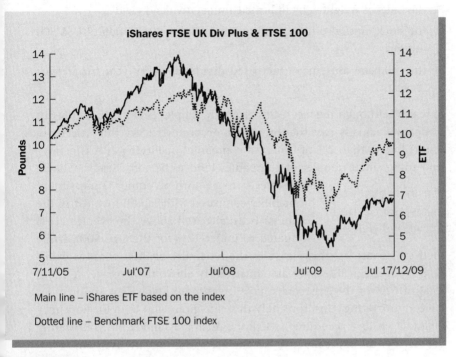

iShares FTSE UK Div Plus & FTSE 100

Main line – iShares ETF based on the index

Dotted line – Benchmark FTSE 100 index

Figure 4.11   **UK Dividend Plus**

Source: www.sharescope.co.uk

The poor, relative performance of this index and the accompanying ETF has prompted many investment professionals to look for more subtle ways of tracking high yielding stocks. Index and research firm Standard and Poor's in the US has introduced a rather novel alternative take on the same idea, this time by focusing on only those stocks that consistently increase their dividend yield over time. Back in 2005 they launched something called the S&P High Yield Dividend Aristocrats index, which according to the developers is 'designed to measure the performance of the 50 highest dividend yielding S&P Composite 1500 constituents which have followed a managed dividends policy of consistently increasing dividends every year for at least 25 years',[12] i.e. only those large companies paying an above average yield, consistently over time.

---

[12] From S&P Research Paper 'The S&P High Yield Dividend Aristocrats Index' by Srikant Dash (www.standardandpoors.com).

For a share to get into the index, the company must pass a simple set of tests which include:

■ the index is weighted by indicated annual dividend yield

■ the stock must also have a minimum market capitalisation of US$ 500 million

■ the *company* must have increased dividends every year for at least 25 years.

In reality, although the test seems elegantly simple, only a tiny number of companies actually pass the thresholds. According to S&P this 'selectivity results in less than 2% of US listed companies qualifying as Aristocrats'. And those small number of companies tend to be very steady, reliable

unsurprisingly this elite group also tend to sport juicy dividend yields

companies – their return on equity (a measure of profitability compared with capital invested in the business) is usually well above the average (15% compared to under 12% for the S&P 500), while their credit ratings (this measures the reliability of their debts as measured by agencies like S&P) are consistently above the average. A grand total of 62% of the Aristocrats have investment grade debt and just 8% have a junk rating. Unsurprisingly this elite group also tend to sport juicy dividend yields – according to S&P the Aristocrats index has consistently delivered yields in the range of 3.2% to 4.2% over the past five years.

The acid test of this kind of simple index though has to be returns. S&P did test it over the five years up to inception in 2005 and found that over those five years the annualised return was over 14% compared to –1% for the wider S&P 500 benchmark index. The risk inherent in these returns – as measured by something called standard deviation – was also much lower than the S&P 500.

Backtests are of course always informative but rarely that useful until the strategy is actually implemented, at which point, curiously, many successful concepts proceed to break down! The S&P Aristocrats by contrast does seem to have been moderately successful in the US. The most recent analysis at the end of September 2009 revealed that the index had fairly consistently beaten the S&P 500 benchmark index, with much less risk (see Table 4.2 for returns and Table 4.3 for companies in the index).

Table 4.2 S&P US Aristocrats Index portfolio statistics

Index performance	3rd quarter 2009	YTD to 30 Sept 2009	12 months	3 years	5 years	10 years
S&P 500 Dividend Aristocrats	19.29%	19.84%	0.56%	−1%	4.04%	2%
S&P 500	15.61%	19.26%	−6.9%	−5.43%	1.02%	0.51%
Standard Deviation	3 year	5 year	10 year			
S&P 500 Dividend Aristocrats	19.18%	15.32%	14.7%			
S&P 500	19.68%	15.96%	16.24%			

Source: S&P Global Strategies Report, September 2009 (www.standardandpoors.com/indices/sp-500-dividend-aristocrats/en/us/?indexid=spusa-500dusdff--p-us----)

Table 4.3 Top ten companies in the index

Name	Weight	Sector
Gannett Co Inc	2.51%	Con Discretionary
Walgreen Co	2.14%	Consumer Staples
Abbott Laboratories	2.12%	Healthcare
Centurytel Inc	2.09%	Telecom Services
Chubb Corp	2.02%	Financials
Questar Corp	2.01%	Utilities
Kimberly-Clark	2.01%	Consumer Staples
Clorox Co	2.00%	Consumer Staples
Avery Dennison Corp	2.00%	Industrials
Sigma-Aldrich Corp	2.00%	Materials

Source: S&P Global Strategies Report, September 2009 (www.standardandpoors.com/indices/sp-500-dividend-aristocrats/en/us/?indexid=spusa-500dusdff--p-us----)

Standard and Poor's have also recently launched a European version of this index[13] called the S&P Europe 350 Dividend Aristocrats. This features a slightly different strategy – two measures feature in the screen through the wider market:

1 Each company must be a member of the S&P Europe 350 index of largest blue chip companies on the mainland and the UK.

2 Each company must have increased dividends for at least ten consecutive years.

The resulting index is equal weighted and constituents are reviewed annually in December. The constituents from this index at the end of September 2009 are shown in Table 4.4.

Table 4.4 Constituents of the S&P Europe 350 Dividend Aristocrats

Name	Weight	Sector	Country
Legal & General Group	2.99%	Financials	UK
Man Group	2.82%	Financials	UK
Novartis AG	2.73%	Cons Stpls	Switzerland
Misys	2.72%	Info Tech	UK
Gas Natural SDG SA	2.71%	Utilities	Spain
Daily Mail & General Trust	2.71%	Cons Discretionary	UK
Abertis Infraestructuras	2.69%	Industrials	Spain
Essilor Intl	2.67%	Healthcare	France
KBC Group NV	2.62%	Financials	Belgium
Scottish & Southern Energy	2.61%	Utilities	UK

Source: www.standardandpoors.com

Intriguingly returns from this European strategy have been noticeably less impressive (see Table 4.5). The index has only been either in backtest or in actual implementation for five years through to September 2009 and although results in 2008 and 2009 were impressive, returns for the first three years were very poor with significant underperformance.

[13] S&P Research Paper 'S&P Europe 350 Dividend Aristocrats' by Aye M. Soe (www.standardandpoors.com) (212) 438-1677 aye_soe@sandp.com).

Table 4.5 S&P European Aristocrats Index portfolio statistics

Index performance	3rd quarter 2009	YTD to 30 Sept 2009	12 months	3 years	5 years
S&P European Dividend Aristocrats	25%	42%	12.88%	–3.5%	6.18%
S&P Europe 350	23.21%	31%	2.6%	2.92%	7.08%
Standard Deviation	3 year	5 year			
S&P European Dividend Aristocrats	25.22%	20.67%			
S&P Europe 350	25.76%	21.54%			

Source: www.standardandpoors.com

The UK members of the S&P 350 European Dividend aristocrats in 2008 are shown in the box below

---

UK DIVIDEND ARISTOCRATS

Barclays	Hammerson	Centrica
Cobham	Legal and General	Next
Capita Group	Misys	Pearson
CRH	National Grid	Rexam
Daily Mail	Scottish and Southern Energy	Royal Dutch Shell
MAN Group	WPP	Tesco
Enterprise Inns	British American Tobacco	Vodafone Group
FirstGroup	British Land Company	

Investment strategies focused on yield – Progressive Dividend Heroes

The problem with many of these special indices and new ideas is that the markets are so fluid and volatile that everything can literally change overnight with the biggest risk, simple non-payment. In the box on page 135 we outline some of the issues facing investors looking for a secure income from dividends. Take a look at the S&P list of British Dividend Aristocrats, for instance, and you might notice banks like Barclay – which stopped paying its dividend in 2009 – as well as property companies like British Land and Hammerson. Investors need to take a backwards look at dividend consistency *and* a forward look at projected dividends growth, otherwise they could find themselves investing in companies like GKN and AngloAmerican where the dividend has been stopped despite many years of heroic consistency.

We've tried to build this thinking into a simple filter – we call it the Progressive Dividend Heroes – which looks at the FTSE 100 universe and then systematically excludes any company that doesn't fit the following criteria:

- We looked at the more recent past – the past eight years for instance – and excluded any company which hasn't increased its dividend year on year over those eight years.
- Crucially we looked at forward projections of dividend growth by analysts and only included those where dividends are set to increase. Bear in mind though that this is only an *estimate* and that analysts could have got it wrong!
- We've also only included companies where there is a stated dividend policy. This will usually consist of a simple commitment to growing real sterling dividends (Pennon for instance is committed to growing it at 3% per annum), or possibly a committment to paying a fixed percentage of earnings.
- Only companies with a proper dividend reinvestment plan have been included.

When this screen was run in late 2009 (September) the resulting shortlist comprised just 16 companies in the FTSE 100 and their details are shown in Table 4.6 alongside some other key measures, including:

- The potential foreign exchange (FX) risk – how much of the business is conducted outside of the UK. If a large portion of turnover is derived in dollars and euros this opens the company up to some risk if the exchange risk goes against them (the opposite has been happening in the past six months). Most companies will aggressively hedge away this exposure but it's estimated that upto 60% of the entire earnings flow in the FTSE 100 is based on foreign earnings.
- We've also included a measure for cash flow per share in the most recent accounts – this shows you how much the dividend per share is covered by operating cash inflows. As long as its above 1 the company can afford the payment and anything above 2 is pretty safe.

■ Pension scheme liabilities also matter hugely. The Pensions Regulator has already warned that companies are expected to sacrifice their dividends before they cut pensions payments, so a company with a high deficit is potentially risky. None of our shortlisted dividend heroes seems to be in too much trouble.

■ Last but by no means least we've also included the level of gearing – this could be an indicator of future trouble if the SocGen analysis is correct, although it's worth cautioning that many utilities have high levels of regulated debt that are comfortably backed by both real assets and growing earnings.

As to returns, it's worth stating one very simple fact: over the eight-year span the FTSE All Share index had declined by just over 11% in total returns terms (dividends included) yet our progressive heroes have returned to investors an average gain of 30% in total. But that average total return increases to an impressive 61% if you have reinvested the dividends paid out by our heroes. You would have doubled your total returns if you had reinvested through the companies' dividend reinvestment plans.

The Weiss Income Screen

Another alternative take on a dividends-based strategy comes from an investment writer based in the US called Geraldine Weiss. Editor since 1966 of newsletter *Investment Quality Trends*, she's been dubbed the 'the Grande Dame of Dividends' and has promoted one simple message – dividends don't lie. She was once quoted as saying 'my father told me that he would never buy a stock unless it paid a dividend. He believed that companies that did not share profits with stockholders in that way were not worth investing in.'[14]

Her belief is that the level of a stock's dividend yield shouldn't just be seen as an income stream (though there's nothing wrong with that per se), but as a measure of valuation. For that reason, she targets stocks with dividend yields at the high end of their historic ranges, and trading at comparatively low prices. But Weiss wants more. Her chosen stocks must also have other favourable characteristics, such as a dividend that is well protected by earnings of some sort, plus a relatively low level of debt. But the key measure for Weiss is something called

the key measure for Weiss is something called the dividend cover

---

[14] In 'The Duchess of Dividends' by Marla Brill (www.fa-mag.com).

Table 4.6 The resulting shortlisted dividend heroes

Name	EPIC	Close	Cash flow per share (P)	Cash cover on dividends	Net gearing %	Total gain without reinvesting	Total gain with reinvesting	Pension deficit
BP PLC	BP	4.5475				5.33%	26.60%	$301m deficit
British Land Co PLC	BLND	4.02	58.6	1.67	74.4	25.80%	38.75%	Na
Centrica PLC	CNA	2.5975	50.9	4.4	26.6	20.47%	40.78%	£97m surplus
Diageo PLC	DGE	8.3	63	1.83	186	33.14%	65.51%	£477m deficit
FirstGroup PLC	FGP	2.6675	87.3	5.13	320	33.97%	58.39%	£89m surplus
GlaxoSmithKline PLC	GSK	11.06				19.31%	34.73%	£285m UK deficit
ICAP PLC	IAP	2.065	43.7	2.79	7.18	65.22%	104.42%	£1m deficit
Imperial Tobacco Group PLC	IMT	16.6	141	2.23	184	65.98%	155.81%	£105m deficit
Marks & Spencer Group PLC	MKS	2.51	59	2.62	128	41.23%	67.39%	
National Grid PLC	NG	6.19	212	6.42	388	27.11%	55.22%	
Pearson PLC	PSON	6.33	64.9	2.05	28.4	13.03%	24.42%	NA
Pennon Group PLC	PNN	4.28	67.6	3.41	275	56.57%	129.98%	£58m deficit
Sage Group (The) PLC	SGE	1.66	19.4	2.69	41.6	6.96%	11.77%	NA
Schroders PLC	SDR	7.01				13.24%	23.66%	NA
Scottish & Southern Energy PLC	SSE	11.27	134	2.21	123	51.18%	111.97%	£211m deficit
Vodafone Group PLC	VOD	1.2265	19.5	2.6	32.7	13.92%	25.06%	
					average	30.78%	60.90%	

over 8 years to 1 March 2009

the dividend cover – it can't be paying out more in dividends than total earnings. Her logic is undeniable: if a company isn't making money, it stands to reason that it will have trouble paying dividends. That means a dividend cover of at least 2 is absolutely essential, i.e. that for every £1 dividend there's £2 of earnings. She's also a fairly unashamed blue chip investor and usually insists on a minimum market capitalisation of at least $100 million or even $500 million. Weiss also stipulates that the share price must not exceed two times book value, and it must sell for 20 times earnings or less.

To get into her elite final selection a stock also has to meet one last crucial criteria – it has to have raised its dividends at a compound annual rate of at least 10% over the past 12 years. Tough but it seems rewarding. Since 1986 *The Hulbert Financial Digest* – the oracle of investment returns based on gurus' musings – reckons her recommended stocks gained 12.2%, beating the 10.9% annualised gain of the Wilshire Index over the same period. Crucially Hulbert reckons her picks were 27% less volatile than the index, and her newsletter performed better than each of the 42 others tracked by Hulbert over the period on a risk adjusted basis.

But Weiss's methods are increasingly not suited to a (US) market that believes dividends are a signal of failure. Over the past decade yields have been steadily falling as companies have stopped paying them. Their defence? Better to take surplus profits and reinvest them in the business to grow profits. As yields tumbled below 6% and then 3%, Weiss grew increasingly bearish. Since the end of the 1990s she has argued that the whole market was overvalued and advised her readers to put as much as 70% of their money into cash. That meant they'd have missed the crash of 2001 and 2008 but also the subsequent massive rallies and bull markets, thus missing out on some huge profits! And Weiss hasn't changed her view since the 1990s. In one recent interview she noted that although 'the yield profile of the Dow has evolved ... There could certainly be a new paradigm for the Dow in which a 1.5% yield signals overvaluation and a yield of 3% would mean undervaluation.'[15] To describe this as a tad bearish is perhaps the understatement of the century. Her view also crucially ignores the increasing importance of share buybacks in the US which some analysts[16] maintain could, if added to dividends as a measure of shareholder returns, double the yield again bringing it back within the normal historical range.

---

[15] *Forbes* magazine (www.forbes.com/2002/02/12/0212adviser.html).

[16] Such as Chris Dillow in the *Investors Chronicle* Op Ed column on 1 October 2004.

A strategy for finding Weiss Blue Chips

Running a Weiss screen in the UK is fairly straightforward, but does involve a few minor alterations from her US-based approach. Investors should focus on a number of key measures or screens:

- The dividend yield should be above the average for the market.
- Dividend cover should be at least 2 – that is dividends are covered at least twice by earnings.
- The minimum market cap should be at least £100 million.
- The PE ratio should be at least positive and there should be some evidence that the firm has been growing earnings per share over the past three to five years, on average.

Turning to the balance sheet, Weiss suggests a number of other crucial measures:

- Net gearing should be less than 50% to avoid companies with too high a level of debt.
- There should be some evidence of positive cashflow at the operating level.
- The current ratio should be above 1.
- The share price should be no more than twice the level of tangible assets.

Armed with an initial shortlist, Weiss then recommends that investors investigate the successful companies in much greater detail, in particular examining whether that crucial dividend payout is viable. According to Weiss investors need to see five years of continuous dividend payments that have been increasing year on year. This is a tough requirement and the vast majority of firms can never hope to meet this but it's a great way of finding firms that take dividends and shareholder rewards seriously.

Weiss wants stocks that simply won't vanish. She wants stability and stature. That means she also wants some evidence that the big institutions like the stock. Her suggested requirement is that at least three big institutions hold above 10% of the stock, or ideally 50%. This last requirement can be a little daunting but most stocks that have passed all these demanding requirements will have heavy institutional backing anyway.

WHAT TO WATCH OUT FOR WHEN HUNTING DOWN DIVIDEND STOCKS!

Dividends may have a great many obvious attractions but they are not without their challenges and concerns. Rob Buckland from Citi reminds his clients that:

> any dividend based analysis should recognise that attitudes to dividends vary between both markets and companies. Companies in some regions place little emphasis on dividends, either because they can't pay them or because they believe investors will be better served through cashflow being re-invested into the business. Furthermore, taxation legislation may mean that stock buybacks are a better and more flexible way to return capital to shareholders (this was the case in the US in the late 1990s when capital gains taxes were only 20% (long-term) versus a 39.5% income tax rate on dividends). Also, buyback programmes can be abandoned more easily than dividend payments. The UK, on the other hand, has a strong dividend paying culture, despite the fact that taxation on dividends is onerous.

Dividends can also change over time – and be suddenly cut back in a recession. Back in 2009 for instance dividend hero General Electric announced out of the blue that it had cut the quarterly payout from 31 to 10 cents a share in the second half, its first dividend cut since 1938. And General Electric was far from being the only major company to cut dividends in a recession – at least three major FTSE 100 companies slashed their dividends in 2009. According to a report from Buckland's team at Citibank Research in 2009: 'the key swing factors in the [FTSE 100] dividend are the oil price, the dollar/sterling exchange rate and the state of the financial system'. According to research by ING Wholesale Banking in 2009 of the 59 large-cap European stocks that had declared dividends by the middle of the year nearly half had either cut their dividends or omitted them entirely. Many in France also cut back cash payments, and brought in scrip payments, where the dividend is paid out in cash instead.

That sudden decline in dividend payments, not unnaturally, caused much concern in the financial markets – and especially in a niche market that trades swap financial instruments which track the estimated dividend payout in any one year. At the end of 2009 this specialist market was pricing in a 31% drop in European dividends from 2008 to 2009, and then a 48% drop from 2009 to 2010. These might seem like disastrous numbers but stockmarket historians are always quick to remind us that previous bear markets have also taken their toll on dividend payouts. As the world reeled from the 1973 oil shock, for example, dividends from companies in the benchmark S&P 500 index fell from more than 60% of earnings in 1970 to 37% in the second quarter of 1974.

Table 4.7 shows total dividend payouts for all FTSE 100 companies over the time period shown.

But it's not just falling or vanishing dividend payouts that investors need to be wary about. They also need to be incredibly careful about an undue concentration on just a few big companies, nearly all of which earn most of their profits in foreign currencies, with more than a few focused on oil (another toxic asset class). According to research from Citibank again, *just seven companies contributed half of the total UK dividend base in 2009*. Their analysis suggests that of the total dividend base 37% is paid in dollars, while about 25% is from the oil sector. Citibank's bottom line: 'A sharp fall in Oil price below $40 a barrel would make the sustainability of the dividends questionable.' Table 4.8 shows the UK dividend base.

▶

Table 4.7 Total FTSE 100 payment falling fast

	Forecast (£)	Exchange rate
Dec-07	72,377	2.0434
Jan-08	68,475	1.9587
Feb-08	69,886	1.9484
Mar-08	71,202	2.0125
Apr-08	71,349	1.9746
May-08	70,582	1.9608
Jun-08	71,451	1.9538
Jul-08	71,330	1.9773
Aug-08	72,702	1.9127
Sep-08	74,881	1.7596
Oct-08	68,402	1.6975
Nov-08	66,735	1.5626
Dec-08	67,329	1.4834

Source: Rob Davies, manager of the Munro Fund

And as for a quick and sudden strengthening in the sterling rate against the dollar – the conse-quences could be cataclysmic. GlaxoSmithKline noted in their 2008 annual report that every 10 cents movement in the cable rate (sterling versus dollar) has a direct 3.5% affect on earnings, even after their extensive hedging operations. With just £620 million of their £19 billion sales made in the UK, one can understand that caution. A run on the dollar which pushed the cable rate back to $2 could directly hit EPS by between 15 and 20%, with possible knock-on effects on the dividend.

Table 4.8 UK dividend base 2008E–09E (£ unless indicated)

Stock	2008	2009	% of 2008 FTSE 100 dividend	% of 2009 estimated dividend
HSBC	6,024	7,395	10	11
BP	5,719	7,392	10	11
Royal Dutch Shell	5,572	7,063	9	11
Vodafone Group	4,101	4,306	7	7
GlaxoSmithKline	3,092	3,354	5	5
AstraZeneca	1,679	2,539	3	4
BAT	1,669	1,897	3	3
BT Group	1,231	724	2	1

Source: Citi Investment Research

And if all this wasn't bad enough the pensions regulatory body in the UK has chipped in with its own (negative) thoughts on the future of the dividend. David Norgrove, chairman of the Pensions Regulator, told managers of defined benefit schemes that: 'There is no reason why a pension scheme deficit should push an otherwise viable employer into insolvency. But the pension recovery plan should not suffer, for example, in order to enable companies to continue paying dividends to shareholders.' (See statement 18 Feb 2009, www.thepensionregulator.gov.uk/Press/PN09-02). So in the Regulator's view, the dividend ranks as less important than the pensions deficit. Investors in outfits like BT Group with huge pensions deficits and equally huge dividends might want to consider just how safe their payout really is.

Investors using a dividend-based stock selection strategy also have to be aware of one last very significant, structural risk – sector bias. Typically, most dividend-oriented portfolios or index funds are dominated by two sectors, Financials and Utilities. For example, the Dow Jones Select Dividend Index and the Mergent Dividend Achievers 50 Index have nearly 60% and 80%, respectively, in these two sectors. According to an S&P note on their US Dividend Aristocrats: 'This is because companies in these sectors have traditionally been the biggest dividend payers, and portfolios focused exclusively on high yields tend to be concentrated in these sectors. While this approach enhances current yield, it poses significant sector risks. Traditionally, Financials and Utilities have done well in stable and low interest rate environments.' This constant bias towards specific sectors can be seen in Figure 4.12 which tracks the composition of one of S&P's own dividend-based indices in Europe – their S&P 350 European Aristocrats.

The bottom line? All these threats to a strategy focused solely on companies that pay out a fat dividend cheque should remind investors that equity is risk capital: their role is to stand first in line when losses are realised. And that means the first thing to go in trouble is usually the dividend!

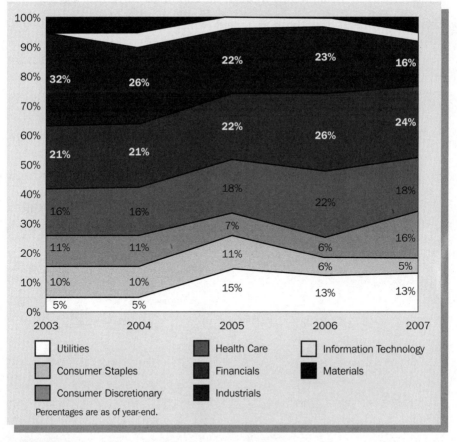

Figure 4.12   **S&P Europe 350 Dividend Aristocrats: sector composition of the Aristocrats over time**

Source: Standard and Poor's

Conclusion

Focusing your portfolio on equities that pay out a generous dividend can be hugely productive – as long as you're very aware of the risks in bearish markets where dividend favourites like banks tend to be disproportionately badly hit. Also investors would probably be advised to focus their search for high yielding stocks using more than just one measure – an above average yield. Some sense of the consistency of the payout and its growth over time is essential, while a focus on balance sheet strength is also probably a good idea. Ideally dividends shouldn't be seen as operating in isolation from the wider balance sheet and cash flow statement. Nevertheless, these caveats aside, if you are going to try to build a portfolio of high yielding shares you'd be wise to use the following simple measures as a way of filtering through the enormous universe of stocks:

- The dividend itself, both as a yield (which is total payout divided by total market capitalisation) and as an actual payout itself over time. Most analysts look for a consistent dividend payout, preferably increasing over time.

- Dividend cover is also popular. This is the ratio between the earnings per share and the dividends per share. If a company produces £2 of earnings and pays out £1 in dividends per share, the dividend cover is 2. Most analysts regard a dividend cover of 1 as the bare minimum, less than 1 troubling (the dividend isn't covered by earnings) and over 2 positive.

- Some analysts take a dim view of stated earnings and prefer to look at cashflow per share at the operating level (after depreciation but before tax, capex and dividends) and then compare this to the dividend payout.

5

Using funds and hybrids to build an income from equities

Introduction

In this chapter we're going to dig a little deeper into the riskier world of shares – equities – and explore a number of alternative ways of generating an income. In the first part of this chapter we'll look at how a wide variety of funds – equity income funds, property funds and infrastructure specialists – have emerged that focus on deriving an income from investing in shares, while in the latter part of this chapter we'll switch our focus to a slightly more exotic investment idea, hybrids. These hybrids come in many different shapes and sizes, are issued by a legion of institutions, and usually sport a confusing array of acronyms but they all combine characteristics of both equity investing and bonds.

This hybrid structure makes them especially confusing to many private investors. These prefs, PSBs and other more exotic creatures pay a fixed income like bonds but they share many of the risks characteristics of equities. However, as we'll discover a little later in this chapter, these hybrids can offer the potential for a superb stream of income payments and even some opportunity for a capital gain, but their inherent complexity does also greatly increase your risk. Investors need to understand both the risks and the opportunity within hybrid structures!

So, to recap, in this chapter we will look at six different income ideas for the private investor, all in some way dependent on equity style returns and risks. They are:

- equity income unit and investment trusts
- real estate investment trusts (REITs) and property funds

- infrastructure funds
- split capital funds
- hybrids – preference shares and the deluge of acronyms: PIBs, PSBS, ECNs, etc.
- convertibles.

We're going to start though with perhaps the most popular equity-based option for investors looking for an income – namely that of a collective fund that invests in high yielding individual company stocks.

Equity income unit and investment trusts

Table 5.1 tells the story of equity income funds much more effectively than any words! This table shows some of the leading unit trusts available through an IFA or direct, operating in a mainstream segment of the funds space called UK equity income. The managers who run these funds are some of the best in the industry and their funds currently offer both an income – around 4% give or take 50 basis points – and the potential for capital gain. Crucially income – the yield – on offer from these funds is much higher than the wider market. The best comparison or benchmark for these funds is probably something like the FTSE 100 index of top companies and as of summer 2010 this collection of Britain's top 100 listed companies is paying out a little under 3.5%.

Table 5.1 Equity income unit trusts: Top ten

	Yield %
Unicorn UK Income A	5.33
Invesco Perp Income Inc	4.07
Invesco Perp High Income Inc	4.07
JOHCM UK Equity Income Ret Acc	4.00
CF Walker Crips Equity Income Acc	4.01
Trojan Income O Acc	3.99
SJP UK High Income Acc	3.80
Halifax UK Equity Income C	3.27
Schroder Income Acc	3.25
SJP Equity Income Acc	3.10

Table 5.2 illustrates the other key virtue of these UK-focused equity income unit trust funds. The top row shows total returns over the five years 2005–09 from a tracker-based exchange traded fund that follows the FTSE 100 index. This is a plain vanilla fund with no active fund managers, low costs and a simple policy of buying the FTSE 100's constituents.

On the third row down, one of the most successful funds in the equity income sector is highlighted – the Invesco Perpetual Income fund which is managed by perhaps the UK's most successful fund manager, Neil Woodford. He certainly boasts some of the largest pools of money under management and looking at his results compared to the FTSE 100 one can understand why he's been so popular with investors. Remember that his fund will tend to produce higher income payouts than its equivalent index-hugging peers yet these results also show that in four out of five years his fund has delivered total capital gains in excess of the FTSE 100 ETF. As is often the way, Neil Woodford has poor years and annoyingly his record for the most recent year – 2009 – isn't stellar, but the overall point remains, namely that Neil Woodford's hugely successful Invesco Perpetual Income fund has delivered higher levels of income and better capital gains than most other fund managers and equivalent ETFs.

Table 5.2 Some of the UK's most successful funds

Fund	2009	2008	2007	2006	2005
iShares FTSE 100 ETF	26.9	−28.6	6.8	13.9	20.3
UK Equity Income SECTOR	22.7	−28.2	−1.1	6.9	20.1
Invesco Perp Income Inc	10.5	−19.9	6.9	27.0	26.0
Unicorn UK Income A	55.9	−32.8	−10.4	16.7	22.2
Invesco Perp High Income Inc	9.8	−19.4	7.0	27.3	27.0
SJP UK High Income Acc	9.8	−16.3	6.4	23.3	23.7
Schroder Income Acc	35.9	−23.3	1.1	16.7	19.9
Halifax UK Equity Income C	30.6	−22.9	6.0	13.7	21.5
SJP Equity Income Acc	34.8	−25.2	1.9	16.3	19.8
Trojan Income O Acc	14.7	−12.1	4.9	16.8	11.7
JOHCM UK Equity Income Ret Acc	40.4	−23.7	−9.9	20.8	23.9
CF Walker Crips Equity Income Acc	30.6	−26.4	2.6	18.1	23.5

It's important to say that Neil Woodford is far from being the only successful manager in this sector. The list in Table 5.2 above features some of the UK's most successful funds and managers including relative newcomers such as Sebastian Lyon at Trojan. Each of these managers has their own distinctive style but by and large they all share a common focus on deriving a consistent and growing income from holding shares in large blue chip companies.

Talk to a fund manager like Neil Woodford – or any of his peers for that matter – and he'd probably identify five key characteristics of his investing style:

- Achieve cautious growth by investing in the shares of larger companies with robust balance sheets, and in sectors regarded by the market as more robust and likely to grow through thick and thin – typical sectors for this last quality might include the big tobacco companies.
- Aim for a decent dividend payout that can easily be afforded by a business that is churning out cash at the operating level.
- Buy companies which are increasing their dividends year in, year out and progressively over time, i.e. increase the dividend cheque every year.
- Diversify sensibly between different large cap, blue chip companies but retain some focus on investing in UK-based companies.
- Avoid flashy, risky stocks that shoot up and down like a yo-yo.

These investing characteristics can easily be discerned in Table 5.3, which shows the composition of Neil Woodford's Income fund in the middle of summer 2010. On the left-hand side one can see his top holdings which comprise boring drug companies like AstraZeneca and GlaxoSmithKline (both of which pay out a huge dividend yield), tobacco companies such as Reynolds and British American Tobacco (BATs to its friends) as well as steady utility stocks like National Grid. To the right of these top holdings you can see the country focus – 87% in the UK (avoiding any big currency risks) and just under 9% in the US. There are also a few boring European countries in there but crucially no Chinese or Russian stocks, in fact nothing that wouldn't sit well in your average 'widows and orphans' fund! If one was especially mean one might call this collection of stocks boring but focused.

Table 5.3 Invesco Perpetual Income – portfolio structure August 2010

Portfolio breakdown

Largest holdings	%	By asset class	%	Sectors	%
ASTRAZENECA PLC	10.3	UK Equities	87.3	Consumer Goods	23.7
GLAXOSMITHKLINE	7.6	US Equities	8.9	Healthcare	21.6
REYNOLDS AMERICAN INC	5.7	Switzerland Equities	2.1	Utilities	16.4
VODAFONE GROUP	5.1	North American Equities	1.7	Industrials	10.5
BG GROUP	5.0	Luxembourg Equities	1.1	Telecommunications	9.6
BRITISH AMERICAN TOBACCO	5.0	American Emerging Equities	0.2	Financials	7.9
NATIONAL GRID	4.9	Finland Equities	0.1	Consumer Services	5.9
BT GROUP	4.2	Money Market	–1.4	Oil & Gas	5.5
TESCO	4.2	Total	100.0	Technology	0.3
IMPERIAL TOBACCO GROUP	3.9			Money Market	–1.4
Total	55.9			Total	100.0

This focus on quality and dividend growth appeals to a huge potential audience of investors and it's little surprise that mainstream independent financial advisors (IFAs) have swarmed around the equity income sector, eagerly buying up funds. Some IFAs go the extra

some IFAs go the extra mile and run their own research and due diligence approach

mile and run their own research and due diligence approach, the most notable of which is probably the White List from IFA firm Principal. Every year its advisers and researchers sift through the universe of equity income fund managers, check performance and then select their White List of 'approved' funds. The advisory firm defines this list as the best 'UK Equity Income funds that offer investors the most attractive potential for long-term income and capital growth, with a measured level of volatility'. This commentary is also usually accompanied by some choice comments from leading fund managers – two of which have been highlighted below... with some key words in italic.

> *I think it is time to move away from a heavy cyclical exposure and it is going to be the* quality *that delivers results.*

(Robin Geffen, Neptune Income)

> *I expect the* dividends *from my portfolio to grow. Up to 10% is a realistic assumption.*

(Neil Woodford, Invesco Perpetual Income)

These managers love talking about 'quality' companies that produce a solid sustainable and growing 'dividend' – this is the motto of great equity income investing. And according to Principal at least, their top rated equity income fund managers have also delivered in terms of results. '[Figure 5.1] compares the income received each year on a £10,000 investment made into Schroder Income, Invesco Perpetual Income and a National Savings Investment Account on 01/01/2000,' says Principal in its 2010 White List commentary. 'Of course, the capital risks in equity investment are significant and cannot be compared to cash. However, for investors with the willingness and ability to take equity market risk, high quality UK Equity Income funds have a proven capability to provide a high, rising and resilient income stream, even through torrid equity markets and falling interest rates.' It's White List is shown in Table 5.4.

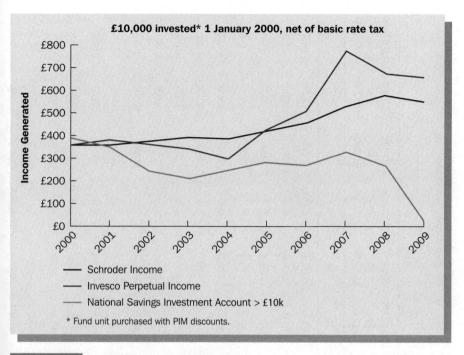

£10,000 invested* 1 January 2000, net of basic rate tax

- Schroder Income
- Invesco Perpetual Income
- National Savings Investment Account > £10k

* Fund unit purchased with PIM discounts.

Figure 5.1   **Annual income payments**

Source: Lipper Handsight, Principal Investment Management

An equity income alternative – investment trusts

There is an equally interesting alternative to these unit trust funds sold by IFAs. This alternative group features almost exactly the same investment philosophy and also boasts a crucial twist, namely that managers use an alternative wrapper or structure, called an investment trust.

Investment trusts are like unit trusts in most respects – they pool together a range of individual company holdings and then sell individual units and shares to private investors. The big difference is that investment trusts are listed on the London Stock Exchange and only issue a limited number of shares to outside investors. These 'closed end funds' can issue more shares periodically via placings, but essentially they're investment companies with a fixed amount of shares in circulation, quoted on the London Stock Exchange: i.e. they are closed end funds compared to open ended unit trusts. Unit trusts by contrast are sold through IFAs or on fund supermarket platforms directly and are essentially open ended – they can create as many new units as they want on a daily basis. These differences may sound small but investment trusts have some distinct advantages – and disadvantages – compared to their unit trust siblings.

Table 5.4 Principal's White List

The White List Top fourteen funds by overall merit	Net Dividend Yield 31/12/09	Net Income 5 Years to 31/12/09	Total Return Capital Growth & Net Income Reinvested					Volatility
Fund		(Based on £100 investment)	31/12/08 to 31/12/09	31/12/07 to 31/12/08	29/12/06 to 31/12/07	30/12/05 to 29/12/06	31/12/04 to 30/12/05	31/12/04 to 31/12/09
	%	£	%	%	%	%	%	%
Artemis Income	4.6	24.5	20.7	-22.7	2.0	18.8	23.9	4.1
Invesco Perpetual Income	4.1	22.9	10.6	-19.9	6.9	27.0	26.1	3.8
Neptune Income	4.3	25.3	23.1	-26.4	5.7	18.5	23.7	4.4
Invesco Perpetual High Income	4.3	22.4	9.8	-19.4	7.0	27.3	27.0	3.8
JOHCM UK Equity Income	4.6	24.9	40.3	-23.8	-9.8	20.6	24.0	5.1
Royal Bank of Scotland Equity Income	4.2	24.4	21.0	-19.2	1.4	17.2	22.1	4.2
Aviva Investors UK Equity Income	4.2	24.2	21.7	-20.0	1.3	18.2	22.5	4.3
Threadneedle UK Equity Income	5.1	24.4	17.4	-23.1	7.5	18.9	19.8	4.1
CF Walker Crisps Equity Income	3.8	21.7	30.6	-26.4	2.6	18.0	23.5	4.4
St James's Place UK High Income	4.0	21.6	9.8	-16.9	7.2	23.4	23.7	3.3
Threadneedle UK Monthly Income	4.9	23.8	15.8	-25.6	6.3	19.9	20.3	4.2
Royal London Equity Income	4.7	23.0	25.6	-28.2	0.8	19.7	19.9	4.4
Schroder Income	4.1	23.9	35.4	-23.3	1.2	16.6	19.9	5.1
Old Mutual Equity Income	4.6	25.1	23.5	-29.8	-0.1	20.3	20.3	4.6
WHITE LIST AVERAGE	4.4	23.7	21.8	-23.2	2.9	20.3	22.6	4.3

Generally speaking, investment trusts are used by larger, institutional investors, and these professionals are reluctant to pay the high fees charged to private investors through unit trusts. Many investment trusts charge between 0.55 and 1% per annum in total fees whereas 1 to 1.5% or more is pretty much the standard for unit trusts. That 0.6% difference in fees, compounded over many years, can make a huge difference.

But the advantages of investment trusts don't stop there – investors can also cleverly take advantage of the discrepancy that can emerge between the market price and underlying net asset value of the shares in the fund. To understand how this works, imagine for one moment an investment company with 100 shares, each issued at £1 per share. That £100 is entirely invested in the equity of large blue chip companies and at the end of the first month the net asset value per share, i.e. the total assets divided by the shares in issue, is equal to £1 a share.

Zoom forwards to the end of year two. The stock markets are suddenly very fragile creatures and investors are not keen to own risky equity assets – that means investors have been dumping all their investments. But our fund has done well and that £100 in total assets has now risen to £150, implying assets of £1.50 per share. But because of market fear, and a range of other more technical factors, the actual price on the stockmarket for each share is just £1.35 – the shares trade at a discount of 15p per share or a 10% discount. Theoretically an aggressive investor could buy up all the shares in issue, and then just sell the underlying assets and make a sudden £15 gain, but in reality these investment trusts require a formal winding up process and lots of time to sell the underlying assets. The long and short of it all is that discounts can open up, become very wide in times of market distress, and persist for many months and years. Crucially though that discount can widen *and* narrow, and sometimes some funds can even trade at a premium if buyers outnumber sellers!

Many professional investors – and more than a few smart private investors – play this discount 'widening and narrowing' process, buying when the discount is very high, waiting for confidence to return, and then selling when the discount narrows.

Table 5.5 Returns from leading trusts

Fund	2009	2008	2007	2006	2005
UK Equity Income SECTOR	22.7	−28.2	−1.1	6.9	20.1
iShares FTSE 100 ETF	26.9	−28.6	6.8	13.9	20.3
Invesco Perp Income Inc	10.5	−19.9	6.9	27.0	26.0
M&G Equity Investment Inc	23.9	−0.1	5.6	22.0	12.8
Edinburgh Investment Tst plc	20.4	−24.6	2.0	23.9	23.3
Standard Life Equity Income Trust	23.3	−22.1	−3.4	26.3	18.6
City of London IT PLC Ord	24.5	−21.4	−4.7	22.1	22.5
Finsbury Growth & Income Trust PLC	33.7	−29.6	−10.3	19.5	29.2
Temple Bar Investment Trust PLC	32.7	−13.8	−10.6	12.7	21.2
Perpetual Income and Growth Investment Trust plc	11.2	−15.0	0	13.4	20.3
Invesco Income Growth Trust plc	15.0	−28.6	1.0	26.3	24.1
Murray Income IT PLC Ord 25p	23.7	−26.2	−6.1	20.1	27.3
Schroder Income Growth	20.3	−12.9	−6.6	15.7	18.0
Dunedin Income Growth Trust PLC Ord	32.3	−36.3	−2.8	27.1	17.8
F&C Capital & Income IT PLC Ord	29.0	−26.4	−0.5	20.3	14.2
JP Morgan Elect Managed Income	23.3	−12.6	−8.8	15.8	18.0
Merchants Trust PLC	28.3	−34.2	−5.8	24.3	22.1
British & American IT PLC Ord	62.8	−34.8	−18.7	21.4	31.1
Securities Trust Of Scotland	19.6	−31.1	−6.1	26.1	18.4
Lowland Investment Company plc Ord	43.3	−49.6	−9.5	24.9	31.8
Shires Income plc Ord 50p	37.5	−38	−16.8	15.8	18.1
Value & Income Trust plc	43.2	−36.7	−18.2	25.6	22.2
Edinburgh New Income Trust plc Uts	14	−42.9	−4.3	23.1	n/a
Troy Income & Growth Trust plc	47.2	−54.4	−25.5	30.8	23.2

Regardless of whether you choose to play this discount game, there's another less obvious advantage to having a discrepancy between the net asset value and the share price – the ability to buy funds at discounts means that you are getting more income-generating assets for your money. For instance, a fund with a 5% yield at NAV would be paying 5.56% if purchased at a 10% discount.

Lower costs , higher income and the ability to make money on the discount narrowing process – these are all great selling points for investment trusts, but there's one last, absolutely crucial advantage, largely ignored by most investment journalists.

According to Charles Cade, an analyst at stockbrokers Numis and Co:

> *Perhaps the key advantage is the security of income due to the ability to smooth dividends by using revenue reserves if required. OEICs/unit trusts are forced to distribute their net income each year and several have been forced to cut dividends this year. In contrast, most of the UK [equity income trusts] have significant revenue reserves, enabling them to maintain or grow their dividends without having to reduce the quality of their portfolios in a search for yield. Investment trusts are able to retain 15% of their gross annual income which enables them to build up distributable revenue reserves over time.*[1]

Those reserves are absolutely invaluable, especially as markets turn down and big companies stop paying dividends. In 2008 for instance many large blue chips stopped paying dividends, badly damaging the equity income payouts of many unit trust funds. The large equity income investment trusts, by contrast, were able to maintain their dividend payouts through thick and thin, by drawing on those reserves.

Equity income on the defensive

The cynical observer may already have worked out the potential flaws to the equity income model – be it within a unit trust or an investment trust. A quick perusal of the top holdings of the Invesco Perpetual Income fund would have immediately identified that the top five companies comprise 33% of all holdings in the fund. That concentration of potential risk on just a few very big companies in a few big sectors is symptomatic of a wider problem for all strategies designed to target high yielding com-

---

'Where to Find Income? Investment companies offer diversity and security of income,' by Charles Cade and his team, 18 September 2009.

the portfolios of equity income funds tend to be dominated by the same stocks

panies – five stocks now make up almost 50% of dividends from the FTSE 350 Index and so the universe for income focused funds is more concentrated than for the market overall (by market cap, the top five stocks represent 32% of the FTSE 350). This means that the portfolios of equity income funds tend to be dominated by the same stocks.

A number of defensive sectors including telecoms and utilities, and tobacco and drugs, also keep cropping up in the portfolios of equity income managers, and although these huge companies usually boast a huge range of underlying international business units, their parent groups are almost always UK listed and based. That focus on the UK is no bad thing as such – the London Stock Exchange is a very wide, deep and liquid market and it's also traditionally tax efficient for UK domiciled funds to pay out franked income from UK dividends, avoiding any potential withholding tax on overseas income. Nevertheless some form of international diversification would seem to be a sensible idea. Some upstart fund managers also suggest looking at new sectors – technology and healthcare are popular amongst some smaller managers – and smaller companies for greater diversification.

Investors also need to be mindful of another risk – fund manager selection and execution. Academic study after academic study has shown that managers who actively pick stocks tend to (a) cost more in terms of charges and (b) deliver less than an equivalent index tracking passively managed fund. The logic here is deadly simple: great managers such as Neil Woodford cannot keep shooting the lights out and over the very long term their performance will 'revert to mean,' i.e. fall back to the long-term average. But all that active management – picking out certain stocks and then researching them – requires lots of time and expense and those extra expenses will eventually produce a lower than average return after fees are allowed for. This is the argument put forward by the fans of index tracking funds and it's hard to dispute the mountain of academic evidence. In a later chapter we'll look at an alternative index tracking approach that focuses on dividends. In this chapter we'll hear from Wisdom Tree, a large American firm and pioneer in this innovative new investment space. We'll look at how an approach that explicitly removes manager interference might be a more cost-effective and rewarding alternative to the traditional equity income actively managed fund.

Overseas dividend growth

Until fairly recently the concept of dividend-centred, equity income-based investing was almost exclusively the preserve of investors operating in developed market economies, particularly the UK and, to a lesser degree, the USA. But the rising yields available on many overseas stock markets (especially on the European continent and in emerging markets) is indeed encouraging many UK-based fund managers to launch international equity income funds. These have much broader geographic exposure, yet can still generate a healthy yield. The investment trust sector has been especially keen to internationally diversify its holdings. The global growth funds segment, for instance, has typically invested around half of its assets in overseas markets. Table 5.6 shows both recent share price performance and yields for the largest global growth funds – many are paying out well over 4% per annum.

Table 5.6 Performance and yields for the largest global growth funds

Fund	Price in p	Discount or premium %	Net yield %	Performance		
				1 year	3 years	5 years
British Assets Trust plc	118.70	2.0	5.21	22.8	5.6	22.8
Eclectic Investment Trust plc	83.50	20.5	0.60	60.1	50.8	41.1
London & St Lawrence Investment Company	255.00	3.1	4.35	16.8	6.0	30.7
Midas Income & Growth Trust	110.25	5.6	5.91	24.4	21.2	2.6
Murray International Trust PLC Ord 25p	847.00	8.7	3.48	31.1	49.5	100.4
Ruffer Investment Company	186.25	2.6	1.61	18.7	80.0	74.7
Scottish American Investment Company PLC	206.00	2.2	4.46	37.6	2.0	29.1
Sector average				27.9	2.0	23.5

Source: Numis Securities Investment Companies Research

But investors shouldn't just focus on these big globally diversified investment trusts – there's also an increasing number of funds now offering above average yields from Asia (see Figure 5.2). Figure 5.3 looks at dividend growth by region in 2008 and 2009, a turbulent set of years in which many European banks in particular cut or axed their dividend payouts. According to Numis 'in Asia, [by contrast] dividends held up better over this period although there have still been a significant number of cuts'.[2]

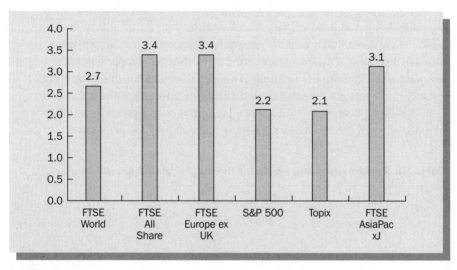

Figure 5.2   **Percentage dividend yields by region**
Source: Numis Securities Investment Companies Research, Datastream

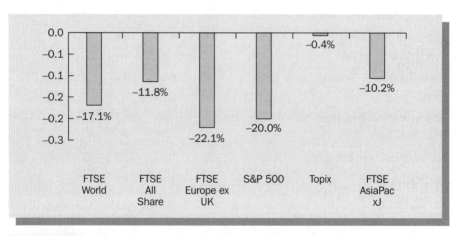

Figure 5.3   **Percentage dividend growth in 2008/09 by region**
Source: Numis Securities Investment Companies Research, Datastream

---

[2] Ibid.

This Numis research also highlighted another key plus – the big global growth investment trusts have even larger revenue reserves than their UK income peers, 'typically representing at least one year's annual dividend payout. The extreme is Caledonia Investments which has revenue reserves equivalent to almost 14 times its current annual dividend.'

REITs and property funds

Over the past decade many investors have turned to more sector specific funds in order to generate an income – perhaps the most popular have been those focused on the commercial property space. Real Estate Investment Trusts (REITs) have, until recently at least, proved immensely popular with investors tempted by the promise of decent, sustained income flows and some potential for a capital uplift.

These REITs are in fact a specific, tax-based structure specially designed to boost the income payable from holding real estate assets (e.g. office blocks, industrial warehouses or shopping malls). REITs have been popular all around the world but were formally introduced into the UK in 2007 and are set up with the specific task of paying out at least 90% of their rental income straight to shareholders through regular dividends. This tax structure also determines that all UK REITs are exempt from tax on income they receive and on capital gains made on the properties in which they invest. Because of these tax structures and other restrictions imposed on REITs – there are also some restrictions on borrowing – total returns for private investors will primarily be driven by dividends and less by share price movements in the long term, which should also help to make returns more stable. It's also worth noting that although the REIT structure is tax-efficient, it's not entirely tax-free. For individual investors any capital gains will be subject to CGT and any income received via dividends may be subject to income tax.

REITs are also popular with many private investors because of their listed status. They're effectively state regulated real estate specific closed end investment trusts, with a primary share listing on the London Stock Exchange. That stockmarket listing – shares are quoted on the market with the price largely determined by the underlying net asset value of the fund – gives investors the flexibility to move in and out of the asset class on a tactical basis, and they can even invest globally in REITs listed on the UK, European and Asian exchanges (largely through exchange traded index tracking funds).

But shares bought and sold on an exchange have some equally important disadvantages – pricing is more influenced by short-term movements in the stockmarket as opposed to changes in the value of direct property investments, and that 'market risk' produces much higher volatility in terms of pricing. And, as with investment trusts, there's always the risk that a discount will open up between the market price and the underlying net asset value per share, although some REITs might trade at a short-term premium if they're especially popular. Table 5.7 lists a number of leading UK REITs as well as some foreign property funds (all European-based) that aren't formally REITs but still pay out a generous dividend. This snapshot shows that most property funds in the summer of 2010 traded at a sizeable discount to their NAV (ING UK Real Estate shares traded at an 18% discount), yet the yield on offer varied between 6.5% per annum and 9%. The last column shows dividend cover, i.e. how much of the dividend paid out was covered by cash income or profits.

Table 5.7 Leading UK REITs and European-based property funds

Name	Ticker	Market cap (£m)	Share price	Discount/ premium (%)	Yield (%)	Dividend cover (%)
UK						
Commercial Property	UKCM	923	77	2	7.0	83
Standard Life Property Inc	SLI	65	62	2	7.0	117
F & C Commercial Property	FCPT	624	92	2	6.5	78
IRP Property	IRP	91	82	0	9.0	69
ISIS Property	IPT	69	91	11	9.0	94
ING UK Real Estate	IRET	165	48	18	8.0	112
European						
Invista Property	IFD	133	41	19	9.0	56
Alpha Pyrenees	ALPH	30	26	13	14.0	Over 100
Axa Property	APT	50	50	36	6.0	Over 100
Invista Europe	IERE	57	22	56	NA	NA
Tamar Industrial	TEIF	44	31	60	4.0	Over 100
Matrix European	MERE	43	120	59	6.0	Over 100

Source: Numis Securities Investment Companies Research

In Table 5.7 you can also see some key statistics for European property funds. These aren't actually structured as REITs but they are frequently off-shore-based and subject to minimal taxes within the structure. After the global financial crisis of 2007 and 2008 these funds collapsed in value and as of the summer 2010 prices have still not recovered to pre-crisis levels. That means that discounts are still huge and yields very high. According to analysis from Numis these 'European property companies have not wit-nessed the same recovery in share prices as their UK counterparts. This largely reflects remaining balance sheet risks, macro uncertainties, smaller declines in European valuations and less transparency on the European market. Given current share prices, companies in this sector are much likely to be seen as value and recovery plays'.[3] Figure 5.4 shows discounts on NAV for some of the leading players in this specialised, European space as at the end of the first quarter of 2010.

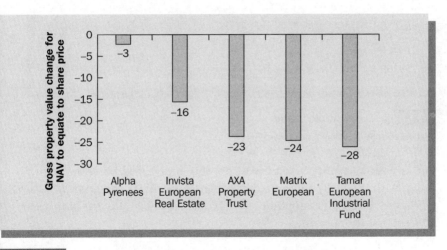

Figure 5.4   **Implied discount on properties from Q1 2010**
Source: Numis Securities Investment Companies Research

With yields across the property sector varying between 4% and 15% (includ-ing European funds) it's little surprise that private investors looking for an income have made some sizeable investments in the leading firms. And these high yields on offer from listed property funds are by no means unusual. Figure 5.5 shows yields over time for the UK property investment companies (the top line) compared to the FTSE All Share index and 5–10 year corporate bond yields. Property fund yields have pretty much consistently been at least twice as high as those on offer from the FTSE All Share index.

Ibid.

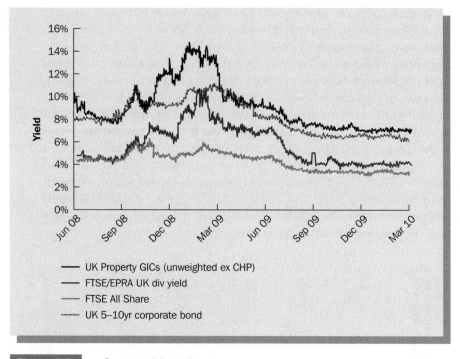

Figure 5.5   Comparable yields

Source: Numis Securities Investment Companies Research

But as with all equity-based investing, this super-sized potential return brings with it equally super-sized risks. On paper, REITs should be a more conservative investment option but in recent years volatility has been sizeable and risk ever present.

Perhaps the most obvious long-term risk is debt. REITs are primarily funded by equity but the property projects they invest in tend to be based around large amounts of debt. The property sector globally has in fact been built on huge mountains of debt, much of it issued by large commercial and investment banks. That in turn sparked a massive asset price bubble which deflated in epic style in 2008 and 2009, prompting prices to fall rapidly. This inherent sector-based pricing volatility has translated into massive share price volatility – and that in turn has prompted many cautious investors to flee the sector, forcing funds big and small to liquidate their holdings so that they can pay out to their fast declining investor base.

perhaps the most obvious long-term risk is debt

In fact many funds found themselves caught in a deadly spiral – under-lying property investments were falling fast in value, rents stopped being paid, NAVs started plummeting and investors started pulling their money out, prompting firesale disposal of assets and even lower prices. Most big REITs have survived but many have had to dispose of peripheral assets, lower their debt levels, and 'make do' with smaller amounts of money under management. That has in turn forced up the cost ratios charged to investors for managing their money and produced consistently high discount levels as wary investors wait until prices have bottomed out!

More fundamentally many private investors have become profoundly disillusioned with listed private equity funds – they look on the underly-ing asset class as very speculative and higher risk because of the relative illiquidity of the properties, i.e. funds can't just sell an office block in a matter of hours to meet investor demand. That relative illiquidity now has a price expressed in the still high discounts, although it's also worth noting in conclusion that many value orientated, longer-term horizon investors also reckon that, that illiquidity discount is an opportunity, espe-cially if you're being rewarded in the short term by a hefty dividend yield!

Infrastructure funds

Over the past decade private investors have discovered the once esoteric delights of infrastructure investing. The idea that private investors would make money from anything as boring as a bridge or even a hospital was once regarded as almost heretical by the more socialist inclined: govern-ments funded public infrastructure, not the private sector. But the fiscal retrenchment of the 1980s and 1990s combined with the wave of pri-vatisations gave birth to a new idea – public private partnerships (PPP) where the private sector would fund a public sector project. In the UK this found formal expression as the PFI – the Private Finance Initiative – but PPP structures have emerged all around the world. In fact PPP projects have been in existence for many decades in countries as varied as the USA, Spain and France. Many of the most successful long-term projects have actually been in the transport space, e.g. private sector own-ership of airports or toll road schemes. These projects have many of the same characteristics of the more recent PFI and PPP structures. They fea-ture a long-term contract by private investors to fund a big project with an agreed inflation-linked revenue structure. These revenues are dependable and paid back, like clockwork, to the investors year in, year out, over a fixed term at which point the project is either sold on, retained by the owners or handed back to the government.

In many respects one can identify these assets as being closer to bonds than equity and most projects are in fact bond funded, with the large banks as major structurers. Dependable income streams, over long periods of time, and regular inflation-linked reviews are typical of many modern bond structures, all with the added benefit of relatively low risk.

The PFI structures introduced towards the end of the 1990s introduced more risk into the equation – if private sector investors were to invest in a public sector hospital they'd be taking on much greater risk. Building and then maintaining hospitals is a riskier enterprise than building and maintaining a bridge, and that extra risk needs to be captured in a potentially higher return. But the government also needs to be reassured that that extra risk is real – that the private sector isn't just 'milking' the public sector. So targets are set to justify those higher returns, and reviews introduced, frequently based around levels of 'service'. As this investment proposition became more complicated new structures emerged, structures that mixed up lower risk bonds with higher risk 'equity' in PFI companies. And as the UK pioneered the space so other countries followed, introducing their own versions of PFI and PPP to fund new public infrastructure.

Not unsurprisingly, new funds and managers have emerged to take advantage of this opportunity, with many based in the UK, although Australian firms such as MacQuarie have also been very active. The London Stock Exchange is now home to a small number of very specialist funds, all of which invest in infrastructure assets in some shape or another. Table 5.8 gives details of the three main players in this space – they all pay out a well-backed dividend to their investors which, as of the summer of 2010, averaged around 5% per annum. Crucially this dividend is well backed by contractually structured income-producing assets and is also likely to grow over time as new assets come on stream, producing extra income. Table 5.8 shows the mix in the underlying portfolios between mature, income-producing assets and earlier stage assets where the income produced is low but there is also some potential for income growth *and* capital gain.

Table 5.8 The three main players' mix of portfolios (as of July 2010)

Fund	Ticker	Price (P)	Market cap (£m)	Yield (%)	Discount or premium (%)	Gearing (%)	Portfolio: mature (%)	Early stage (%)
International Public Private Partnership	INPP	115.5	533	4.80	2.2	6	69	31
HSBC Infrastructure Company	HICL	117.0	535	5.59	8.1	10	100	0
3i Infrastructure	3IN	112.0	914	4.88	−3.2	NA	86	14

These infrastructure investments all boast a number of common characteristics:

■ The underlying projects owned by the funds are all of long duration, usually matched by attractively priced long duration debt. Banks are usually more than willing to lend at low rates to a government customer over 20 or 30 years.

■ Cash flows tend to be stable and usually have some form of inflation protection built in.

■ They are generally low-risk investments, producing a solid income – but there's also likely to be less chance of a capital gain.

■ The funds will tend to invest in a mixture of assets – mostly UK-based PFI projects but increasingly some foreign assets. There will also be a mixture of early stage and late stage assets and some funds might also boast some less conventional infrastructure assets such as utility companies: for example, the 3i Infrastructure fund not only invests in emerging markets infrastructure projects (more risk, less income but the potential for capital gains) but also invests in UK-based water companies (less risk, more income).

■ These are all listed, closed end funds and like their REIT siblings they can trade at a discount or a premium. The more cautious and defensive funds such as the one from HSBC tend to trade at a premium while the riskier ones such as 3i tend to trade at a big discount.

The decision about whether to invest in infrastructure companies is a relatively simple one – their lower yields of around 5% are much more secure than the dividends paid out by traditional equity funds but they're only just above those on offer from investment grade corporate bonds. Is the extra 0.50% to 1% worth the extra risk? You are investing in government-run assets which could be negatively affected by changes in political philosophy or policy. That said, the risk of government's tearing up contracts is still small, and these structures do boast inflation protection, not available on fixed rate investment grade bonds. Also directly owning an investment grade corporate bond might directly give you between 4% and 5% with only the costs of purchasing the bond to add on top. These funds are complex creatures and require a lot of specialist staff and that cost is reflected in the fees charged by the managers, all of which come out of the funds' income payment and NAV. On balance most investors would probably conclude that infrastructure funds have some role in a diversified fund – they just need to be aware that these funds are stockmarket listed and regarded as quasi-equity, making them vulnerable to shorter-term market risk and pricing volatility.

> most investors would probably conclude that infrastructure funds have some role in a diversified fund

Split capital funds

In a later chapter we'll look in much more detail at a deceptively simple investment idea around which has been built a whole industry that issues what are called structured products. This fast growing sector has emerged out of a simple insight: that the returns from investing in equities come in many different ways (dividends which produce an income, increasing share prices producing capital gains) and that the requirements of investors are also many and varied. If some investors only want an income, why not just give them that income but with no potential for capital gain? Equally some income investors might not want their income every year but are willing to roll up their returns as a single lump sum payment many years hence, and along the way draw some profits by selling units in a fund. Last but by no means least, some investors only want the prospect of big long-term gains if equity markets shoot up: in effect they want an option on rising share prices. Why not build a structure that accommodates all these aspirations and different sources of total return?

It was exactly this question that motivated fund managers in the last century to develop a complex ecosystem of what were called split capital investment trusts – and it's the same idea that still motivates structured product providers. In essence split capital investment fund structures offered a series of defined returns, i.e. an income, a fixed annual capital gain or an upside option on booming stockmarkets, in return for taking a series of defined risks. The underlying investment was still equities – in this case large cap equities which produced a decent dividend income – and many of the funds first emerged from investment houses that had traditionally excelled at equity income investing.

The structure built to accommodate all these different requirements was actually fairly simple and comprised of three classes of share, with varying levels of risk:

■ The zero dividend share which did not pay a dividend/income but paid out a fixed sum in a number of years in the future when the fund matured (e.g. over a five-year period each 100p share would accrue a 5% gain and at maturity in five years' time would pay out 125p). These would be the lowest risk and would be paid out after any loans on the fund had been paid back.

■ The income share where an income would be paid – these would be slightly riskier in that their final capital payment would only be repaid in full at maturity if the zero dividend final payment (our notional 125p) had been paid.

■ The capital shares would receive whatever was left in the fund after the income and zero dividend shares had been paid. In effect this operates as a longer-term option on rising share prices, i.e. if shares boom in price, they go up in price very quickly whereas if shares collapse in value they could be worth nothing.

If we step back from this structure we can immediately see the attractions – different classes of investors receive different forms of returns, sliced and diced up within a split capital structure. In booming equity markets this structure can produce decent, reliable returns for shareholders either in the form of an income or a defined return, and potentially massive returns for the capital shareholders. In dismal, sideways moving markets the capital class is wiped out and some lose much of the original principal invested.

To understand how they work let's imagine a simple example.

Split capital investment trust example

Our equity income fund manager builds a portfolio of high-yielding, reliable blue chip equities averaging a payout of 5% per annum. The manager might also take out a loan on which interest costs just 5% per annum. In total, equity of £100 million is invested alongside £50 million of loans (£150 million in total). The interest bill is £2.5 million per annum and the dividend income is 5% of £150 million or £7.5 million. The manager also then assumes that over the long term equities rise by about 5% per annum in value, compounded. Over five years the manager anticipates that the £150 million will be worth 27% more in value, or £191 million in total – which after the £50 million loan is repaid equates to £141 million.

The fund managers now get down to the job of structuring the returns. Of our £100 million in equity raised the fund is split up as follows:

- £50 million from a zero dividend class of shares – 50 million £1 shares are issued which in five years' time pay £1.33 which is the equivalent of a compound annual return of 6% per annum. These are the least risky and must be paid out first.

- £40 million from income shares paying out 7% a year (i.e. £2.8 million per annum) – 40 million £1 income shares which will only get 100p back in five years' time. These are next in line for a payout after the zero dividend shares.

- And £10 million from capital shares. These will only pay back anything if the zero dividend and income shares have been repaid first.

Over the next five years our dividend fund must pay out £2.5 million in interest on the loans and £2.8 million in dividends to the income shares – a total of £5.3 million paid from the dividend income of £7.5 million (any remaining income is paid in fund management costs and fees or kept in reserve).

In five years' time if the fund does indeed produce a capital return of 5% per annum, our £191 million is used to pay back the £66.6 million owed to the zero dividend capital shares, the £40 million owed to the income shares, and the £50 million loan. The remaining £34 million is kept by the capital shareholders, who have made a massive return on their initial £10 million investment.

But what happens if returns are nowhere near 5% per annum? What happens if the capital doesn't grow at all? If our £150 million fund is still worth £150 million in five years' time? Our £50 million loan must be paid back first, and then our zero dividend shareholders – leaving just £33.33 million for our income shareholders (remember they invested £40 million) and nothing for the capital shareholders. And if the shares actually decreased in value, our income shareholders would be even harder hit, with losses possibly extending all the way into the zero dividend class.

Falling stockmarkets spell unmitigated catastrophe for nearly all shareholders – remember that the loan had to be repaid before all other classes and even relatively safe classes of shares could find their final payout jeopardised. And disaster did indeed strike in the years 2000 to 2002. Equity markets across the world dived in value as a consequence of the 'dot.con' fiasco and suddenly equity income funds found themselves in a massive storm, as split cap managers were forced to sell their holdings, pushing values down to even lower levels. The following box explains in a little more detail how this fiasco was made worse by the structure of these funds, but the end result was nearly terminal for this very specialised sector. Many normally conservatively inclined investors who had invested

---

WHAT WENT SO WRONG WITH SPLIT CAP FUNDS?

The crisis in 2000–02 very nearly destroyed the split capital funds sector. But what went wrong? The simplest answer is that the sector became vulnerable to systemic risk – the underlying funds were heavily invested in equities, in a market which started selling off equities. But the crisis was made much worse by the combination of a number of dangerous structural issues:

- Lots of cross fund holdings, i.e. funds owning shares in each other – this added to the total costs charged to shareholders and helped to push the whole sector close to the edge as equity prices overall plunged downwards.

- Bank debt – a 50:50 debt:equity became commonplace. When share prices plummeted loan covenants were breached and many funds were forced to sell their assets, pushing net asset values down even further.

- Bad fund management – too many funds started to diversify away from the traditional UK equity income portfolios and started buying everything from tech stocks to junk bonds.

- Fees were too high – charging fees on gross assets encouraged the fund managers to take out high levels of debt. These high fees levels also ate into final returns.

- Poor transparency – according to one analysis of the fiasco, from Numis: 'Although a lot of data was available on splits, much of the analysis was based on static, simplistic measures such as cover and hurdle rates which ignore differences in portfolio yield and did not allow for option-like payoff profiles. There was also too little information available from fund managers on the nature of the portfolio or on the performance of the fund's assets as a whole. People began to ignore the differences in the quality of assets and there was a widely quoted fallacy that the price of split capital funds would be supported by their yield, irrespective of the underlying asset performance.'[4]

---

[4] Cited in 'Split Capital Funds – Making a Comeback?' by James Glass, 24 November 2009 (a private report).

huge sums in the income and zero dividend classes, expecting rock solid returns, suddenly found the payments stopped and the capital principal threatened. Many split capital funds closed, a huge investigation into the sector was launched, and compensation was paid out in the more extreme cases. But the sector didn't completely die – a small number of split capital funds did survive and in Tables 5.9 and 5.10 we list both the surviving zero dividend share classes on offer (with gross redemption yields based on 0% growth in the underlying basket of equities) as well as the much smaller pool of income shares (with running yield).

Table 5.9 The surviving zero dividend share classes on offer

Fund name	Windup	Mid price (p)	Redemption Price (p)	NRY 0%
Aberforth Geared Income ZDP 2017	29/06/2017	105.00	159.70	6.19
Ecofin Water & Power Opportunities ZDP 2016	31/07/2016	112.25	160.70	6.08
Edinburgh New Income ZDP 2011	31/05/2011	133.75	141.85	6.70
Electra Private Equity ZDP 2016	05/08/2016	109.75	155.41	5.88
Equity Partnership ZDP 2011	31/07/2011	126.00	139.30	9.80
F&C Private Equity ZDP 2014	15/12/2014	105.75	152.14	8.52
JPMorgan Income & Capital ZDP 2018	28/02/2018	108.75	192.13	7.25
JPMorgan Private Equity ZDP 2013	28/06/2013	62.75	73.00	5.20
JPMorgan Private Equity ZDP 2015	31/12/2015	60.75	87.30	6.82
Jupiter Dividend & Growth ZDP 2017	30/11/2017	72.50	150.00	1.57
Jupiter Second Split ZDP 2014	31/10/2014	29.75	40.50	7.39
JZ Capital Partners ZDP 2016	22/06/2016	250.75	369.84	6.73
M&G Equity ZDP 2011	08/03/2011	76.75	100.00	4.62
M&G High Income ZDP 2017	17/03/2017	69.50	122.83	6.03
NB Private Equity ZDP 2017	31/05/2017	109.50	169.73	6.55
Premier Energy & Water ZDP 2015	31/12/2015	159.75	221.78	6.16
Premier Renewable Energy ZDP 2010	31/12/2010	383.50	392.00	4.55
Utilico ZDP 2012	31/10/2012	159.75	177.52	4.64
Utilico ZDP 2014	31/10/2014	129.50	167.60	6.14
Utilico ZDP 2016	31/10/2016	108.75	192.78	9.47

Source: www.splitsonline.co.uk

Table 5.10 The surviving income shares on offer

Fund name	Windup	Mid price (p)	Redemption price (p)	Estimated NAV (%)	Net flat yield (%)
Aberforth Geared Capital & Income	31/12/2011	111.00	100.00	100.72	11.35
Equity Partnership	31/07/2011	81.25	100.00	100.00	15.37
Global Special Opportunities	31/05/2011	47.50	120.82	47.29	0.00
JPMorgan Income & Growth	30/11/2016	60.25	103.40	70.34	6.64
Rights & Issues Income	25/07/2011	445.00	29.07	578.39	5.73
Rights & Issues Preference	25/07/2011	85.50	100.00	100.00	6.43

Source: www.splitsonline.co.uk

A new dawn after 2010...?

Back in 2008 and 2009 the split capital sector seemed to be one step away from death's door. As one report from Numis in 2009 noted:

> It is no coincidence that the split capital funds that survived had little or no bank debt and more mainstream portfolios with no cross-holdings. However, these funds have been reaching maturity and the universe has continued to shrink. As a result, it seemed likely that the split capital market would simply wither away... at the start of this year, the market capitalisation of the entire sector was just £2.2bn.[5]

Yet a new decade brought some indications in 2010 that life may be about to return to the sector (the structured products sector has grown enormously over the same period – more on that in a later chapter). A small number of specialised funds have started re-issuing new tranches of split capital shares including zero dividends and income shares. A number of factors seem to be powering this tentative rebirth including the difficulty some specialist funds (private equity in particular) experience in finding new sources of debt. Zero dividend shares and income shares by contrast

---

[5] 2009 private research paper by Numis.

are a low cost source of fresh capital even at 6% per annum. Investors also seem open to the idea again. Interest rates are low and 6% defined returns even from a higher risk private equity fund look appealing. Also the current tax structure seems to be working in split caps favour. The change in capital gains tax (CGT) for UK investors from an individual's marginal rate to a flat 28% has made any fund that offers a capital roll-up through zero dividends especially attractive (particularly given that there is also an annual current CGT allowance of £10,100).

> the current tax structure seems to be working in split caps favour

Hybrids

In an earlier chapter we observed that bond investors and equity investors seem to inhabit two almost completely distinct worlds! Bond investors increasingly rule the roost and trade in much bigger, more liquid global markets that can be capitalised in the tens of trillions. Bond markets have continued to produce solid returns in the first decade of the 21st century whereas equity markets have been enormously volatile and failed to advance overall. Equity markets are also increasingly taking their lead on perceptions of risk from the bond markets, reinforcing a growing sense of inferiority compared to the bond vigilantes!

But that there is this binary distinction between bonds – perceived as low risk – and equities – higher risk – is only partly true. There exists a small but important hinterland *between* these two worlds, inhabited by a myriad gaggle of hybrid structures that share elements of both bond investing and equity investing. Crucially these hybrids – with many different acronyms used to describe them – are much riskier than many bonds, and share some of the same risk characteristics of equities. But that greater element of risk also means that they tend, on average, to pay a much higher yield than either mainstream bonds or equities.

To understand the nature of this risk it's first important to understand who issues the great majority of these products – banks and building societies. As we'll see in this discussion of hybrid structures there are other insititutions and companies that do offer structures such as preference shares and convertibles, but it's also true that this is largely a private investor, retail market, comprising income investors looking for 'yield enhancement'.

The crucial point is that all these hybrid structures are technically not bonds, but a type of risk capital – by risk capital we mean money invested in an organisation that bears some risk. In the case of building societies and banks that will mean the hybrid will only be paid out after the more 'senior' investors have been paid, i.e. the senior corporate debt and any money owed to depositors or the government. In large corporations the hybrids issued – in this case convertibles and preference shares – take on extra risk because they will only be paid after all other secured creditors have been paid including the corporate bond holders.

That extra risk is compensated for by the issuer – they pay out a higher income of yield. But this (largely though not exclusively) fixed income coupon is *fixed,* i.e. the investors don't get anything more than the principal repaid and the regular income. Because of this fixed income structure these hybrids behave in a manner similar to bonds. They also share many of the same terms applied to bonds, including coupon, price, yield and other features such as calls. It's also worth noting that like mainstream bonds these hybrids can be adversely affected by sudden changes in interest rates: if interest rates generally go up, their value goes down, but if interest rates fall, their value rises.

Bond market cynics might counter that the extra risk involved in hybrids isn't worth the extra reward. Traditional bond investors sit on rock-solid guarantees whereas risk capital such as convertibles or building society PIBSs (see over) only get paid after the more senior bonds have been paid out. Equally they don't receive any of the upside that equity investors receive – that coupon payment is fixed (unlike dividends which can and do increase over time in many companies) and that the final payment sum is also fixed (with the exception of convertibles which do have some upside potential).

This mix of risk and return makes many mainstream investors nervous and cautious. Many institutions avoid this sector and that makes the markets for hybrids fairly illiquid (more so with PIBSs and PSBs (see later), less so with convertibles) and subject to frequent bouts of risk aversion (investors withdraw their money from all assets perceived to be risky). But many private investors think the trade off in risk and return is worth it. Over the past few decades hundreds of thousands of smaller, usually older and wealthier, investors have bought a range of these hybrid structures, particularly those regarded as the 'safest'. (It is often noted that no building society, for instance, has ever defaulted on its payments to investors in PIBS.) Investors in banking sector prefs and PSBs had also been reassured by this fact but the credit crisis of 2007 delivered a nasty surprise – rescued banks such as Lloyds stopped paying coupons on their preference shares whilst the government effectively destroyed the value of PSBs held in rescued former building society turned bank Bradford and Bingley.

Which hybrids can you invest in?

Until fairly recently the most popular hybrid structure was something called **Permanent Interest Bearing Shares (PIBSs)**, a type of instrument issued by UK building societies. These fixed income securities are usually issued at fixed interest rates and quoted on the stockmarket (although a few building societies have issued floating-rate PIBSs in which case the interest rate varies based on general interest rates).

All PIBSs are permanent and have no maturity date, although some PIBSs do allow something called a call where the society can redeem the PIBS early, on a specified date. But it's important to understand that the investor has no right to repayment on the call date. PIBSs have been enormously useful to building societies as a source of long-term funding at fixed rates – both wholesale money markets and savings accounts boast fairly volatile rates. PIBSs provide the building societies with a wonderfully easy and simple form of long-term risk-bearing capital – remember that they can't issue shares in the traditional sense to raise capital. The risk is obvious: if the building society runs into problems it can stop making the coupon payment and PIBS investors would be last in the queue to get their money back, i.e. all other investors including bond holders, depositors and the government would get their money back first. And although additional PIBSs can be issued instead of a cash coupon payment, interest payments are non-cumulative, so in the event that a society fails to make a payment, no obligation is carried forward. PIBS holders are also not covered by the Financial Services Compensation Scheme, although holders of PIBSs are regarded as members of the issuing building society, and entitled to full voting rights.

Interest payments on PIBSs are made gross – free of tax – although the investor will subsequently have to pay income tax on those payments (usually twice yearly), and they are traded without interest, so any accrued interest has to be settled separately.

OTHER QUESTIONS COMMONLY ASKED REGARDING THE WORLD OF HYBRIDS

What's the difference between a cumulative and non-cumulative security?

A **non-cumulative** hybrid such as a preference share is one where if the income is not paid, the lost payments are never paid. A **cumulative** fixed-income security is one for which any skipped coupons are accumulated to be paid in the future.

What does callable mean?

A callable hybrid such as a PIBS is one where the financial institution has the right (but not obligation) to redeem, usually at par, a security at a fixed date in the future. If this does happen the coupon will usually be set at a new level.

Most PIBSs, bank subordinated bonds and many bank preference shares are callable, and prior to the banking crisis it was a convention that they would exercise their right to call at the first call date.

It seems that many preference shares are traded at something called the dirty price – what does this mean?

The dirty price means that when you buy a bond or hybrid you're also buying the accumulated or accrued income coupon up until that point in time after the last coupon or ex dividend date. The price excluding accrued interest is sometimes known as the 'clean price'. All PIBSs and PSBs trade at a dirty price as do all gilts and most preference shares. Where you purchase a security which trades 'clean' and pay accrued interest there will be added complications for entering the interest correctly on your tax return.

Many investors have also found themselves almost without choice invested in another hybrid structure similar to PIBSs called **Perpetual Subordinated Bonds** (PSBs). These PSBs were actually originally PIBSs and were issued by building societies that decided to demutualise – issue shares on the stockmarket. The PIBSs were turned into PSBs but in all other respects they operate like PIBSs, and investors in the PSBs rank ahead of the equity investors in any wind down but after more senior bond investors.

An equally large number of private investors have also invested in **preference shares** and especially bank preference shares. This is a special class of equity share that pays a fixed rate of interest. They rank higher in terms of payment than ordinary shares in any liquidation or wind down and their dividend is fixed as a regular payment. A company can be put into administration if it fails to pay interest on its debt, but preference dividends, like ordinary dividends, are paid at the discretion of directors. Also remember that the upside is limited as well – if profits increase the preference shareholders still only get that fixed coupon whereas the ordinary shareholders may not only see an increase in the value of their shares but also an increased dividend. It's also worth noting that you are not allowed to put preference shares in an ISA, so you will pay tax on the interest. Preference dividends are paid net which means that for basic rate taxpayers there is no additional payment. Most UK listed preference shares pay dividends twice annually and purchases of preference shares, like ordinary shares, are subject to 0.5% stamp duty.

One last absolutely crucial observation which has particular relevance to the small army of investors in bank preference shares: a company will not be able to pay an ordinary dividend until preference dividends have been paid first, although a small number of preference shares are cumulative, which means that the company must pay any dividend arrears from previous years before it can pay an ordinary dividend. Sadly most of the big banking group preference shares were non-cumulative – that means any missed payments will never be paid out but their dividends must be restarted before any dividend can be paid to the ordinary shareholders.

Obviously the global financial crisis had a huge impact on these banking sector preference shares – Lloyds, HBOS and RBS all had substantial preference share programmes. These fixed income shares all ranked lower than senior bank corporate bonds and were deemed to be 'risk capital'. (See the following box for the new tiers of risk capital.) As soon as dividends on ordinary shares were stopped, regulators ordered the banks to stop paying dividends on preference shares as well. Many in government, perhaps rightly given the size of the bank rescues involved, felt that the taxpayer should be paid back before any more dividends were issued. Some banks, and in particular Lloyds Banking Group, reacted to these moves by not only stopping preference share dividend payments for a number of years but also issuing a new form of hybrid structure called **Enhanced Capital Notes (ECNs)**, also known as CoCos or Contingent Convertibles. These are a new form of fixed income security that's emerged to fund the 'capital at risk' funding gap on some banks' balance sheets.

The idea here is actually deceptively simple: the international banking regulators want the big international banks to have greater capital reserves, i.e. reserves of at risk capital that can be used as bad debts pile up. A greater reserve of this 'at risk' capital should imply a smaller chance of complete failure, i.e. a lot more shareholders' money can be burned through before the taxpayer is forced to intervene. In this new world of greater capital strength banks need to raise more money but traditional sources have dried up – many equity investors are reluctant to invest more until they know the banks are safe and producing an income. The more reliable institutions can issue conventional corporate bonds but there's an understandable worry amongst many bond investors about the true risks lurking on bank balance sheets. This fear doesn't preclude any bond issuance but it certainly implies a higher yield for the extra risk.

ECNs are a classic hybrid compromise – there's a much higher yield on offer but there's also a risk. If a bank destroys its capital base, then these ECNs are converted into ordinary equity with a very strong likelihood of no future dividend payments. In the case of Lloyds, their ECN carries coupon rights but there's also a mandatory conversion into those ordinary shares if the Core Tier 1 capital ratio of the bank falls below the 5% level (known as the trigger). In principle there might be a continuing ordinary share dividend but in practice such a trigger is likely to occur in times of heightened financial risk, i.e. the worry would be that the government would nationalise the bank, destroying all equity value.

What is the risk of default in a financial sector hybrid?

The first and perhaps most important thing to say is that no bank (or building society) has ever forced repayment of a conventional hybrid at par, for example in the event of takeover, demutualisation or winding up. But as we've seen, banking sector preferences have experienced stopped dividend payments and even in the building society sector one institution (The West Bromwich) did force through a conversion of PIBSs into a newer form of risk capital that's structurally close to an ECN with a much lower income yield or coupon. So although no bank or building society in the UK has ever defaulted in the classic sense of the word, there have been some fairly drastic 'conversions' which have had huge effects on the value of the hybrid.

Investors in PSBs issued by former UK building society turned bank Bradford and Bingley (B&B) have had the worst experience so far. In September 2008 B&B was forcibly nationalised by the government, which proceeded to break it up into a number of constituent business units including a 'good' savings bank – sold to Santander – and a 'bad' mortgage lending operation where the government has continued to fund mortgage and personal loans. The nationalisation was essentially structured around an £18 billion loan of which £14 billion was provided by the Financial Services Compensation Scheme (FSCS). A further £4 billion loan was provided by the Treasury under a scheme in which the taxpayer is both above and below the subordinated bondholders including owners of PSBs. Incidentally the FSCS is also regarded as being above the subordinated bondholders.

This 'ranking' of claims matters hugely. In the case of the B&B, PSB investors face the near certainty of being wiped out. The Treasury has already said that it is no longer paying any coupons on the PSBs, although more senior bondholders are being paid out (at present at least). In effect the government has arbitrarily ranked itself (the Treasury and the FSCS) ahead of subordinated bondholders in settlement. In legal terms this subordinated debt is capital which remains the investors' property and is a loan. But because it is subordinated, in a winding-up it ranks only one step above the ordinary shareholders, and the government has decided to 'make an example'. In January 2010, for instance, the government issued a notice advising subordinated bondholders that interest payments were not guaranteed and each payment would be subject to the availability of money, while in March of the same year the government stopped the repayment of bondholders' bonds. Most analysts now expect no further payments and very little chance of future capital repayments.

WHAT ARE THE TIERS?

A bank's capital comprises ordinary share capital issued, built-up profit reserves and a range of hybrid structures including ECNs (enhanced currency notes), all divided on the basis of their characteristics into Lower Tier 2, Upper Tier 2 and Tier 1.

Tier 1

Tier 1 is a bank's core capital which consists of ordinary shares, retained profits and perpetual (undated) non-cumulative preferred stock (Tier 1 preferred). This is the most 'at risk' category and investments in this class might see stopped dividends and are also non-cumulative.

Upper Tier 2

These comprise perpetual deferrable sub-lower tier 2 capital ordinated debt (including debt convertible into equity) and can be cumulative.

Lower Tier 2

Dated preferred shares (normally having an original maturity of at least five years).

Convertibles

In recent years a relatively innovative form of hybrid has begun to emerge on private investors' radar, courtesy of a number of specialist fund launches. Convertible shares have been popular with professional hedge fund managers for decades but it's only the last few years that investors have woken up to the potential of this debt/equity crossover structure – many have begun to appreciate these hybrids as a safer way of gaining exposure to a particular share whilst also drawing an income.

A convertible loan stock is effectively a fixed-interest bond that offers the chance at some point in the future to convert into ordinary shares. It pays an income, like a bond, and offers the chance to convert into the ordinary stock. A company might, for instance, offer a 4% convertible over the next ten years with the chance to convert into ordinary shares at a predetermined ratio as long as the share price rises by more than 20%. If the share price rises above that 20% target level, the convertible begins to acquire some 'equity' value in addition to its bond-like value. If the shares don't rise by this amount, the investor simply uses the convertible as a form of loan stock and pockets the income.

To understand why a company might use these structures consider the plight of American investment bank Goldman Sachs a few years back. Chaos seemed to be engulfing the financial community and the big investment banks suddenly found it difficult to raise extra capital. Goldman's in particular was keen not to go cap in hand to the US government so it needed to raise hard cash, fast! It approached a good, old friend of the bank, a certain Warren Buffett, boss of investment company Berkshire Hathaway. He was offered a form of preference share-based structure with a coupon of 10% plus the chance (or option/warrant) to buy ordinary shares in the bank at a predetermined price or conversion ratio. This combination of a fixed coupon loan stock plus an option or warrant to buy the ordinary shares was a form of synthetic convertible and exactly like ordinary convertibles issued every week in both the US and the UK.

In the technical language beloved of bond traders and hedge-fund managers, convertible bonds are in effect corporate bonds with what's called an embedded equity option and often with embedded (issuer) calls and/or (holder) puts. The bonds can switch into the underlying ordinary shares at a conversion ratio which is at a premium to the underlying equity spot price at issuance. Crucially, convertibles typically boast a lower yield compared to a straightforward corporate bond – that embedded option value comes at a cost! Convertibles also come in all sorts of shapes and sizes including 'plain vanilla' convertibles (e.g. five-year convertible, around 2–3% coupon, 20–40% conversion premium callable after two years and puttable after three), floating rate coupons and perpetual convertibles.

> crucially, convertibles typically boast a lower yield compared to a straightforward corporate bond

Should private investors be considering buying convertibles? The short answer is ... maybe, depending on your inclination towards risk. These hybrids generally tend to be more volatile in price than conventional bonds and the higher the option value (the equity component) the greater the volatility. The yield will nearly always be much lower than those available on conventional bonds, and remember that convertibles rank much lower on the 'rankings' system in event of a default. But for some investors looking for the certainty of an income return plus the potential for capital gains, convertibles can be an ideal middle house, offering the best of both worlds, i.e. the potential for capital gains and a steady income.

ARE OFFSHORE FUNDS WORTH THE BOTHER?

Many investors are tempted by the idea of offshore savings and bond structures. They imagine a world of tax havens where they can escape paying tax on savings accounts and money market funds. Sadly for the evaders, Her Majesty's Revenue and Customs (HMRC) takes a dim view of using offshore structures to evade paying tax on the income generated by investment structures. Tax inspectors have gone out of their way to make sure that UK investors do not achieve a tax advantage by choosing to invest in offshore funds as opposed to UK funds (commonly known as the offshore fund rules).

This determined spade work by tax inspectors hasn't stopped offshore funds of course – there are plenty of perfectly legitimate uses for these accounts, not least the demand for them by expats. Offshore investment funds are for the most part structured in much the same way as their onshore equivalents but with one key difference: offshore funds are tax resident in jurisdictions with low tax rates or tax havens and hence the funds themselves do not pay tax.

The key distinction to look out for is one between funds with and without something called distributor status. If an offshore fund has distributor status – and thus distributes 85% of its income – a UK investor is liable to UK capital gains tax (CGT) on the gain realised when they dispose of the investment. Additionally, the investor will pay UK income tax annually on the dividend that they receive from the offshore fund.

If a fund doesn't have distributor status UK taxpayers will probably find themselves in something of a bind. You can't pay capital gains tax on any gains or income but must instead pay income tax on all returns including those paid through dividends. But there are some gains to be made because the point at which tax is payable can be deferred until the investment is sold and the investor gets the benefit of being able to reinvest the return while the investment is held.

This distinction between distributor and non-distributor status matters less for non-UK resident individuals – the tax liability on any income element is limited to the tax deducted at source, if any. It's also important to realise that offshore funds should be entitled to receive income from UK investments free of UK tax, provided appropriate arrangements are put in place.

Offshore life assurance bonds are also popular as tax is usually only due when the funds are withdrawn. This allows assets to be reallocated between the underlying investments without incurring a potential CGT liability. For non-UK residents there is no charge to either UK income tax or CGT. It's also worth noting that with offshore bank accounts, deferred interest accounts may be an attractive proposition. They pay out all accumulated interest only when the account is closed, so that savings can roll up until it makes sense to declare them. Savers will eventually need to declare interest, but they can choose their moment carefully, with the declaration hopefully timed to coincide with a lower marginal tax rate, i.e. as they approach or enter retirement.

6

Using retail structured products

by Christopher Taylor

Introduction

In the previous chapter we introduced readers to the idea of structured products through our discussion of equity-based split capital funds. The idea was and is simple behind all structured investments – provide some form of defined return, a structured risk/reward payoff and maybe even add in some extra income. The split capital sector never really recovered from its self-inflicted wounds but the structured investment or product space has expanded incredibly quickly over the past decade. That growth has prompted a huge range of new products to emerge, many of which have focused on providing an income. In this chapter Christopher Taylor, CEO of one of the largest structured investment providers in Europe, InCapital, explains how these funds or products are constructed, the key features to watch out for and how they can be used within a diversified portfolio.

Structured investments: 'income solutions'

Investing for income is more often than not a matter of need and not wealth creation.

Typically, the need for income is often driven by the fact that many income investors are in or approaching retirement, when the interest is usually straightforward: the need is for high and reliable income with an obvious desire to preserve what will usually be hard earned and irreplaceable capital.

However, with interest rates in the UK at a 300-year low – and with the economic backdrop looking likely to keep them low for a considerable period of time – demand for income 'solutions' is not restricted to just 'typical' income investors, i.e. those in or approaching retirement. In the current environment of derisory interest rates and rising income tax just about anyone with savings is likely to be seeking 'superior income' returns to those available 'risk free', i.e. via cash. But, at the same time as interest rates are painfully low, equity and most other asset class volatility is high: and the economic backdrop is also looking likely to keep it high for a considerable period of time.

Spot the obvious challenge – and dilemma – for investors!

Generally, whatever is driving the need/desire for income, the requirement of most investors is straightforward, i.e. yield optimisation and wealth preservation: or, more simply put, a decent 'return *on* capital' with 'return *of* capital'. But, as this book self-evidences, the choices available to investors to potentially 'solve' income requirements mean that deciding on 'optimal' income investment strategies is not necessarily so simple.

So, what can structured investments (more frequently referred to as structured 'products', but an immediate 'flag' that discerning investors would do well to think about) offer investors – and how close can they get to solving the fundamental interests of income-seeking investors?

Structured investments first surfaced in the UK in the early to mid-1990s. Innovative, even revolutionary, they brought a new dimension to an otherwise tired investment world, offering investors something different to 'traditional' investment funds that mutual fund companies had been flogging since the 1930s.

The industry has enjoyed notable periods of success, and growth in the UK has been exceptionally strong over the past 10–15 years, evolving from days when only 10–20 providers were active in the UK, raising little more than £1 billion per year, to nearly 100 providers, issuing nearly 1,000 'products' and raising nearly £14 billion in 2009. Structured investments are coming of age – in the UK and globally.

The first part of this chapter will do away with textbook theory and technical jargon and consider what investors themselves genuinely seek and want – and what, conceptually, they would design for themselves, as investment solutions, if they could. The answer to this hypothetical scenario will immediately highlight why structured investment use has surged in the UK retail market in recent years – nearly 50% growth in 2009 alone – with no sign of abating. The simple fact is that structured investments can meet the primary interests of many

structured investments can meet the primary interests of many – if not most – investors

– if not most – investors, which the industry data irrefutably highlights: investors are voting with their feet and, more pertinently, their funds in selecting structured investments.

The second part of this chapter will introduce structured investments and describe how they work. The chapter will go 'under the bonnet' to look at the building blocks of construction and highlight points of detail that savvy investors should be aware of and ensure they understand. Specific structured investment income strategies will also be highlighted. The chapter will, of course, also carefully detail risks that investors should be aware of and be alert to – as well as highlighting one or two 'tricks of the trade' that some providers might prefer prospective investors didn't know or recognise.

To be clear from the outset, there are two key risks for investors to understand when considering investing in structured investments:

■ **Counterparty risk.** Usually an individual bank or financial institution is providing the assets, or securities, that underpin a structured investment – and this bank/institution, known as the counterparty, must remain solvent during the investment term, until maturity.

■ **Stockmarket risk.** If a structured investment is not fully protected from the performance of the underlying market or asset that it is linked to (bearing in mind that it is possible for market/asset risk to be entirely removed through some types of structured investment), if that market or asset breaches any defined level of protection provided then capital may be at risk and potentially reduced at maturity.

Over the past decade, the importance of understanding these risks has been highlighted through industry events, in certain structured products. There have been two notable periods or events when both of these risks have been shown to exist, for some investors in certain providers' products. Key words for investors therefore include 'knowledge', 'understanding' and 'differentiation'. Investors need to know how to sort the wheat from the chaff, to avoid the potentially duff providers and products, and identify and potentially utilise the value-adding providers and propositions: especially as like in any industry 'best of breed' is in a minority.

Ultimately, this chapter will highlight the compelling scope to use structured investment intelligently to meet income needs, whilst also providing balanced, commonsense 'points of sanity', including facts such as:

■ **Differentiation is essential.** Like any industry, whether it is mutual funds (active or passive), investment advisers (independent or 'tied'), or indeed financial publishers and publications (including books like this one), differentiation is essential.

The structured investment industry is anything but one uniform, homogenous industry – and the difference in approach, calibre and value of different providers and their products is marked. Knowing how to sort the wheat from the chaff is critical.

■ **Working knowledge and understanding of structured investments is essential.** There's simply no such thing as the perfect investment. But working knowledge and understanding of structured investments will facilitate how investors can benefit from the best that this sector can offer.

■ **Better informed investors make better investment decisions – independent professional advice is always recommended.** Independent professional advice (notwithstanding the statement above, i.e. differentiation in the advice sector is just as important as it is in the funds/product provider sector) can be invaluable, not only for assistance in identifying and selecting the optimal structured investment propositions available at any point in time (the section on differentiating will highlight just how important this is), but because expert professional advice should also focus upon and result in sensible portfolio construction, i.e. diversification.

As with any investment option, prospective investors must understand both the risks and returns of structured investments and figure out how to use them within a broadly diversified portfolio, alongside other asset allocation/portfolio options.

Conceptually, what would investors design for themselves... if they could?

As suggested in the introduction, let's start with the absolute basics in terms of thinking about what investors need and want from their investments, and what they would design for themselves if they were empowered to, before considering the specifics and potential value of structured investments.

■ **Fact:** savers and investors need 'real returns', over and above cash and inflation.

■ **Fact:** savers and investors therefore need 'real assets', for market/asset-based returns.

■ **Fact:** few investors would describe themselves as anything other than cautious to balanced – whilst the risk of most market/asset-linked investments is usually 'variable', at best.

> The most pertinent fact, however, is that these facts don't reconcile themselves terribly well against each other. In fact, the inference of these facts is that most investment options, if looked at in the cold light of day, are akin to investors putting square pegs in round holes.

But, an army of respectable investment professionals, not least the mutual funds industry, has spent decades and millions of pounds 'educating' investors to tolerate/accept market/asset risk. Well-worn explanations seemingly make sense, such as *'the relationship between market/asset risks and returns is unbreakable – but risk can be managed or reduced through diversification and time'*. No doubt, many readers have heard such 'mantras' many times. But recent history proves that neither diversification nor time always work as a means of genuinely managing market/asset risk – let alone controlling investor's exposure to it:

■ First, in times of market stress/distress pretty much all markets and asset classes fell in value, and no amount of diversification prevented portfolio losses as 'correlation' between markets and asset classes converged.

■ Second, the FTSE 100 is still some 1,500 points below its record high of nearly 7,000 points, seen on 30 December 1999 – over ten years ago – and the five-year time horizon many professional advisers advocate as sufficient to mitigate market risk has been shown to be woefully inadequate on at least two occasions in this past decade: in the Technology, Media and Telecoms (TMT) led collapse of 1999–03 and in the more recent 2008–09 financial crisis.

So, what if we dispense with the 'traditional' investment industry's rule book and apparent 'education' and ask *'What would investors design for themselves, if they could?'* I have asked this question of groups of advisers and investors for many years and, whilst many micro-points often come out, three main answers consistently emerge. Most investors, no matter how cautious or sophisticated, would:

1 **Pre-define investment risk.** Let's face it, no one takes investment risk 'for the sake of it'.

2 **Pre-define investment return.** Let's also tell it like it is, we'd all 'have our cake and eat it too', i.e. have all the upside, commensurate with risk profiles, if we could.

3 **Remove any charges.** And, if we admit, it, we'd all like it for free – low or even no charges are on 'the wish list' of most investors.

Take a step back and consider this properly. It's conceptual and simplistic – but, at the most fundamental level, this combination of investment features is surely what 'uneducated' investors would design for themselves, as the 'utopian investment', if they were empowered to. Now ask yourself, 'What investments do I know that come close to all this?'

Investments, product providers and advisers, need to empathise with and meet the real and actual interests of investors. It's difficult to argue that the three points of hypothetical investor interest above *don't* reflect the common interest of many, if not most, if not all, investors. But, it's also difficult *not* to conclude that most 'traditional' investment options/providers/products therefore fall fundamentally short of meeting the primary interests of most investors.

In particular, no investor chooses investment risk for the sake of it – especially income investors, as explained in the introduction. Yet nearly all traditional investment funds carry implicit and varying degrees of investment risk, despite the main investment concern for most investors surely being nothing more complicated than the basic risk of losing money.

In a nutshell, having defined the utopian investment, it seems fair to suggest that it doesn't look or feel anything like a mutual fund – and, conceptually at least, structured investments appear to come strikingly close.

Introducing structured investments

Structured investments are not alchemy – a phrase that will be repeated throughout this chapter: they do not make investment risk disappear. The key to understanding the appeal of structured investments for investors, however, is recognising the direct balance they provide between risk and return. In addition, the sector is unparalleled by any other in the investment universe, in terms of its ability to innovate and its scope to meet and deliver against the real interests and needs of many investors. This cocktail of unique benefits and advantages should make this chapter enticing and enlightening reading for income-seeking investors.

Structured investments come in many forms. At their simplest, structured investments offer investors a choice of the basic propositions:

- growth
- income
- income and growth.

Growth investors generally seek superior, more efficient, risk/return profiles than are available through passive/active funds or direct investment in markets/assets. Income investors generally seek superior/above market (cash, equity, bond) yields/coupons, with the lowest risk profile possible. Income and growth investors, rather obviously, generally seek 'hybrid' investments, offering a potential mix of both income and capital growth.

In the UK in 2009 nearly 100 retail (i.e. excluding institutional, pension, etc.) providers issued nearly 1,000 products, accounting for nearly £14 billion of investment. Because of the scope of structured investments, i.e. the variations in design, definitions vary even amongst providers themselves, but let's start with as close as we can get to a useful 'definition':

General definition

Structured investments are usually fixed term investments (albeit the best ones come with liquidity, i.e. access to capital invested is possible during the investment term), linked to underlying markets/asset classes, providing growth or income, with pre-defined parameters (i.e. levels and type) of both risk and return.

Let's also identify some 'characteristics' of structured investments that will be useful in helping recognise investments as 'structured':

General characteristics

Structured investments are usually 'formula-driven' investments, employing 'financial engineering' to optimise the risk/return profile of, usually passive, underlying investment links (to markets or asset classes).

'Formula driven' means structured investments precisely define risk and return parameters: there are no 'grey areas'. The levels of risk and return are contractually, legally stated, via the terms of a bond: they are not 'aims' or 'promises', as per the active fund management world. In the structured investment world, investments always do 'exactly what they say on the tin', subject 'only' to credit, or counterparty, risk, which will be given the appropriate level of attention needed in this chapter.

It's worth highlighting, in stating that structured investments do 'exactly what they say on the tin' and demonstrating that this chapter will be pitching the case for 'best of breed structured investments' (not structured investments per se), that not all providers are as good at labelling their tins as they should be – and that not all investors are as good at looking for and understanding the labels as they need to be. This chapter will devote overt space for detail on risks and sensible due diligence considerations that prudent investors should take into account in evaluating structured investments generally, or indeed any specific provider/proposition.

On this matter, it is timely to point out that it is patently simplistic for providers, advisers, commentators or prospective investors to think of and describe/label structured investments as 'low risk'. It is factual that structured investments can be 'fully protected' from underlying market/asset class risk. But, just as frequently – and usefully (perhaps more usefully) – they can also be 'contingent protected', i.e. come with defined exposure to the underlying market/asset class risk, in order to enhance returns.

The first point of common sense to stress, therefore, is that *structured investments are not simply about and should not all be thought of as low risk* – not least as the definition of risk in this context is usually only focused on one of the key potential advantages of structured investments, their ability to remove, reduce or at least define exposure to 'market' risk. Equal importance and prominence must be attached to the key risk that always exists in structured investments, 'credit', i.e. counterparty, risk.

Providers should treat prospective investors as 'adults' and be grown up in the language of discussing risk and return profiles – as opposed to letting non-investment driven marketing teams focus overtly upon positioning headline rates, with marketing gimmicks and toys, to attract investors, especially non-advised or ill-advised investors.

But, let's round off the introduction to structured investments with immediate high-level 'observations' that will help start highlighting some of the key benefits and advantages of the sector:

General observations

The 'financial engineering' employed in structured investments can re-position risk and return, without any active fund management (process or risk).

Market risk can be removed entirely, reduced or at least pre-defined, but it is exchanged for credit risk – otherwise known as 'counterparty risk' (which must always be understood).

Understanding structured investments: differentiation is essential

Before moving on to the specifics of how structured investments work – and in particular income strategies – it's important to highlight high level general points that prospective investors should consider with regard to structured investments, if they want to get the best value possible from the sector.

All of the references made throughout this chapter are to structured 'investments', as opposed to structured 'products'. In reality, they're both pretty much the same thing – but intelligent prospective investors surely want to discuss investments as 'investments', and assess risk and return profiles as they would any other investment option, and references to 'products' just seem to dilute the obvious importance of this fact. So, let's talk investments not products. This might sound like a rather vague notion – but this section of the chapter will explain the difference between 'easy structured products' and 'intelligent structured investments', and highlight why differentiation is essential.

differentiation is essential

Let's start by thinking about who 'the players' are, in terms of the functioning of the structured investments market. There are four 'key players' to take into account:

■ **Investment banks.** First, 'investment banks', known as counterparties, usually provide/issue the assets/securities underpinning particular plans.

■ **Providers.** Secondly, providers, who work with the investment banks, generally decide on, arrange, develop and market the investment/ investor proposition, and are responsible for shaping the investment strategy/value on offer.

■ **Advisers or 'sales forces'.** Thirdly, advisers or salesforces play their part. Independent providers usually operate through independent professional advisers, who in turn are responsible for identifying, selecting and advising on the best structured investments on merit, based upon suitability for their clients. High street banks and building societies, on the other hand, usually operate through their branches and 'tied' salesforces, and 'sell' their own products.

■ **Investors.** Fourthly, yes, it's you, the investor – self-evidently investing the capital.

The sector is a rapidly growing one – it will pass through £50 billion in AUM (Assets Under Management) soon, but the UK structured investment industry is anything but one uniform market. With nearly 100 providers active in 2009, issuing nearly 1,000 'products' and raising nearly £14 billion, of course not all providers or products are the same. But, sweeping statements and generalisations do abound with regard to this sector.

However, when it comes to structured investments 'distribution dynamics' have shaped the industry, and how it has been thought of over the years, more than 'financial engineering' capabilities. The reason for taking the time to explain this rather general background is that the calibre and value of a structured 'product' provider or its propositions often depends more upon the type of provider distribution 'channel' than the provider's manufacturing capabilities. Frankly, most providers could probably manufacture better 'products', but not all of them – in fact few of them – choose to or are motivated to do so. The obvious question is, Why?

The answer is that, generally, the market polarises between two fairly distinct types of provider and products. Approximately 75–80% of the UK's structured investment sales are currently 'big brand' bank and building society, including NS&I, driven. Let's call them 'High Street Institutions' (HSIs). The balance, about 20–25% of industry sales volume, is through 'independent' providers and asset management firms.

The main difference between HSIs and independent providers is the fact that HSIs 'own' proprietary distribution, which means 'captive customers', often anything between, say, 1 and 10 million of them. In addition, HSIs usually own 'advisers' – although this is often a euphemism for tied 'salesforces/branch staff'. Independent providers/asset management firms, on the other hand, usually own no distribution, i.e. customers, and are wholly dependent upon independent wealth management firms identifying merit in specific investment propositions and using them based upon client suitability... or unsuitability.

For HSIs that own customers and salesforces (and that are owned by shareholders), the 'name of the game' is simple: profitably sell as much product as possible, to as many clients as possible, as quickly as possible. That might sound basic, but it's also difficult to refute. Imagine the chairman of a major bank standing up at the AGM and telling shareholders that management had focused on building warm relationships with their customers during the year, which should yield profits in future years... but hadn't in the previous 12 months!

Basically, the ideal game plan for 'big brand' institutions is 'one size fits all', or as close as it's possible to get, in terms of building the sales scale and volume that is wanted. This leads to standardised 'fast food' product strategy, which means customers are offered what they're most likely to buy, as opposed to 'à la carte' fine dining. Now this may not sound like such a bad thing, apart from the fact that what an uninformed, unadvised or ill-advised customer is likely to buy might be a world apart from what the best investment might be if à la carte choice and client-centric independent advice was provided.

In the independent intermediary channel, independent providers and asset managers cannot 'get away' with standardised products that might suffice on the high street. Such products simply don't 'cut the mustard' and impress free-thinking and opinionated independent advisers.

Independent wealth managers/IFAs are research-driven, asset allocation focused and client-centric. Robust due diligence processes are employed to assess investments and to identify investment integrity, purpose, relevance and merit. One-size-fits-all sales are not possible, as independent wealth managers/advisers have no interest whatsoever in whether or not a provider maximises sales.

In essence, the point of differentiation being highlighted is as follows:

- **Easy structured products** are generally designed by providers who 'own' distribution, both customers and salesforces, in order to maximise sales and profits.
- **Intelligent structured investments** are more likely to be developed by independent providers, working with independent wealth managers, to drive investment integrity and client-centric value.

It may be harsh, but plain vanilla 'easy structured products' promoted by 'big brand' institutions are often designed to optimise sales... not investment propositions for investors. This is not to say that plain vanilla FTSE 100 offerings, as often seen on the high street, are poor value, per se. Indeed, for inexperienced investors, plain vanilla structured investments can be a sensible 'stepping stone' towards equity-linked investing. But, low participation rates/low caps on growth or low income is not necessarily good value for more experienced or better advised investors.

The problem/obstacle to better value, however, is that 'intelligent structured investments' won't/don't maximise sales for HSIs that own customers. Not only may customers fail to quickly and easily pick up and invest in something that has a slightly more demanding 'investment story' to it but – more disturbingly – the HSI's own staff might struggle to readily pick up and understand anything more challenging than a simple offering.

In differentiating 'easy structured products' and 'intelligent structured investments', there is an irony that should be apparent. Notably, big brand institutions, that have global asset management companies in their midst, have the resources to offer better 'products' – but choose not to and do the least with their resources, while the firms that most need research capabilities – the independent providers who need to impress independent wealth managers – often don't have the resources.

The upshot of this is that many structured investments – both on the high street and in the independent intermediary channel – aren't as intelli-

many structured investments aren't as intelligent as they need to be

gent as they need to be. And most certainly there is far too little inclination across the industry to undertake or demonstrate meaningful research-backed investment thinking, which is what savvy investors should be looking for, and far too much

preference for simplistic 'headline rate driven' product marketing, that savvy investors should be avoiding.

The point of this section is to highlight that not all structured investments are virtuous – and to explain why. More importantly, however, the main point is that differentiation is as essential with structured investments as it is with any other investment sector, or indeed industry.

The good news for the sector – and investors – is that professional advisers are increasing their working knowledge of structured investments, through industry education that is increasingly being provided, and the audience of receptive but selectively supportive wealth managers is steadily increasing.

Some advisers still dislike and don't use any structured investment, with no attempt at or consideration of differentiation between the providers and their propositions. But it doesn't take a rocket scientist – and it shouldn't need the UK regulator (the Financial Services Authority) – to tell advisers that either like and use, or don't like and don't use, an entire £50 billion industry, that a 'marmite' approach, with no differentiation between 100 providers issuing 1,000 products a year, is inadequate.

Intelligent structured investments, however, add indispensable value for investors. Knowledge and differentiation is essential, as 'best of breed' providers and propositions will always be in a minority – but that's no different to the mutual fund industry, where most wealth managers don't use more than 1–200 funds out of a possible 2,000.

Fundamentally 'passive' investments

Before we go 'under the bonnet' of a structured investment and detail what goes on 'behind the scenes' in an investment bank issuing structured investments, there is a critical aspect of structured investments that needs to be highlighted – one that many investors and advisers do not fully recognise. Structured investments are fundamentally passive investments. Not only are risks and returns usually contractually pre-defined but, importantly, the vast majority of structured investments are not subject to any form of active fund management process or risk.

Most commonly, structured investments are constructed upon 'passive' underlying investments, i.e. they use indices, such as the UK's FTSE 100 index (the index reflecting the performance of the 100 largest UK-domiciled 'blue chip' companies that are listed on the UK's London Stock Exchange) or the US's S&P 500 Index (the index reflecting the performance of the 500 leading listed 'large-cap' companies in the major industries and sectors of the US economy). But, significantly, unlike most passive index funds or ETFs, both the risk and return of a structured investment can be financially engineered, i.e. optimised, to improve the risk/return profile – in a manner that active or passive fund managers could only dream of but, by definition, could never deliver.

Fundamentally passive investments

Structured investments generally operate on passive investment principles, linking to underlying markets/asset classes through indices (including ETFs), i.e. without any active fund management process or risks.

Significantly, unlike most index funds or ETFs, both risk and return can be financially engineered, i.e. optimised, in a structured investment to improve the risk/return profile.

It is also worth noting, for fans of passive investments – and there's a seemingly daily growing belief in passive investing *vis-à-vis* often expensive and often unsuccessful active fund management – that with a structured investment the replication of index returns is 'perfect', i.e. devoid of any tracking error that is normally unavoidable through the various stock replication processes and charges.

One important counterpoint to note is that structured investments normally link to indices on a price return, not total return, basis. So, whilst structured investments provide a defined level of growth or income potential, there is no participation in any dividends linked to the stocks that comprise the underlying index. But this is not always as critical as it sounds – and will depend upon the market, asset class and structured investment terms on offer. As always, knowledge, understanding and differentiation remain the key words.

Inside a structured investment

A common assertion that still abounds – amongst structured critics/sceptics – is that what's 'under the bonnet' of a structured investments is complex. Actually the building blocks of a structured investment are really quite straightforward. In fact, if an adviser suggests – or even protests – to an investor that they don't understand structured investments – as is still sometimes the case – it might be better for the investor to conclude that they've just learnt more about the calibre of that adviser than they have about structured investments! It might even be a useful litmus test for investors needing to select an adviser!

Pertinently however – and also recognising that the above statement might be viewed rather subjectively – the more important and irrefutable fact is that whilst it may be interesting (for some folk!) to know what goes on behind the scenes of manufacturing a structured investment, the details are basically irrelevant to an investor, in terms of them understanding the actual risks that they will be exposed to and the prospects of successful future returns.

The reason for this is that any risks under the bonnet of a structured investment are borne by the counterparties – not investors. This is very distinct from, say, investing in a mutual fund – let's say an 'absolute return' strategy – where what the manager does, how they do it, and their skill and success in doing it (or lack of), will have a direct and material impact on the investor, because mutual fund managers only 'aim' to deliver what they claim or 'promise'. If they fail to perform, as so many do, they bank their initial and annual charges and simply write an annual statement report explaining their underperformance, usually with lots of reference to 'relative' performance versus benchmark and/or peer group, i.e. they may have lost money but so has the benchmark and all the other fund managers!

Not so with structured investments.

> With structured investments, not only are the underlying investments usually passive and the risk and return parameters precisely pre-defined, the counterparty, i.e. the investment bank providing the assets that underpin the investment, is contractually and legally obligated, through the terms of the securities they have issued, to deliver what has been promised.

Usually, therefore, the only circumstances in which a counterparty will not deliver what has been stated in the terms of the securities it has issued are 'legal default' – which, in practice, as will become clear when the underlying securities are explained in more detail, usually means they must be insolvent.

But, notwithstanding the above explanation, let's look at the 'building blocks' of a structured investment, i.e. the component parts that the investment banks piece together to make the investments work. There are actually only two basic components for investors to be aware of:

■ First, capital repayment/protection from market/asset risk is typically ensured through the construction of a 'Zero Coupon Bond'. This requires the bulk of the principal amount invested being put into a deposit, which with interest added will equal the full amount originally invested at maturity.

■ Second, the structure participates in market/asset growth or creates income through the use of 'financial instruments'. The majority of the balance of the principal capital, not used for the Zero Coupon Bond, will be used to purchase (or potentially sell) call (or put) options.

Zero coupon bonds	*Options*
A zero coupon bond (sometimes called a ZCB or 'zero') might sound 'technical' but, in practice, it's little more than a deposit.	On the other side of the equation, with the 'zero' taking care of repaying capital invested at maturity, the counterparty must create 'the payoff' for investors, i.e. the 'growth' or 'income' potential.
Usually, approximately 75% of the amount invested in a structured investment is used by the counterparty to create a 'zero coupon bond'.	'Options' give investors exposure to underlying markets or assets at a fraction of the price of the asset – and the counterparty will generally spend approximately 20% of the amount invested in a structured investment on options.
Essentially, a 'zero', in this context, is akin to an institutional deposit, placed by the counterparty's structuring team with the counterparty's treasury team.	
As with any deposit, interest is generated as a result of this transaction.	There are many different types of options, which are also known as derivatives, or 'financial instruments'.
But as the structuring team is creating a fixed term investment they do not want regular and/or variable interest during the investment term, so they 'swap' the variable interest during the investment term for a fixed interest payment at the end of the investment term.	Generally, 'call options' are bought, by the counterparty, to create growth potential, i.e. upside. And 'put options' will be sold, by the counterparty, to either increase growth potential or to create income streams. ▶

Zero coupon bonds	*Options*
Because the deposit, or 'zero', doesn't generate any interest or coupon, it is known as a 'zero coupon bond'. The amount placed on deposit, in the 'zero', is simple in theory. It is calculated so that when the fixed interest payment is paid by the treasury team at maturity, the total amount, i.e. the 'zero' plus the interest, equals the capital invested in the structure.	Options are highly flexible, and can be used by counterparties to create innovative growth or income strategies on virtually any investment market or asset class, with a multitude of investment features, over virtually any investment term, in virtually any currency, including creating access to markets or asset classes that investors might not otherwise be able to access through 'traditional' investment funds.

Protection barriers – exposure to underlying market/asset risk

As alluded to, some structured investments seek to provide superior growth or higher income returns, by providing protection from a defined level of stockmarket risk, as opposed to full protection from market/asset risk.

For instance, an investor's capital might be protected unless the underlying index (or indices) falls by more than 50%, from its starting (strike) level during the investment term or at maturity. If this is the case, i.e. if the index breaches the protection barrier level, then the investment will not repay capital in full at maturity, and investors will lose capital, on a one-for-one basis, in line with the performance of the index/indices.

This risk to capital is the result of the counterparty selling a put option, which introduces market/asset risk to an otherwise potentially fully protected investment, where it did not exist before (as opposed to buying a put option, which introduces protection). So, why do it?

Simply, put options are sold and risk to capital introduced to certain types of structured investment because this process generates premiums received in return for writing/selling the put, which can be used to buy more call options, in order to enhance growth potential or to optimise an income stream.

this process generates premiums received in return for writing/selling the put

In practice, most providers do *not* seek to maximise the value of the put, rather they seek to maximise the protection it provides, or at least to strike an optimal balance between the two sides of the coin. For instance, in the

UK, most 'down and in' put options (as a put that requires the underlying asset to fall is termed) utilised within capital at risk structured investments are sold with 'deep' falls in the underlying index/indices needed (i.e. 50%, as opposed to, say the 10–15% levels seen in the US) before the protection barrier is breached.

The answer, therefore, as to why some structured investments offer only 'contingent/defined levels of protection' is simple, but also critical in demonstrating that structured investments are not alchemy and do not provide returns that are 'too good to be true' and therefore to be avoided (as some commentators like to assert – frustratingly perpetuating ignorance in others who might actually think such comments are credible). The growth or income subsequently produced as a result of having a defined protection barrier is a simple – but irrefutable – matter of economics, determined by the value of the put option, i.e. the premium it generates. The more risk the put carries, for instance by linking to an underlying market or asset class that might be more volatile than others, or by setting the barrier level higher than, say, 50%, the more value in the put and the higher the growth or income.

There are different types of barrier used by different counterparties and providers – but the good news is that the main choices are fairly common.

Continuously observed (including 'intra-day') (known as an 'American' barrier)	Continuously observed (daily closing prices only) (known as an 'American' barrier)	Non-continuously observed (known as a 'European' barrier)
Continuously observed barriers are monitored every minute of every day throughout the investment term – and can be breached at any point, including 'intra-day'. Intra-day movement can be significant (+/–10% in a day), even on mainstream indices, especially in the current environment, so this barrier carries greater risk to capital. It is also the least transparent.	Identical to intra-day continuously observed barriers, apart from the important fact that intra-day monitoring is excluded. The barrier can be breached at any point during the investment term, from Day 1 until maturity, but based only upon the closing prices of the index/indices at the end of each trading day.	A notable improvement over either of the American barriers, a European barrier transforms the risk usually associated with a market/asset-linked investment, by only assessing the index/indices level at maturity – which may be 5–6 years after the strike date.

▶

Continuously observed (including 'intra-day') (known as an 'American' barrier)	Continuously observed (daily closing prices only) (known as an 'American' barrier)	Non-continuously Observed (known as a 'European' barrier)
Some providers favour this type of barrier, as it is the most profitable, in terms of the value of the put option that is sold to create the risk. But, this value is rarely used to enhance returns sufficiently to justify the extra risk – so it seems to be used more by providers who like maximising their own margins!	This reduces risk considerably, particularly during times of market stress. It is also more transparent. This barrier has less put premium for providers, but offers better risk/return value for investors – and 'deep ' barriers can be an 'astute' way to 'use' or 'exploit' risk for experienced investors.	A 'European' barrier cannot be breached during the investment term – it is not even monitored. Assuming it is also set deeply this reduces market risk considerably. It is extremely transparent and easy to understand. However, European barriers offer the lowest put premium to providers – and, for this reason, are not always viable/possible – but they should be favoured by investors, when available.

The obvious point to highlight, having delved 'under the bonnet' of a structured investment is that both the zero coupon bond and options (whatever type they are) are provided by a counterparty – usually the same counterparty. Counterparty exposure is therefore a critical aspect of structured investments for investors to understand – arguably the single most important aspect. Most importantly, investors must understand that the repayment of any capital invested in a structured investment and any potential growth or income returns depend upon the solvency of the counterparty at all times.

But, that said – and forcefully so – let's make another point immediately: a commonsense point. Investors fundamentally understand deposits and 'counterparty risk' attached to them: it's just that they don't call it or know that it's called 'credit risk'. But savers and investors do, generally, understand the principles of credit risk. For instance, they know that if they want to sleep at night, if they place their deposit with the biggest, safest banks in the country/world, they will receive less interest than they might if they place their savings with a smaller bank, regional building society or overseas bank.

In fact, most savers and investors also probably intuitively understand why this is so, i.e. major banks are big enough not to need investors' money and safe enough not to have to pay much interest to attract it; whilst smaller banks want investors' money more and have to pay more interest to attract it – and to make up for the fact that they're small, i.e. that they carry more 'credit risk'.

That said, despite suggesting that savers and investors might already understand 'credit risk', given that it is one of the most important risks of structured investments, this chapter will comprehensively explain sensible due diligence processes for prospective investors to think about when assessing structured investments and different counterparty options.

Pricing parameters

Two particular factors determine the structured investment manufacturing capabilities of providers – and are therefore worth highlighting given the recurring reference made in this chapter to structured investments not being alchemy.

■ First, the level of interest rates clearly dictates the percentage of principal capital that needs to be placed on deposit, in the 'zero coupon bond', in order to create 100% repayment of the full principal capital amount at maturity.

■ Second, the level of volatility in the underlying market/asset dictates the cost/value of call/put options, that determines the level of growth or income that can be produced.

These factors are 'black and white', and act as parameters that all providers need to operate within – notwithstanding the fact that 'credit risk' can be used – or 'abused' – by providers seeking cheaper 'zero coupon bond' options, so that they can create higher growth or income payoffs.

Discerning investors should therefore seek providers that utilise counterparties that are highly rated and regarded, taking into account various and combined factors (factors detailed later in this chapter). Higher headline rates on structured investments can be achieved by providers who utilise (or are internally linked to) weaker counterparties – but investors should always differentiate between headline rate driven products and potentially better value investment integrity.

In addition to any 'absolute charges' in a structured investment, savvy investors should also think about the 'relative costs' of investing in a structured investment.

This may include considering the cost of pre-defined protection from market risk (including the potential removal of it altogether) and pre-defined returns potential (including potentially unconditional, i.e. fixed and non-market-linked returns) and weighing up these potential benefits against possible/probable lack of participation in dividends, if the underlying market or asset carries them, and/or low participation rates and/or capped returns: though neither of these points is always the case.

CHARGES/COSTS

For readers keeping a tally on how much the counterparty has 'spent' under the bonnet of our example, it will be apparent that only 95% of the total 'asset price' of the structured investment has so far been accounted for: 75% on the zero coupon bond and 20% on the options.

In addition to the zero and the options, the third aspect, or 'component', of building a structured investment, that investors should take into account, is the level of charges/costs that are included. In this example, circa 5% has been set aside for internal charges.

Sometimes charges won't be disclosed by the provider, and this might be explained with reference to the fact that there are no 'explicit' charges. This means that the returns of most structured investments are stated *after* allowing for any internal charges, including administration fees and expenses and any commissions: unlike traditional mutual funds, active or passive, there are no direct deductions from an investor's capital, either initial or annual.

100% of any investment made in a structured investment will usually benefit from the growth or income potential and any protection from market/asset risk that is provided.

However, charges are clearly an important aspect of any investment – and structured investments clearly carry charges (or providers wouldn't be in the business of offering them!). So, notwithstanding the fact that most structured investment returns are stated after allowing for charges, investors should always look for and expect to find/be provided with total transparency with regard to the charges of any investment.

Progressive providers will proactively detail their implicit/internal charges, without being asked. Opacity is only likely to appeal to providers motivated by and concealing high margins. As a fairly obvious rule of thumb, if charges aren't readily apparent it's probably best for investors to assume that they're more distasteful, i.e. higher, than they could or should be. Any charges, implicit or explicit, should always be disclosed, by any provider – but, again, less than client-centric providers might hide this important 'big point in the small print'.

In the example illustrated here, charges of 5% have been used. It should be noted that for a retail proposition this is likely to be competitive, i.e. good value for investors. Many providers, particularly HISs, may work with charges of up to twice this level – and hence offer inferior propositions via their high street channels than investors could access via independent advisers and independent providers.

Lastly, however, it is worth remembering that protection from market/asset risk and greater certainty over returns has a cost because it has a value, for many investors.

Introducing structured investment income strategies

As stated early in this chapter, income is a matter of need for many investors. Indeed, income investors may sometimes need to be reminded that they are – or should be – cautious investors.

Responsible, 'client-centric' providers need to demonstrate that they understand this. Despite the fact that interest rates are low and demand for income options is therefore high, cautious investors are likely to require security and familiarity for their savings and investments – and, for many, this may mean that deposit accounts must be seen as the best fit/best advice solution. But, that said, deposit accounts – particularly with rates at their current levels – have an opportunity cost, as well as a value, and certain investors may not only want but need a level of income that can only be achieved outside of deposit accounts.

> certain investors need a level of income that can only be achieved outside of deposit accounts

Choice is a good thing, as is innovation – and the structured investment industry is rightly famed for providing both. But innovation and simplicity/transparency should not be opposing forces, particularly in solving income solutions for 'typical' income investors, where a cautious approach is always likely to be a prerequisite.

For all that is good about structured investments – here's that phrase again – it must be remembered they are not alchemy. They cannot and do not make investment risk disappear – and there will always be a trade-off in balancing the level of income with the level of protection from market risk.

The simple fact is that it is not possible to deliver superior income, over and above the risk-free rate of the market (which is, of course, where the investment banks/counterparties price the financial instruments that are utilised in the construction of a structured investment) without introducing some risk – either to income or capital, through either market or credit risk. This fact should be obvious – but it is often overlooked or forgotten, not least as some providers (anxious and willing to exploit the need and demand for income) exhibit an unshakable propensity to use 'smoke and mirrors' and to hide big points in the small print.

The bottom line is that:

- Low/lower risk (to capital and/or income) income strategies will offer low/lower premiums over and above the risk-free rate.
- High/higher income options will carry greater risks (to capital and/or income streams) in return for the higher potential rewards.
- And 'specialist' investments (for instance, strategies linking to higher risk, or possibly multiple or esoteric, underlying market/asset indexes or indices) are likely to carry higher risks than investments considered more 'mainstream'.

For the purpose of this book and its potentially broad reader base, the main focus of the small number of examples provided will be regarding more mainstream options.

1 Plain vanilla 'protected' income strategies

The starting point on the plain vanilla curve of structured investment income options is strategies that are fully protected from underlying market/asset risk. (100% capital protection, as many providers would describe such investments/products – although 'capital protection' as a phrase neglects the fact that counterparty risk is not explained – so is a phrase providers ought to consider more carefully.)

As explained previously, structured investments cannot create fixed and unconditional income, over and above the risk-free rate, without incorporating risk somewhere in the equation. So, the immediate point to make, in respect of 'plain vanilla' fully protected income strategies, is that you can't have your cake and eat it too. If this were possible, structured investment providers would be building product quicker than investors could buy it!

In fact, in order to create an income stream with any meaningful premium over and above the risk-free rate possible, the income stream of a protected plain vanilla proposition needs to be made conditional in some way – most obviously through linking it to the underlying market/asset.

A typical protected income proposition, therefore, might offer, say, 5.5% income per year, over a five-year investment term, paid each year if the FTSE 100 is at or above its starting (strike) level. This is a pretty reasonable and transparent condition. If the index is at or above its starting (strike) level then 5.5% income is payable annually – or, if the index is below its starting level on any anniversary, no income is payable that year.

Twists on this theme can occur in several ways:

- It might be possible to build in a 'memory' feature, that will remember if a coupon is missed at any anniversary (because the index is below its starting level trigger condition), and to pay any missed income as a backdated coupon at a subsequent anniversary, if the index is then above the trigger level.

- It might be possible to build in a 'trigger' that removes the index condition *if* the index has risen at any anniversary by, say, 25%. This would convert all future income payments remaining to fixed and unconditional: a 'neat' outcome.

- A 'roll-up' option might be offered, allowing any income generated during the investment term to be 'reinvested' until maturity. The advantage of this might be that it is possible to offset the 'income' against capital gains tax allowances at maturity.

2 'Contingent/defined level protected' income strategies

Moving along the plain vanilla curve a little, in recognition of the fact that for some investors the premium on the income stream in the first example wasn't sufficient to justify putting the income stream at risk through the index condition that applied – despite the simplicity of the condition and the full protection of capital from market risk – the next step is to introduce a barrier (described above) that repayment of capital will be linked to.

For instance, full protection from market risk may be linked to the UK's FTSE 100 index, contingent upon the index not falling by more than 50% during the investment term. In this way, the income that had previously been both conservative and conditional might be enhanced to, say, 6.5%, and be fixed and unconditional throughout the investment term.

The 'downside' of such a strategy, however, is that capital is at risk should the FTSE 100 fall and 'breach' the protection barrier level. It will depend upon what type of barrier was used as to whether the barrier will be monitored during the investment term or only at maturity – but this will also affect the level of income provided. A continuously observed (daily closing prices only) 'American' barrier might result in 7% fixed annual income. Whilst the lower risk, but less valuable, 'European' barrier might leave the income at 6.5%, for example.

The same twists that applied above might also be possible with this strategy option. In addition:

■ It might be possible to build in a 'trigger' that would remove the contingent barrier condition and convert the investment strategy to one that benefits from full protection from market risk *if* the index has risen at any anniversary by, say, 25%. Again, a 'neat' outcome.

These 'capital at risk' income strategies are known in the structured investment/derivatives industry as 'reverse convertibles', because they reverse the principle of starting with protection from market/asset risk and endeavouring to maximise growth or income and have instead secured the income stream first and linked repayment of capital to the market/asset.

3 Range accrual income strategies

A little further along the curve, in the pursuit of higher and more compelling income propositions/solutions (for wealth managers/professionally advised investors seeking them) let's look at a strategy known as a 'range accrual'.

Still conceptually straightforward, but now linking both the income stream and the repayment of capital at maturity to an underlying market/asset, a typical range accrual might currently offer 7.5% income per year, payable each year, based upon the market/asset index being at or above, say, 60% of its starting (strike) level – with repayment of capital at maturity linked to the same index condition.

At each anniversary, income might be paid for each week that the market/asset index is above 60% of its starting level. The 'range accrual' feature is interesting because income will only be missed for any week where the index is below 60%: but if, say, the index was below this level for ten weeks at the start of the year, but then 'back up' for the remainder of the year, the income accrual would result in 42/52 of 7.5% for that year.

Strategy	Description	Possible investment applications
Range accrual	Generates an enhanced yield by taking a view that the underlying asset will stay within a pre-determined range. Interest will be accrued if the underlying asset is within this range. Underlying assets options are typically equities, indices, interest rates or foreign exchange.	Investors can generate potentially higher yield than cash by taking a view on the trading range of the underlying asset(s).

Range accruals can be simple and transparent, with 'deep' conditions applying to both income and capital repayment – i.e. they are unlikely to be breached unless there is a significant/dramatic sell-off in the market/asset.

Twists on this strategy include the potential to:

■ Introduce an upper 'cap' on the range, so that the index must stay within a range of, say 40% below the strike level or 40% above the strike level. This might allow the income coupon to be increased to, say, 8.25% per year – a fairly significant premium over and above the risk-free rate.

Such a strategy might appeal to and suit a wealth manager or experienced investor who has a specific market view that the index will trade in a range for the foreseeable future, i.e. +/–40%. In index terms this range is quite wide – based on a current FTSE 100 level of about 5,500 points, the bottom of the range would be 3,300 points (below the trough of the bear market of 2003, following the collapse of the TMT bubble) and the top of the range would be 8,800 points (significantly above the market's all time high of about 6,900 points, seen many years ago).

4 Auto-call (or 'kick-out') strategies

Innovative strategies that have been highly popular and successful in recent years are the 'auto-call' strategies, as they are correctly called in structured investment/derivative parlance (or 'kick-outs' in structured 'product' flag lingo). They create potentially high, fixed growth returns and provide automatic early closure with full repayment of capital, at any anniversary, based upon the underlying market/asset simply being at or above its starting level. No market/asset growth is required.

If the strategies don't auto-call at the first anniversary, the coupon/growth payment is 'rolled up', or accumulated, and is paid at the first subsequent anniversary, based upon the original market/asset condition, i.e. the market/asset must simply be above its original starting level – but no growth is needed.

Because the strategies may – and often do – successfully 'call', i.e. close early, at the first anniversary the growth payments of such strategies have been looked on by some advisers/investors as 'quasi income', with the benefit of being taxed as capital gains – a significant benefit, especially given the high coupons/growth being generated.

Strategy	Description	Possible investment applications
Auto-call ('kick-out')	The level of the underlying asset will be monitored on a pre-agreed frequency (e.g. annually, semi-annually, monthly, etc.). If the level of the underlying asset is at or above a pre-agreed threshold, the structure is 'called' automatically, repaying 100% of the investment principal plus a fixed return. Underlying asset options are typically equities, indices, commodities or foreign exchange.	Investors can generate a high fixed return, potentially higher than the return of the underlying assets, even if the underlying asset(s)' performance is flat – quasi income, albeit not necessarily reliable as an income stream.

Auto-call coupons/growth payments have been as high as 15–18% per year, or more, although 10–12% per year currently is more the norm (as market volatility has decreased, thereby decreasing the value of the put options).

With the no market/asset growth condition, if investors believe that in the medium to long term markets will rise, then the longer the strategies continue 'uncalled' the more likely auto-call becomes – and the higher the payoff.

An additional benefit of 'auto-call' strategies, from a portfolio perspective, is that early auto-call ensures successful repayment of capital and a solid investment return, but also facilitates potential repositioning of portfolios and investment strategies, at a time when the economic backdrop may have stabilised to make other investment options more attractive than might have been the case when the auto-call was selected.

5 Diversified income strategies

A final illustration of potential structured investment income strategies is a 'diversified' income strategy that was 'put together' as a bespoke solution for professional investors in the recent credit crunch/financial crisis period. This is a relatively simple strategy example that utilises the basic 'reverse convertible' strategy explained in the section on 'contingent/ defined level protected' income strategies above – but in fact it is an example of something that not all providers are capable of offering or delivering for investors. The 'twist' of the diversified income strategy was giving the high net worth investor access to a simple income strategy but with multiple counterparties providing the underlying assets, in order to diversify, i.e. mitigate, credit risk.

As a strategy example this highlights the flexibility of independent structured investment providers to offer investors non-prescriptive investment solutions. Working with a specialist wealth manager and a sophisticated professional investor the 'investment mandate' was to deliver fixed and unconditional income of about 5%+ per annum, over a short investment term of three years, with a barrier 40% below the strike level, but to do so with a choice and combination of leading (generally AA rated) global investment banks as the counterparties, as opposed to just one solitary asset provider.

The investment mandate was met – and exceeded – through offering the wealth manager and investor, and his trustees, a list of ten due-diligence screened AA rated institutions, allowing them to screen these further themselves, at their total discretion, and to select three for the 'diversified income strategy' solution. Further, the 'plan' is that each year, over a five-year period, the investor will repeat the exercise, selecting three different banks and different underlying investment strategies each time, in order to build a truly diversified, albeit straightforward, investment portfolio.

In fact, this example highlights an interesting and important point. The best structured investment income strategies don't have to be the most challenging. The best structured investment income strategies can be, basically, 'boring': but boring can be good. In fact, often the more boring the better when it comes to income – given our starting point of 'typical' investors in income investments.

boring can be good

Key risks with structured investments

Structured investments expose investors to risk. Careful consideration should be given to the risks of any investment – and it's no different for structured investments – even when, as explained earlier, some providers might let their marketing teams have a field day with references to capital protection and low risk claims, etc.

The investment terms of a structured investment are defined and fixed at the outset and there is no active investment management, which means that investors know before investing exactly what growth or income potential is provided and the extent of potential investment risk that is presented. But it is essential that prospective investors understand and accept that there is always 'counterparty risk' – and there may also be 'stockmarket risk' (although in some propositions market/asset risk can be entirely removed).

Counterparty/credit risk

This relates to the risk of the investment bank that is providing the assets/securities that a structured investment is based upon (or backed up by) not remaining solvent until maturity and defaulting upon its obligations. Usually the likelihood of a major financial institution failing to be able to meet, or honour, its commitments in this way can be considered small – but the risk should not be ignored or misunderstood by investors.

Stockmarket risk

If an investment is not fully protected from market/asset risk then the performance of the underlying index will determine the level of capital repayment at maturity. Some structured investments do not remove market or asset risk, although they may offer a defined level of protection, i.e. protection is offered unless the market or asset falls by a certain amount and breaches a particular barrier level. As with counterparty risk, even if the barrier is 'deep' and the risk of breach reasonably considered small, investors should ensure they are aware of and understand the risk.

A point repeated throughout this chapter is that structured investments are not alchemy – they do not make investment risk disappear, so any risks in any investment must be fully understood by prospective investors. Risks can be explained in straightforward terms by providers – and they should always be clearly and fairly described, both in terms of the actual risks and the consequences of the risks – not least as low probability events can carry high impact losses for investors.

The following section therefore offers comprehensive guidance on the key risks within structured investments, and potential due diligence considerations for prospective investors.

Counterparties, counterparty risk and counterparty assessment

In addition to any risk to capital or growth/income returns through underlying stock market or other asset class links, most structured investments depend upon the solvency of the financial institution, known as 'the counterparty', that is providing or issuing the securities that deliver the stated investment returns.

The securities that counterparties issue are usually medium-term notes, warrants or other securities which are similar to corporate bonds and other debt instruments – often referred to generally as 'bonds'. In effect, an investment in a structured investment is a loan to the counterparty in exchange for the growth or income returns.

Bonds have been explained in detail in Chapter 3 and the principles are no different when it comes to structured investments. Counterparties must meet the contractual terms of the bonds that they issue – and their ability to do so largely depends upon their solvency.

The risk that they might fail to meet the terms of their bonds is known as 'counterparty risk', sometimes also referred to as 'credit risk'. A counterparty failure during the investment term of a structured investment plan, for instance through insolvency, such as bankruptcy, administration or liquidation, is likely to cause a 'default', i.e. the counterparty will fail to make payments due during the investment term and/or to repay their debts (i.e. the bonds) at maturity. Usually the risk of a major financial institution failing to be able to meet its commitments in this way can be considered small, but a default or failure puts a structured investment, and any growth or income potential it provides, at risk – so the risk must be understood by investors and assessing the financial strength of prospective counterparties is an important aspect of evaluation and selection.

There are objective and recognised methods of assessing the financial strength of an institution, i.e. measuring their 'creditworthiness'.

Credit ratings are recognised indicators of the financial strength of an institution. They are assigned by independent organisations known as credit rating agencies, and the three leading agencies, designated as Nationally Registered Statistical Rating Organisations (NRSROs) by the US Securities and Exchange Commission (the SEC), are Standard and Poor's, Moody's and Fitch Ratings.

Credit rating agencies assign ratings based upon views of 'worst possibilities' in the 'visible' future, as opposed to the past record or the present status of the institution/bond. Ratings are normally in the form of letter designations, such as AAA, A+, BB, C, etc. These provide investors in the debt securities of these institutions, such as a bond, with an indication of the institution's strength and ability to meet its obligations in repaying both the principal capital and any income due from the security.

Credit default swaps

In addition to credit ratings, another instrument used to assess the credit strength and quality of bond issuers is Credit Default Swap (CDS) spreads. CDSs are credit derivatives that were introduced relatively recently, in 1997, in the 'over-the-counter' market (where buyers and sellers of derivatives trade directly with each other, rather than via recognised exchanges).

Generally, a CDS is a swap agreement/transaction between two parties, in relation to loans, bonds or other debt instruments issued by a company (often called the reference obligation). At a basic level, the buyer of a CDS usually owns the reference obligation (e.g. the bonds of a counterparty) and pays a fee to the seller, for a CDS, to get protection, i.e. insurance, against credit risk. In exchange for paying this fee, the buyer of the CDS will be compensated by the seller if a credit event impacts upon the reference obligation. Potential credit events include default, bankruptcy, debt restructuring, etc. If such credit events occur, the seller of the CDS will receive the reference obligation (now in distress) and the buyer will receive cash to compensate the credit loss. CDS providers include financial institutions, for example banks and hedge funds.

Credit default swaps are quoted in the market in the format of an annualised spread, over LIBOR, known as the CDS spread, similar, conceptually, to the premium paid for an insurance contract. For example, the CDS spread quoted for a bond issued by XYZ company may be 100 basis points (1 basis point equals 0.01%). If the CDS buyer wants to protect a £10 million investment in XYZ bond, then the buyer has to pay the CDS seller an annual fee of £100,000 (typically paid quarterly).

As a CDS provides protection, i.e. insurance, against a credit event impacting upon a debt instrument, the CDS spread should widen (i.e. increase) if the credit derivatives market perceives that the credit strength/quality of the issuer of the debt will deteriorate; and vice versa, if the market perceives the credit strength/quality of the issuer will improve it should narrow (i.e. decrease). This makes economic sense – the CDS will cost more if the perceived risk of a credit event, e.g. a default, in respect of the reference obligation increases (or vice versa).

Credit analysts use CDS spreads as an additional indicator and tool to assess the credit quality of corporates, including financial institutions that issue structured investments. Structured investments are often issued as debt on a bank's balance sheet, and hence the CDS spread is a relevant parameter to examine, within an overall analysis of the credit strength of counterparties.

It is important to note, however, that just like credit ratings, CDS spreads should not be relied upon in isolation in assessing the credit risk of a counterparty (especially bearing in mind that credit quality is only one factor that can affect the CDS spread).

Credit ratings and CDS levels as complementary research tools

Regardless of recent criticisms of credit rating agencies, as a result of the financial crisis, when broadly speaking the agencies 'missed' Bear Stearns, Lehman Brothers and still had AIG as a AAA rated institution (before American tax dollars were used to give it a lifeline), consensus opinion still holds that credit ratings are a leading indicator of an institution's financial strength. It is also worth highlighting that some of the loudest critics of credit rating agencies appear to be either institutions or individuals in institutions who suffer most at their hands, i.e. institutions carrying lower (i.e. worse) credit ratings than they might like. Especially in the structured investment industry this is a noticeable dynamic! That said, however, it's fair to recognise that rating agencies are generally viewed as focusing on the 'longer term' picture and being 'potentially slow' to react to unfolding events, at either a macro top-down or micro bottom-up level.

There is also an obvious conflict of interest, as ratings are commissioned and paid for by the institutions issuing the bonds that they are provided upon: although regulators oversee the activities of the agencies and this risk should be mitigated.

Credit default swap spreads, on the other hand, are anything but slow to react – and are a function of entirely conflict-free credit derivatives market economics. CDS spread levels can and do react to events incredibly quickly and can be acutely short-term focused – which is both good and bad.

The bottom line is that credit ratings and CDS levels both have nuances and potential shortcomings – but as lead indicators of financial strength/creditworthiness of an institution they are both valuable. The obvious conclusion to draw is that if both are assessed and used in tandem then their respective strengths and weaknesses are ironed out – and, certainly, a more comprehensive assessment of credit strength/risk is obtained.

An interesting aspect of CDS spread levels, for many observers, is that they can be used as a 'sanity check' on the ratings agencies, to see if they're 'on the money' with their ratings, or whether they appear to be 'behind the curve', according to the credit derivatives market. For instance, if a AA+ rated institution had a CDS that was markedly lower than a AA– institution then some further 'digging' and thinking might be sensible, or at least a little caution employed.

Financial 'fundamentals'

Credit ratings and CDS spreads are both important indicators of the credit quality and financial strength of counterparties. However, over-reliance on either indicator, especially in isolation, is potentially short sighted, and both should be taken into account, with similarities, differences and/or anomalies considered and assessed.

In addition to assessing headline indicators of corporate strength (i.e. credit ratings and CDS), prospective investors should consider financial 'fundamentals' and wider aspects of a counterparty's background.

Financial fundamentals means thinking about an institution both quantitatively but also, to some extent, qualitatively. Jurisdiction for regulatory purposes, the strength of the sovereign state (where relevant), market capitalisation, Tier 1 capital ratios and share price movement can all be considered.

Of particular relevance, at this time, is the question of a banking institution's 'systemic' importance. Generally, the obvious consideration in this respect is the extent of a bank's retail operations, as opposed to its 'casino' operations. Banks holding extensive retail deposits, on behalf of Joe Public, are far more likely to be deemed systemically important, notably by the relevant government/central bank, than an investment bank that might have previously been primarily concerned with proprietary trading and active risk taking/profit making in its activities.

The first question is whether or not a prospective counterparty is likely to be deemed systemically important if future problems arise for the financial sector or the individual institution. But the second question – 'Where is the institution systemically important?' – is equally applicable. At the bottom line, there's little point in identifying a bank as systemically important, perhaps because it's a major retail bank somewhere, if it doesn't happen to be domiciled somewhere that is capable of supporting its system. Think Icelandic banks and the point should be apparent.

Access to credit ratings and CDS levels

Whilst many independent providers of structured investments provide details of credit ratings for the counterparties underpinning their products, this is not always the case for banks or building societies issuing products in their own name, backed by their own credit risk.

Accessing credit ratings and CDS levels is not necessarily easy for retail investors. So, it is worth highlighting the Incapital Europe 'Counterparty Platform' (see Figure 6.1), which has become well known amongst wealth managers for carrying credit rating and CDS level information for many institutions that are leading providers of securities used in structured investments or that are active issuers of structured products in the UK. The credit ratings ascribed by each of the three main agencies, including the date and direction of the last change and the outlook (positive, negative or stable), are shown. In addition, five-year credit default swap spread levels are highlighted, based upon various time periods. Finally, details are updated on a monthly basis.

Counterparty (data at 31-03-10)	Credit rating			Indicative 5 year spread
	Standard & Poor's	Moody's	Fitch Ratings	
Barclays Bank	AA– ↓ NEG	Aa3 ↓ STB	AA– ↓ STB	87.16 105.8 85.55
BNP Paribas	AA– ↓ NEG	Aa2 ↓ STB	AA ↑ NEG	70.19 82.66 60.21
Citigroup	AA ↓ NEG	A3 ↓ STB	A+ ↓ STB	155.58 211.24 172.56
Rabobank	AAA ↔ NEG	Aaa ↔ NEG	AA+ ↓ STB	69.19 83.22 72.05
Investec Bank	– – –	Baa3 ↓ STB	BBB ↓ NEG	– – –

Figure 6.1   **Incapital Europe Counterparty Platform**

Source: www.IncapitalEurope.com

Consider the benefits of counterparty exposure

As suggested earlier in this chapter, investors have been 'educated' over many decades, by the traditional investment funds industry, to accept or tolerate a multitude of 'naked' investment risks, including stockmarket downside/volatility, investment/market timing and active fund management risk.

The often overlooked benefit of counterparty exposure in structured investments, as opposed to the risks that are so acutely focused upon, is that structured investments exchange a multitude of 'traditional', variable, investment risks, for contractually pre-defined risk and return parameters, via the terms of a bond or security. Investors only need consider whether a counterparty is likely to go bust or not. If counterparties remain solvent they are legally obligated to deliver the returns stated in their bonds/securities.

Many investors find it easier to consider whether a major bank is likely to be solvent in 5–6 years' time than what may or may not happen to the stockmarket and all the variable risks of 'traditional' investment funds.

No investment is perfect: but consider the benefits – as well as the risks – of structured investments. Counterparty can be looked at as a benefit. Some

counterparty can be
looked at as a benefit

'clever stuff' may be going on – removing market/asset risk and pre-defining returns in market/asset-linked investing is obviously challenging – but counterparties carry the risks of the 'clever stuff', i.e. the investment process, not investors. This is significant and in stark contrast to mutual funds.

Conclusions on counterparty risk

In addition to the specific aspects of 'understanding counterparties', in terms of their role and relevance in structured investments, and regarding sensible consideration of counterparty due diligence and assessment, two general points are worth highlighting in conclusion:

- **'Flight to quality'**. Discerning investors should seek providers and structured investments that utilise counterparties that are highly rated and regarded, taking into account various and combined factors in a balanced approach. Higher headline rates on structured investments can be achieved by providers who utilise (or are internally linked to) weaker counterparties – but investors should differentiate between headline rate driven products and potentially better value investment integrity.

- **Diversification**. As with any type of investment, prudent investors should also seek to diversify their portfolios – which in terms of structured investments most importantly means considering the underlying counterparty, and limiting or diversifying exposure to or reliance upon any single counterparty. Independent providers offering unfettered access to all counterparties, with no bias to any, facilitate potential diversification of counterparty exposure that cannot be offered by individual banks, or accessed only by investors dealing directly through their retail bank.

Investors must adopt a balanced approach in their consideration of structured investments, assessing counterparties sensibly, carefully and prudently.

What are the stockmarket risks?

Whilst most structured investments do not invest directly in the underlying index or indices that they link to, or the companies that the index or indices represent, repayment of capital at maturity and the growth or income potential of structured investments are usually determined by the performance of the underlying index/indices, during the investment term.

As already explained, some structured investments can and do remove market/asset risk entirely. This is a simple fact – investors are not exposed to the performance of the market/asset should it fall during the investment term and be below its starting level at maturity, although investors are always exposed to counterparty risk, as this chapter makes abundantly clear. Other structured investments, however, provide superior growth or income returns by only providing protection from a defined level of market/asset risk. For instance, an investor's capital might be protected unless the underlying index (or indices) falls by more than 50%, from its starting level, during the investment term or at maturity. If this is the case, i.e. if the index/indices breaches the protection barrier level then the investment will not repay capital in full at maturity, and investors will lose capital, on a one-for-one basis, in line with the performance of the index/indices. 'Barriers' have already been explained in this context.

Figure 6.2 helps explain the protection and risks of structured investments that utilise 'barriers' or 'soft protection', using a 50% barrier example. This highlights the risk to capital that exists if the market/asset index should fall from its starting level by more than 50% at maturity.

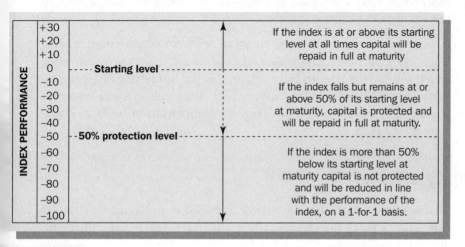

| Figure 6.2 | A 50% barrier example |

It should be noted that the market/asset protection features of most structured investments only apply at maturity, not upon early redemption by investors during the investment term.

What are the additional risks?

In addition to the key risks of 'counterparty risk' and 'stockmarket risk', prospective investors should also consider and ensure they understand some additional, though perhaps more generic, risk factors, including: **liquidity risk** which concerns investors' limited access to capital during the investment term.

Structured investments are not the same as bank or building society accounts where capital is guaranteed and, with instant access accounts, readily available without penalty. Structured investments are generally designed to be held until maturity and, although access during the investment term is possible, with certain providers the full return of capital is not assured.

The early redemption value of a structured investment during the investment term will depend upon a number of factors (including internal charges, market movement, interest rates and market conditions such as volatility and credit spreads) which are likely to result in a capital loss, particularly in the early years.

Investors should also consider the potential impact on these liquidity factors during distressed market conditions, when the prevailing value is likely to be lower than usual, in the event that they may need or want to redeem early in such circumstances.

It should also be noted that the Financial Services Compensation Scheme (FSCS) does not cover performance related issues in respect of investments, which means that counterparty default, i.e. the insolvency of a counterparty, or significant falls in a market/asset index/indices and a breach of a protection barrier, would not result in **compensation** being available through the FSCS.

Sanity checks

'Best use' of the financial engineering employed in structured investments can bend or break the theoretically linear link between risk and return. Structured investments can actually 'use' risk astutely to create and enhance returns that might not otherwise be achievable, including returns in range bound, sideways trading or even falling markets. Structured investments can deliver risk/return profiles that active fund managers could only ever dream of delivering: but, by definition, in practice never could.

A key benefit and advantage of structured investments – and a point of particular appeal for the increasing audience of receptive advisers and investors that are utilising them – is the unparalleled scope for innovation in meeting specific investor requirements, including investing for income, vis-à-vis any other sector of the investment universe. Advancing knowledge of structured investments will extend the range of investment options for investors at a time when value-adding investment solutions have never been more needed.

However, structured investments are not suitable for everyone. And prospective investors should always ensure that they refer to the full literature in relation to any investment, and ensure that they understand it thoroughly – in particular, any risks that may apply to capital or investment returns, and any important features, terms or conditions.

The checklist below details some general points that may help highlight whether an investment might be appropriate or suitable, based on individual circumstances. However, investors should always consider their own individual circumstances carefully to assess suitability – including the need to diversify their investments in order to achieve a sensibly balanced investment portfolio. Suitability always depends upon an investor's individual circumstances and attitude to risk.

CHECKLIST

A structured investment plan might be suitable if investors:

- Do not expect to need access to the funds invested before maturity.
- Have sufficient funds available for emergencies.
- Are investing as part of a sensibly diversified investment portfolio.
- Want a 'structured' investment linked to the underlying stockmarket/asset class, with no active investment management.
- Want a 'structured' investment, with returns delivered by warrants, issued by a single institution.
- Understand the features of the investment, including how the growth or income potential is determined.
- Understand and accept that capital invested is at risk – and may be lost in part or in full.

▶

In addition, a provider's marketing material (the brochures, etc.) for a structured investment should always:

■ Be clear about where money is invested, i.e. in the bonds/securities issued by a single institution.

■ Be clear about relevant counterparty risk, including the specific counterparty.

■ Prominently state that capital is at risk.

■ Use language that investors can understand.

■ Not describe a product as 'protected' or 'guaranteed' if this is inaccurate or misleading.

■ Explain the circumstances when FSCS coverage applies, and when it does not.

Professionally advised investors should, by definition, be better informed investors, making better investment decisions that can impact positively upon long-term investment performance. Many of the best structured investment propositions are available exclusively through independent wealth management firms and investment advisers, who select investments on merit to meet precise investor needs and interests, so savvy discerning investors should always discuss their investment needs with an IFA before making investment decisions.

7

Putting it all together in portfolio terms

In the next two chapters we'll pull together our discussion about different products and structures into a coherent strategy that should help the reader put together a portfolio of investments that might generate an income. In this chapter we've asked one of the country's leading financial planners, James Norton of Evolve Financial Planning, to outline how he approaches the challenge of building a successful investment portfolio that might also help produce a sustainable income.

by James Norton

Newton's third law of physics states that 'for every action there is an equal and opposite reaction'. If Newton was around today and was analysing financial services, I am sure he would tell us that risk and reward go hand in hand. If you want higher yield, whether through fixed interest or equity holdings, this comes with increased risk to your capital. I doubt Newton would have been a fan of the financial alchemy that is so often peddled today.

My role as a Chartered Financial Planner is to help my clients make sensible decisions about money. It is about asking them the right questions so that I can help them create a personalised strategy. It is not about selling them products. For many of my clients, increasing their retirement income is a key part of this strategy and I want to share with you some of my thought processes when creating this strategy. It may sound like a bit of a cliché but we are all different. Therefore, there will be aspects of this chapter that don't apply to you but if you come away with one good idea, the investment of your time in reading this chapter will have been a worthwhile exercise.

The financial services industry likes to pigeonhole us and the reason it likes to do so is that it can sell us its products rather than design personalised solutions. I wonder how many readers of this book have been given the bland classification of a 'low-', 'medium-' or 'high-' risk investor, or the marketing-speak 'income', 'balanced' or 'growth' investor label. Have you or a family member ever been party to the following (abridged) conversation:

> **Bank Manager**: 'I have noticed that you have a lot of cash in your account. Would you like to increase the income you are getting on this?'
>
> **Customer**: 'Sounds good. Who wouldn't?'
>
> **Bank Manager**: 'We have an excellent investment bond that allows you to draw a 5% p.a. tax-free income. I'll send you a recommendation.'

What you probably won't be told is that the 5% p.a. income is really just a return of your original capital, it is tax-deferred not tax-free, the investment bond is far less tax-efficient than an ISA and the bank earns a 7% up front commission.

As a firm we meet hundreds of investors every year and are always amazed by the lazy 'advice' that some many people are offered. Part of the problem is the culture of many of the larger players in financial services and part is because many 'advisers' are simply not very good and ask the wrong questions. If you ask a stupid question like 'Would you like more income?', you'll get a stupid answer!

If you think about it logically, very few people who are still working need their investments to produce an income. What they want is for their investments to produce a good return. Of course, the income that the funds generate may well be a very important part of that return and for certain investments, like cash savings, the income is the return. However, the fact remains that investors require a total return, not just an income. Who would want an investment with an impressive 8% p.a. yield that made a less than impressive capital loss of 9% p.a.?

> very few people who are still working need their investments to produce an income

If you need your investments to produce an income whilst you are working and trying to accumulate money, you are either spending too much or earning too little. By drawing an income from your investments you are effectively dipping into your retirement savings fund. It is only when people have stopped working that they should really need their investment portfolios to start producing an income.

What 'accumulators' really need is a strategy to help them accumulate so that they have an *appropriate* (not the biggest) pot of money at the point of retirement to provide for their spending requirements. This is all that's important. When they retire they need to think about how best to use the pot to fund their spending. I stress the word *appropriate* because, as we will see later, many people end up with too much money when they retire which means that they could have retired earlier, or worked in a less stressful job, spent more time with the kids, taken less investment risk, or spent more money in the accumulation stage, and still achieved the *right* level of retirement income for them.

What 'decumulators' need, on the other hand, is a strategy to help them make the most of that pot of money as the opportunity to increase it through saving excess earned income disappears on the day they retire.

Now, given that not all people reading this chapter will be in the decumulation stage, and as we'll see later, many decumulators don't actually want to decumulate, let's first look at a strategy to accumulate money. We could call this 'investing so that you can achieve the desired level of after-tax income in retirement in the most efficient manner'. Admittedly, it doesn't roll off the tongue as well as 'investing for income', and wouldn't fit neatly on a billboard in the London Underground, but surely it's exactly what accumulators want?

The importance of reinvesting income

Tables 7.1 and 7.2 illustrate the importance of investment income as part of the overall return. Table 7.1 shows the result of investing £100 in 1899 without reinvesting the income. If this was invested in equities, in real terms (i.e. taking into account inflation) it would only be worth £139 at the end of 2008; however, in nominal terms it would be £9,129. In the case of gilts, the erosive power of inflation is startling with the £100 investment falling to £1 in real terms at the end of the period.

Table 7.1 Value of £100 invested in 1899 at the end of 2008 without reinvesting income

	Nominal	Real
Equities	£9,129	£139
Gilts	£49	£1

Source: Barclays Capital Equity Guilt Study 2009

When income is reinvested, whether this is through dividends on equities, or interest for gilts, the picture is very different. The real value of the equity investment rises to £17,571 and the gilt investment increases to £365. Although in absolute terms the impact on equities is much larger, the difference for fixed income is still huge at over 300 times (see Table 7.2).

Table 7.2 Value of £100 invested in 1899 at the end of 2008 reinvesting income

	Nominal	*Real*
Equities	£1,152,944	£17,571
Gilts	£23,916	£365

Source: Barclays Capital Equity Guilt Study 2009

What the above figures help to demonstrate is that income yield is an extremely important part of an investor's return and if it is reinvested, the longer the time frame, the more important it becomes. That's the power of compound returns. The best way to have a good retirement fund is to save as much as possible as early as possible, remembering that the income is a vital component of the total return.

An accumulation strategy

In the accumulation stage it is important to have a strategy. Conventional wisdom states that 'there is no such thing as a free lunch' but that's not true. The financial world is full of free lunches and it's one of my jobs as a Chartered Financial Planner to help clients spot these. The more free lunches you can eat, the fatter your retirement fund will become.

EXAMPLE

Let's look at a very simple example. Take a husband and wife. He earns £60,000 p.a. and she earns £30,000 p.a. They have £100,000 in cash savings in a joint account. This earns 3% p.a: that's £3,000 p.a. He gets taxed at 40%, she at 20%. The aggregate tax rate on their cash savings is 30%. 30% of £3,000 is £900 tax. If they move the £100,000 to her name that's still £3,000 p.a. interest but at 20% tax: 20% of £3,000 is £600. The difference between £900 and £600 is quite a lot of free lunches, year on year on year.

Let's now look at a slightly more complex example but one that will be relevant to any reader of this book who is still an accumulator and is a crucial part of the 'How can I maximise my retirement income?' equation. If you are already retired and have children, your children might like to read the following few hundred words!

Which is best, a pension or an ISA?

On the face of it, this seems like a straightforward question, and indeed, given that pensions and ISAs form the bedrock of most people's retirement plans, you would hope that the relative merits of each would be easy to understand. However, as with most financial decisions, the answer to this question depends entirely on your personal circumstances.

A simplistic answer to this question would be that pensions are better because of the tax relief. £10,000 invested into an ISA, returning 7% p.a. after charges, would be worth £54,274 after 25 years.

A basic rate taxpayer paying £10,000 into a pension would see their contribution grossed up to £12,500. Using the same returns basis as the ISA, this would be worth £67,842 after 25 years. This is clearly a bigger number but you are tying money up until at least age 55 and remember that this could well be changed upwards in the future. To me, this doesn't seem particularly compelling. Yes, the fund is bigger and yes you get 25% of the fund back as a Pension Commencement Lump Sum (otherwise known as 'tax free cash'), but the income the remainder generates is taxable and is often quite inflexible too. Most people will end up buying an annuity which some would argue offers poor value for money and, more importantly for many people, it is a very large asset which can no longer be left to their children. The reality is that for most people their pension is their largest individual asset after their house.

But, what if you are a 40% taxpayer when you pay money into a pension? After you have received your tax relief, £10,000 out of your pocket buys you a gross pension contribution of £16,667. If this returns 7% p.a. after charges, it would be worth £90,459 after 25 years. Imagine also that you are a 20% taxpayer in retirement. 40% on the way in and only 20% on the way out is an altogether more attractive proposition. In this scenario there is a real tax arbitrage opportunity.

The figures are more pronounced still for 50% taxpayers and for those people with income over £100,000 who can reduce their taxable income to under £100,000 and thus recover their lost £6,475 personal allowance.

For the income bracket £100,000 to £112,950 this gives an effective rate of income tax relief of 60%. How many people would turn down the opportunity of converting £4,000 into £10,000 overnight? £4,000 in an ISA returning 7% p.a. after charges would be worth £21,709 after 25 years but £10,000 in a pension would be valued at £54,274. The difference, £32,565, buys a lot of free lunches.

Many employers will offer staff bonus sacrifice and salary sacrifice opportunities and generous employers will add their employer NI saving back into the employee's pension pot. Employer NI is currently 12.8%. If you have a salary of £90,000, get a £10,000 bonus and your employer will rebate their full 12.8% NI saving, that's £11,280 in your pension versus £10,000 if you hadn't asked your employer about bonus sacrifice. That's another free lunch or ten!

The point here is that you need to challenge the conventional wisdom. The accumulation phase is about building wealth as efficiently as possible. Saving for retirement is not just about saving into pensions. Our view at Evolve would be that almost all taxpayers should make the most of what is on offer via their employer in respect of pension contributions. If your employer is prepared to pay into a pension for you, bite their hand off for it. If they will match any further contributions you make, most people should take advantage of this. It's yet another free lunch. But beyond this, most basic rate taxpayers may be better off with ISAs simply because 20% tax relief doesn't really compensate you for tying the money up for the long term especially if you are paying 20% income tax when you draw it. Having money in a pension isn't going to help you buy a house or fund your children through university. One point that should not be overlooked though is that the discipline of money going into a pension direct from salary is probably the easiest way to save and, for many people, not being able to access the pension until retirement will be a real bonus!

Looking at it ruthlessly, most people should make an annual decision based on their personal circumstances and the tax rules at the time. If you are a 20% taxpayer now but expect your income to rise, it could well make sense to defer pension contributions in favour of ISAs until you are able to obtain 40% relief. In an ideal world you would do both, of course! Reality is such that most people want simplicity and we are strong advocates of that. Spreading your investments between pensions and ISAs makes a huge amount of sense. The most important thing is to save, start saving early and do it on a regular basis in a tax-efficient way. We will look at the powers of long-term saving in more detail later in the chapter.

What I am trying to demonstrate here is that before you have even decided on what holdings to put in your portfolio, you need a strategy. That strategy needs to be reviewed when tax rules change and when your personal circumstances change. If you get the strategy right you will have a lot more money in the portfolio to start off with and surely that has to be the best possible way to start a strategy of 'investing so that you can achieve the desired level of after-tax income in retirement in the most efficient manner'.

The next step is to work out how that money is to be invested. It's all very well making the right decision in the pension v ISA question at age 30 but if you leave your pension or ISA in cash until retirement, and trust me, there are people who inadvertently do, you'll most likely regret it!

What is income?

Let's now leave the pre-retirement market and look at those people who are in retirement who sagely saved money into PEPs, ISAs and other investments in the accumulation years, to top up their pension income.

According to Wikipedia, income is defined as 'the sum of all the wages, salaries, profits, interests payments, rents and other forms of earnings received... in a given period of time'. This sounds like common sense and fits with what anyone would think of as income. Put another rather simple way, it is the money that comes into our bank account and what we are then able to spend on living.

For most people the majority of their retirement income is in the form of pensions, either from company defined benefit ('final salary') schemes or annuities. However, many people will supplement their pension income with investment income from a number of different sources, such as bank and building society interest, rental income or a more traditional portfolio comprising equity and fixed income investments, hopefully in ISAs. Indeed, for some people, investment income is their largest single source of income and therefore managing the investments in the correct way is of imperative importance.

Traditionally, investing for income has revolved around building a portfolio of equity income funds and fixed interest funds with the aim of generating as much dividend and interest income from a portfolio, which can then be spent. Our view is that the natural income a portfolio generates is largely irrelevant. The primary driver of how much an individual spends should be determined by their disposable wealth and the total return of their portfolio, not the income alone. To demonstrate this, let us consider Mr Jones.

EXAMPLE

Mr Jones is in the fortunate position of having an investment fund of £250,000 and he has expenditure of £15,000 per annum that he needs to fund. Does it really matter if he spends £15,000 from income, £15,000 from capital, or a combination of the two? Assuming all other things are equal and the fund generates a total return of 6% per annum after tax and charges, there is absolutely no difference. At the end of the year Mr Jones will have had his £15,000 income and the portfolio will still be worth £250,000. In fact, the main difference in net outcome is to do with how income and capital are taxed, with drawdowns on capital often being the more favourable of the two depending on marginal tax rates.

If the portfolio generated more than £15,000 per annum should Mr Jones spend this? Well if the capital was maintained, maybe he could, but if the capital base is being eroded, the high income would in effect be an early drawdown on future years' income. What about if the income yield on the portfolio was only £10,000? Does this mean that Mr Jones cannot spend his required £15,000 per annum? Well, again it depends on the investment return and what has happened to the capital. It could be that the portfolio has grown by another £10,000 meaning he has more than enough to spend, but it is the total return that should determine this, not just what is generated in income.

The really important point is whether over rolling periods of time Mr Jones's spending rate is sustainable and is meeting his requirements. This is largely down to investment performance and therefore the structure of a portfolio is of vital importance.

I am very aware that retirement is a major milestone. Along with getting our first job, getting married and having children it is a key defining moment, a life-changing event. Given current demographics (and the budget deficit) it is likely that the moment where one ceases accumulating wealth and starts spending may well become more of a transition period as retirement becomes less formal and the over 65s work part-time. However, a key characteristic we have found is that once an individual has retired, they find it very hard to spend capital. Retirement for many is a moment of finality, when their ability to generate new wealth suddenly ends and as a result there is an understandable fear that they will run out of money. The ability to go out and get a job to bridge any shortfall reduces or disappears altogether depending on the nature of the individual's career. Consequently, there is often an unhealthy fixation on income, the general belief being that 'as long as I don't touch my capital, I will be fine'.

But why is this important? Well, from an investment point of view it narrows down your options and forces us to take a blinkered view that equity income funds and corporate bond funds are our only options due to the yield they produce. This gives us an unhealthy fixation on large cap UK equities and can also tempt us into taking more risk on the bond aspect of our portfolio than we are really comfortable with. Just look at the performance of equity income funds in the credit crunch with their over-dependence on the banking sector.

Consider the Sterling High Yield Sector average returns of +44.4% in 2009 (wow!) but –25.8% in 2008 (whoops!) (source: Trustnet). Is that really the sort of volatility that you expect from the supposedly less risky part of your portfolio? Some of you may think that looks like a really good return over two years. After all, who wouldn't want a 44.4% return in one year? However, you cannot simply add the return of the two years together as the rise has come after a large fall so is worth considerable less. In fact, the total return over two years is just over 7% or about 3.5% compounded, with massive volatility.

Maintaining capital may sound like a worthy goal, but this is too simplistic an approach. Our experience is that many people who are moderately wealthy seem to overestimate what they spend in retirement. The result is that even in retirement they are net savers. Part of this may be due to the fear of running out of money, but for many it is simply that they have not planned their finances and don't require as much money as they thought. It may sound prudent to try to be a net saver in retirement, but is there any point? Funnily enough, when we go through the same exercise with younger clients, they generally underestimate what they spend. Perhaps that's a topic for a psychology PhD!

Surely it is better to either spend it or give excess income or capital away to family, friends and charitable causes than to have it clobbered with 40% inheritance tax on death? How many readers of this book believe that the government will make a better decision about how to spend their hard-earned, already heavily-taxed, life savings than they can? The answer should surely be none, but if you are a net saver in retirement and don't have an inheritance tax planning strategy running alongside this, this is exactly what you are doing and, of course, this is illogical!

There is then the issue of inflation. What is the reason for wanting to maintain a notional capital sum? It is meaningless since in real terms it is changing year on year as a result of changes in inflation, whether that be the Consumer Prices Index, the Retail Prices Index or a more bespoke index for the elderly for whom it is often suggested that inflation runs at close to twice the national average. It merely acts as a comfort blanket unless that capital sum has some express purpose.

In addition to our ingrained bias towards income, I would argue that the main reason so many people invest in this manner is that the financial services industry tells us to. It goes back to the pigeonholing point I was making earlier.

Portfolio management – the basics

If we accept that the natural dividend/interest income from a portfolio is really not important, we need to look at how to manage money. Whilst this section will specifically look at how to manage an investment portfolio to generate 'income' in retirement, the strategy is just as suitable for someone aged 40 as it is for an 80-year-old who is living off their investments. Before we look at the specifics of how to manage an investment portfolio for income it is important to get the basics right. There is a plethora of books on how to manage investments so this will by no means be a comprehensive guide: however, it will explain four key pillars of portfolio management which are critical if you are going to stand a chance of success. The four pillars are:

- risk
- the role of fixed interest,
- costs, and
- rebalancing of portfolios.

Risk

Risk is traditionally measured by fund managers using standard deviation. This is a statistical measurement of risk and whilst it may be meaningless to the average investor, it is very important as it provides a way of measuring something that to many may be subjective. A less mathematical definition might be the fear associated with seeing your investments rise and fall over time.

Figure 7.1 shows the returns of the FTSE All Share from January 1956 to December 2009 and shows the best and worst returns from this index over various time frames.

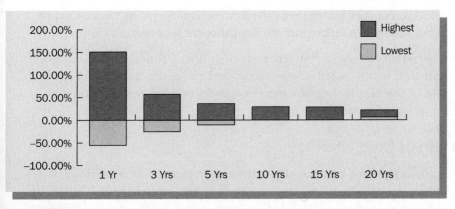

Source: FTSE

Figure 7.1   **Best and worse returns FTSE All Share – annualised rolling return (monthly Jan 1956 to Dec 2009)**

It can be seen that the risk of holding equities for one year is huge, with the largest loss in the period being 55.84% in 1973. The corresponding upside is just as great with a rise of 151.41% in 1975. Think about these two figures when we look at portfolio rebalancing later. However, as the timeframe lengthens to say five years, the worst annualised loss falls to 10.58% and for a ten-year period the graph shows a breakeven picture. Extending the timeframe even further it can be seen that the worst return is actually positive at almost 7% per annum compared to the best return of just over 23%. The purpose of this is to show that the risk of investing in equities is real, but also that it reduces over time.

I would argue, however, that the main risk for those seeking income from their portfolio is inflation. The cost of living generally rises faster for those in retirement. For a 40% or 50% rate taxpayer, there is no chance of keeping up with inflation if all of their financial assets are held in cash. At the time of writing, in August 2010, the Retail Price Index (the most sensible measure of inflation) is around 5%. Most fixed term deposits are paying no more than 2.5% gross which nets down to 1.5% for a 40% taxpayer. This 'real' loss of 3.5% p.a. may not make a big difference over one or two years, but compounded over 15 or 20 years it could make a real difference to someone's standard of living.

> the main risk for those seeking income from their portfolio is inflation

So why does risk matter? It is important because it helps investors set the framework for their portfolio. Provided investments are going to be held for the long term, the fear of losses cannot be written off, but can be reduced. But this fear of losses needs to be considered in the context of inflation and how much of an issue the investor believes it to be.

Only when an investor understands their own attitude to risk can they start to construct a sensible portfolio, and by far the biggest decision to take in this area is the proportion of equities to fixed interest in a portfolio, as looked at below.

The role of fixed interest

It seems intuitive that the higher the equity exposure in a portfolio, the higher the expected long-term returns and the greater the risk. Indeed, a golden rule of investing is that risk and return are inextricably linked. Don't believe anyone who tells you otherwise. Financial alchemists in the big banks, insurance companies and fund houses are constantly trying to dream up products that break this equation. Of course we all want high return with low risk, and investment products that purport to offer this are a marketing man's dream. With-profits funds, precipice bonds, zero dividend preference share... they all go wrong in the end.

Table 7.3 shows a very simple portfolio that invests in the FTSE All Share and one month treasury bills. It can be seen very clearly that as the equity component of the portfolio increases so does the standard deviation or risk of the portfolio. Such figures are easily distorted by the date range chosen, so we have used the longest data set possible. Some of you may be thinking of your own investment experience of the past decade wishing it would have matched even the most risk averse of the portfolios below.

Table 7.3 Risk and return on equity and gilt portfolios from January 1956 to December 2009

	100% gilt	75% gilt 25% equity	50% gilt 50% equity	25% gilt 25% equity	100% equity
Portfolio return	7.7%	9.3%	11.1%	13.0%	15.3%
Standard deviation	3.6%	6.9%	12.9%	20.0%	28.6%

Source: Data is based on UK Treasury Bills and the FTSE All Share. The Portfolio Return is on an annualised basis.

It can be seen that holding fixed interest reduces risk (and return) of portfolios. It is therefore vital that the right type of fixed interest investments are held. Our view is that investors should concentrate on holding high quality corporates, supranational and sovereign debt and not chase yield. Remember, risk and return are correlated so the higher the yield, the higher the risk of default. Whenever you risk forgetting this, just remember what happened to all the Icelandic banks paying interest rates that seemed too good to be true! We also believe it is important to hold short-dated bonds (less than five years to maturity if possible) as this greatly reduces the risk with only a modest reduction in the long-term expected returns.

The cost of investing

An index fund is just the more modern way of describing passive funds or index trackers. Evolve, like a growing number of investment managers and advisers, only construct portfolios using index funds. So why is this? Put simply, costs matter.

Table 7.4 Returns on a £250,000 portfolio over time assuming expenses

Maturity	Annual expenses		
	1%	2%	3%
5 years	£333.453	£316,949	£301,105
10 years	£444,764	£401,826	£362,656
15 years	£593,232	£509,434	£436,790
20 years	£791,260	£645,858	£526,078

Table 7.4 shows the return of a £250,000 portfolio over various timeframes assuming expenses of 1%, 2% and 3% p.a. with a 7% p.a. growth rate before charges. It is worth pointing out that it is not at all unusual to find portfolios with expenses of 3% per annum or more. When private bank or stock broking discretionary fees are added to fund charges, custody costs and commission, fees rapidly rise. The problem is that even total expense ratio figures don't properly evaluate total expenses. In Table 7.4, it can be seen that a 1% cost portfolio returns over 10% more than a 3% portfolio after only five years. This amounts to a staggering £32,348. When this is rolled out over 20 years, the difference is £265,182 or 50%! That's the miracle of compounding in reverse. What better way to reduce your retirement income than to let the investment industry take an unnecessarily large chunk of it.

The fact of the matter is that there are volumes of academic research showing that active managers as a group underperform the main market indices and therefore underperform the best index funds, which charge as little as 0.15% per annum with no up front fees. Don't be put off by active managers' billboards showing top quartile or top decile performance over short timeframes – it is meaningless. How often do they advertise their many funds with third and fourth quartile performance? It is simply marketing and gives no indication whatsoever of future performance.

Anyone, even a chimpanzee, can outperform in the short run; however, it is the long run that is important. In his landmark publication *A Random Walk Down Wall Street* (Norton [1973], 2003), Burton Malkiel states: 'A blindfolded monkey throwing darts at a newspaper's financial pages could select a portfolio that would do just as well as one carefully selected by the experts.' In fact, you and I could be running and marketing a top decile fund in 12 months' time. All we need to do is set up the Red Fund and the Black Fund. We then take a trip to the casino. If red comes up trumps we market the Red Fund as having doubled in value in 12 months. The money will pour in based on a 100% one year return! Naturally, we quietly close down the Black Fund. I don't mean to sound flippant but fund advertising material is worthless. In fact, it is worse than worthless because when push comes to shove, it is you the investor who is bearing the brunt of it. It is paid for out of your investment returns. With a red fund and a black fund, the investment house (the house) always wins.

Rebalancing of portfolios

Rebalancing is all about portfolio maintenance. Just as we advocate using low-cost index funds, it is vital not to 'play' with your investment portfolio too much. If you construct a portfolio that is appropriate for you with the correct level of risk, it needs very little work. Just as the stockbroker or fund manager is unlikely to know which stock is best to hold, BP or Shell, the chances of making the correct call about switching into or out of the US, increasing or decreasing fixed income, or taking a punt on a new hedge fund are about 50:50. Sometimes they will make the right call and sometimes the wrong call. However, it is guaranteed to cost the portfolio every time – this is a real drag on performance.

Once you have set up the portfolio, it is best to leave it. You have arrived at your attitude to risk and this should not change unless your personal circumstances change. If someone invests in a 'balanced' portfolio with, say, half invested in fixed interest and half in equities it is wrong to start changing this. Human nature is such that when the stockmarket rises investors want more of the action. At Evolve we put this down to greed, not a change in attitude to risk. Likewise when stockmarkets fall many want to sell equities and hold more secure assets. This is fear. Now, have a look back at the equity return figures for 1973 and 1975.

Investor behaviour is largely defined by these emotions of greed and fear, but it is wrong to let them interfere with a long-term investment strategy. That is why we rebalance portfolios. This brings discipline into the process and removes the chance for emotion to take over.

EXAMPLE

Taking a simple example of a £250,000 portfolio with half in bonds and half in equities. After a good year, equities may have risen 20% and the bonds 5%. Equities will then make up 53.3% of the portfolio. That is not a problem but if this continues, equities could be upwards of two-thirds of the portfolio. That may seem good if all you are interested in is making money, but what happens when the stockmarket suddenly falls 50% in one year? Investing simply is not just about making money: money is irrelevant in isolation. What is important is achieving your lifetime goals, and funding your spending requirements.

So, in the example above, we would sell some equities and buy more fixed interest to get the portfolio back to the 50:50 weighting. What is important is to maintain an appropriate risk in the portfolio. This forces us to buy low and sell high which is the opposite of what most people actually do in practice.

Some people argue that rebalancing reduces overall return as in the long run you are generally going to be selling equities that should have the best long-term potential. However, it is not as simple as that. This discipline of selling assets that have done well and buying assets that have underperformed has to be stuck to in all market environments. Discussing this with clients back in March 2009 when the FTSE All Share hovered around 1,800 was not easy. The market was down almost 50% and we were asking clients to buy more equities. It may have been tough to do at the time, but it was the right thing to do. What it meant was that portfolios were up to weight in equities when the stockmarkets did bounce back, greatly enhancing the returns.

We all overestimate our abilities: we all think we are better than average. This is human nature. However, when it comes to investing, the evidence strongly suggests otherwise. Data from the Investment Management

investors, both retail and professional, let emotions rule

Association shows that inflows into unit trusts peak when the market does and outflows rise when the market is falling. This is the wrong way round because investors, both retail and professional, let emotions rule.

Managing the portfolio for income

So far, everything in this chapter has been hypothetical. It does not actually tell anyone the reality of how to live off their investments. The truth is that when investments form a major part of your retirement income, you must be prepared to take the rough with the smooth. When equity markets are good, your returns are likely to be higher than your requirements, but conversely there can be very difficult periods. The past 10–15 years have not been kind for those living off investments. Although fixed income investments have performed well, the main driver of investment returns, equities, have performed poorly and there is very little anyone can do about this. You have to just take it on the chin.

What we can do, however, is to try to reduce the volatility of income that is generated, and more importantly try to protect the capital from falling too much, by managing the investment fund in a simple way. We recommend that our clients do this by having two separate portfolios, a liquidity portfolio and an investment portfolio.

Apart from an inappropriate asset allocation, i.e. either taking too much or too little investment risk, the biggest mistake that investors can make is selling their holdings when they are low. One thing we know about equity markets is that they are risky. They go up and down. It may be reasonable to assume a long-term equity return of between 7% and 9% per annum but we know this is not going to be smooth. In the past 50 years the FTSE All Share has fallen more than 15% per annum on six occasions and there have been 14 years where returns have been negative. Fortunately, it has risen by more than 15% per annum on 21 occasions. What we want to avoid doing is selling investments when the market has dipped. If you do this, not only do you get less for your investments, but you are reducing your exposure to the risky 'growth' assets which are likely to rise fastest when the market recovers.

The aim of the liquidity portfolio should therefore be to hold a certain level of future projected expenditure in cash. Perhaps three years' worth of expenditure for example. This is not an exact science but it should help reduce the risk of selling low. When we look at three-year annual-ised rolling returns of the FTSE All Share, there are only seven periods that show negative returns. The message is simple – time reduces risk. Having this liquidity portfolio guarantees that you will have sufficient spending money to meet all your requirements for three years and therefore pro-vides important peace of mind. The liquidity fund should be held in cash or near cash. It would be reasonable to tie some up in term deposits of varying maturities, and even to hold some ultra short-dated bonds which may squeeze a little extra return out.

Running alongside the liquidity fund should be the investment portfolio. In nearly all cases, a portfolio of low-cost index funds that invest across all geographic regions, balanced with a good fixed income weighting should be sufficient, as described earlier in this chapter. Leave this portfolio to get on and do its job. Don't look at it every day unless you are investing as a hobby and certainly don't trade it every day. It is designed to capture the long-term returns from equities and fixed interest securities in a manner appropriate to you.

Action really only needs to be taken annually on the investment fund. Income from the dividends and interest from the bonds will have topped up the liquidity fund throughout the year, but for most investors, the natural income will not be sufficient to satisfy their expenditure require-ments. With interest rates so low at the moment, high quality fixed interest yields very little and the historic yield on the FTSE All Share is around 3%. Most overseas stock markets yield significantly less than this. So the chances are that part of the portfolio will have to be sold to top up the liquidity fund. Assuming an income of 6% is required and the port-folio only generated 3%, then 3% of the portfolio will have to be sold. Whilst raising that 3% to top up the liquidity fund, the portfolio should be rebalanced. This is part of the ongoing portfolio maintenance. Put simply, this is to return the asset allocation back to the level at outset. The reasons for this are simple and I will reiterate them. First, it maintains the risk of the portfolio at a level that is appropriate for you and secondly it forces a discipline into the management of selling assets that have per-formed relatively well and buying those that have done less well. In other words, it brings in discipline of selling high and buying low, in the full knowledge that you are unlikely to ever get the top or bottom!

So, in order to raise funds that are needed to top up the liquidity portfo-lio this should be done as part of the rebalancing process. If fixed income has performed well this should be reduced to raise the necessary funds, and if equities have performed well the equity component should be used. Whilst rebalancing, it is also useful to do some other basic housekeeping measures. Part of our investment philosophy is that we believe it is important to trade on portfolios as little as possible so as to reduce costs, so if everything can be done in one go, all the better. Rebalancing is therefore the ideal time to raise additional funds to subscribe to an ISA, and it may be worth crystallising some capital gains at the same time in order to keep the portfolio nimble. Investors currently have a CGT allowance of £10,100 p.a. and the more that this can be used the better.

The simple things

Hopefully by now we have helped to show that investing for income is just a phrase used for convenience rather than anything else. In fact, when done properly a number of simple measures are likely to have the greatest impact on what you can spend in retirement and I am going to share some of these with you now. Remember, the main factor that determines how much you can spend is the size of the investment fund, not if that investment fund is invested in gilts, corporate bonds, PIBS, equities or anything else.

This section will help to demonstrate how a few simple measures can have a dramatic impact on your income. The most powerful way to illustrate this is through graphs (which have been created using our proprietary program), but to do this we need to paint a scenario, so here goes!

EXAMPLE

Let us consider a married couple called Mr and Mrs Smith. They are both aged 60 and Mr Smith has a final salary pension of £15,000 per annum and both Mr and Mrs Smith have State pensions of £5,000 per annum. They hold £100,000 in cash, part of which was the pension commencement lump sum ('tax-free cash') that Mr Smith received on retirement and a further £500,000 in investments in a managed portfolio, all of which are held by Mr Smith as he has dealt with the finances. They spend £40,000 per annum.

For the purposes of the example, I have assumed that the cash earns a return of 4% per annum. This is high compared to current rates but wouldn't have been seen as high two years ago and if interest rates go up, seems like a better long-term assumption than current rates. The investment portfolio is assumed to generate an annual total return of just under 7%.

Figure 7.2 shows the value of the Smiths' wealth, starting at £600,000 (cash plus investment portfolio) and being steadily eroded by the surplus expenditure over income. Based on the assumptions used, as you would expect, there is a steady erosion of their capital base to the extent that by the time they are 96 they have run out of funds. In many respects, this is perfect planning, as there will be little to leave to the Chancellor in inheritance tax, but most people are not comfortable running down their wealth to this extent. For many people an important objective is to pass some wealth on to family members and, under this scenario, it will simply not be possible.

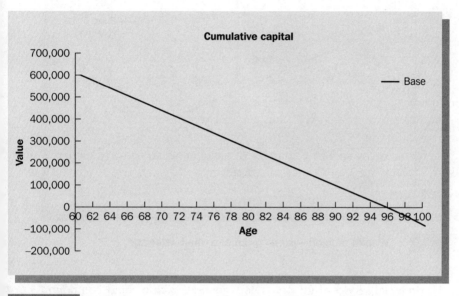

Cumulative capital

— Base

Value

Age

Figure 7.2   **Wealth erosion – running out at age 96**

The cost of investing

So what can Mr and Mr Smith do to ensure that they run out of money later, other than spending less? The first thing we can look at is reducing the cost of investing. In the above example (which I have called the base scenario), I have assumed a high cost of investing of 3.5% per annum. Although this is deliberately on the high side, many people are paying these kinds of expenses when using a discretionary stockbroker charging a 1% Asset Management Charge (AMC), underlying funds with a total expense ratio of 1.65% and commissions and custody charges on top. Multi-manager and fund of fund investors may face similar charges. In Figure 7.3, I have brought the cost of investing and advice down to 2% per annum. Using index funds I would hope that most people would pay considerably less than this, and all of our clients certainly do, but all I really want to do is demonstrate a point. The graph shows that rather than running out of investments at age 96, there will probably still be enough to keep going until around 105.

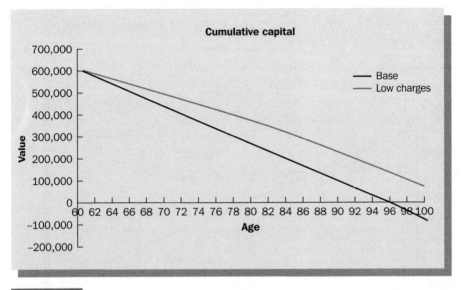

Figure 7.3   Wealth erosion – running out at a much later age

The financial services industry is very good at talking about compound returns, but it's less good at talking about the effect of the compounding of costs. That is what is shown in Figure 7.3, and I would hope it would be enough to get most investors to seriously examine their charges.

ISAs

The next big thing for Mr and Mrs Smith is to use their annual ISA allowance each year. In the 2009/10 tax year this stood at £10,200 each and is due to rise annually. Many potential investors I meet feel that ISAs are not worth using as the stockmarket delivers poor returns (yes, it has over the last decade) so why bother with this extra tax wrapper. The simple reason is that you keep more of the return. Glance back to the beginning of the chapter which talks about the importance of dividends. If equities are not held in an ISA, all of that dividend income will be taxed, whereas in an ISA it is virtually tax-free (the 10% tax credit cannot be claimed back but there is no additional tax to pay). All of the interest on fixed income securities is

the icing on the cake is
that all capital gains
are exempt

tax-free and this should not be underestimated for those in retirement where fixed income should be a reasonably large part of their portfolio. The icing on the cake is that all capital gains are exempt so when the stockmarket does start rising it is one less thing to worry about.

Figure 7.4 may not look dramatic but this simple move that is probably cost-free will extend the cash flow by three years when compared to the base scenario. The graph shows that it takes a few years for the benefits to accumulate. We are starting on the assumption that Mr and Mrs Smith don't have any ISAs at the moment. In reality, most people who have large investment portfolios should start switching to ISAs as early as possible in which case the benefits only get larger.

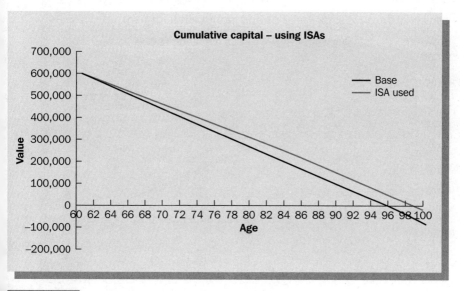

Figure 7.4   Extending the cash flow by three more years

Capital Gains Tax (CGT)

The next point to consider is using the annual capital gains tax allowance. The annual allowance currently stands at £10,100 per person with gains over that level being taxable. Given recent stockmarket history, it does take a bit of a leap of faith to assume that such an allowance will be used every year; however, it is not unreasonable to expect that such a portfolio will grow over the long-term.

The benefit of using the capital gains tax allowance is that this can be used to generate an 'income' and a very tax-efficient one at that. Rather than pushing the portfolio down the direction of high yielding bonds and equities and paying income tax on everything, have a well diversified portfolio with a more modest yield, but take some capital out tax-free. This is one of the free lunches referred to at the start of the chapter. For most people it simply does not make sense from a tax perspective to load a portfolio full of high yielding investments (which may be higher risk due to the high yield) to generate an income when they will pay additional tax for doing so.

This simple measure extends the cash flow by another four years when compared to the base scenario.

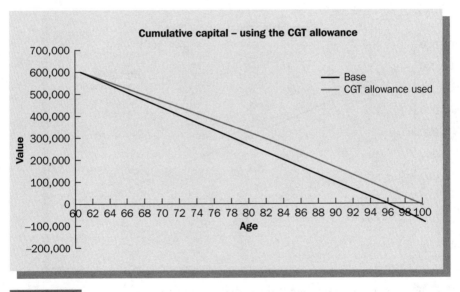

| Figure 7.5 | Extending the cash flow by four more years |

Use your spouse's tax allowances

There are many other scenarios we could look at but for the purposes of this chapter, the final stage of this process is simply to make sure that as many assets as possible are held in the name of the lower tax paying spouse. The simple fact is that in most families it is usually the husband who has gone out to work and has the largest income in retirement. This is certainly the case for Mr and Mrs Smith. If Mr Smith is going to pay 20%

tax on all income, it makes no sense at all for him to hold the cash and taxable investments when Mrs Smith is currently paying no tax and would only pay tax on some of the income if the assets were put in her name.

Many clients think there is something nice about holding joint bank accounts but the only person it is being nice to is the Chancellor! In this example, Mr Smith holds all of the cash and all of the investments. He should simply transfer all of them to Mrs Smith's name and from day one it will start to save them money. Figure 7.6 shows this extends the cash flow by around 18 months. Again, this is not huge, but that is simply because of the example we have created. If Mr Smith was a 40% or even 50% rate taxpayer and Mrs Smith had no pension income the difference would be much more striking, but as it stands an extra 18 months' worth of cash for doing virtually nothing is not bad!

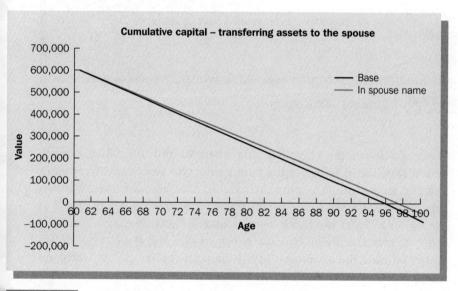

Figure 7.6   Extending the cash flow by 18 more months

Putting it all together

I would be the first to agree that whilst all of the above graphs are interesting, none of them is exactly radical. None is life changing. Extending the line by a year or two here and there is not that exciting and many people might even wonder if it was worth the hassle or the cost of using a financial planner.

But, if Mr and Mrs Smith were clients of Evolve and had taken our advice, then the cumulative effect of all the changes can be seen in Figure 7.7.

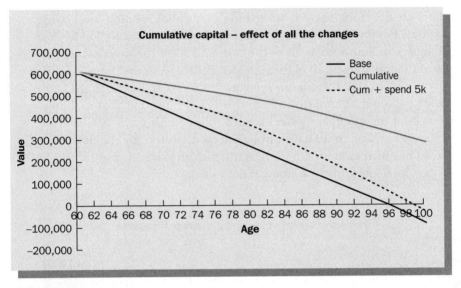

Figure 7.7   Effect of all the changes

Figure 7.7 shows the same base line when Mr and Mrs Smith took no action. The top line shows the cumulative effect of lower investment charges, saving into ISA, using their annual CGT allowance and transferring the taxable assets to Mrs Smith. Rather than running out of capital at age 96, Mr and Mrs Smith now have around £335,000 at age 96. *To achieve this extra return the Smiths have had to take no extra risk at all.* It is simply a matter of using the advantages in the financial and tax system which are available to them anyway.

The middle line on the graph above, shows another scenario. This assumes that the Smiths have implemented all the recommended changes, but rather than save the extra money, they have been able to spend an additional £5,000 per annum. This is an increase in their annual expenditure of 12.5% per annum so could make a real difference to their retirement. Alternatively if Mr and Mrs Smith wanted to, rather than spending more, they could switch to a lower risk portfolio to try to achieve a more dependable return.

It is important to remember that the above illustration is only an example, but the numbers are reasonably accurate with tax computations taking place in the background. However, the whole success of a strategy of living off retirement income is dependent on taking the rough with the smooth – when investment returns are good you take more but when bad, you may have to cut back. Go to a stockbroker or fund manager and they will try to convince you that that they will achieve higher returns. They may do, but most do not. When they do, they are generally taking a higher level of risk. But what is really important to remember is that the benefits in the graphs are real and tangible and, in this example, don't even involve taking any more risk. Even in this very simple example, Mr and Mrs Smith are able to boost their retirement income by £5,000 p.a. for more than 35 years, without even taking any more risk, and still be better off than before.

Conclusion

Hopefully this chapter has dispelled some of the myths of what is an extremely important subject. Don't invest for income. Invest for total return and make sure you get the basics right. Maybe to some of you this chapter has been a bit boring but that is okay because investment should be boring. If you want some fun, go to the casino but if you want a degree of certainty in a very uncertain world, it is important to follow a tried and tested strategy.

if you want some fun, go to the casino

Have clear goals about what you want to achieve and need to achieve (these are different) and construct a low cost portfolio using index funds with a level of risk that is appropriate. Don't listen to your friends on the golf course and their latest great investment, as they have not told you about all the other ones that have gone wrong, and avoid tips in the weekend press, and execution only brokers who want to increase your trading and their commission. All of this is 'noise' and will put you off course. Remember the simple example of Mr and Mrs Smith above who increased their retirement income by 12.5% per annum for 35 years taking no extra risk at all. All of these are simple, easily implemented strategies. The most important skill that you need to carry it through will be discipline. Remember that we are all driven by fear and greed and all too often these emotions get in the way of us making a success of our investments.

8

Building some model income portfolios

In this chapter we're going to try to draw together some of the threads of this book – equities, bonds, hybrids – into a number of different sections that should help an investor build a robust portfolio. Before we start looking at how an investor might put together different asset classes and ideas into a single investment portfolio, it's absolutely worth articulating some portfolio basics – simple ideas about investing that should inform the construction of any portfolio. That means that first we'll look at a number of key issues facing any investor: why diversification is so important, whether you should attempt to carefully time your purchases and sales in the bond and equity markets, and whether you should use funds that passively track an index or consider using actively managed funds run by a manager.

After we've established these portfolio basics we'll move on to look at how an investor could divide up the huge range of income-producing assets into three bundles based on risk. We'll then conclude by looking at two very idealised, model portfolios which might help inform an investor looking to build a collection of their own income-producing assets. Remember that they are just models and that every investor will have their own risk thresholds, their own concepts of return and their own income requirements. So experiment and tinker to your heart's content with these basic structures but don't take the allocations and ideas as gospel! Finally we'll introduce readers to our service that monitors the full range of income-based investments – it's constantly updated and is available online.

Portfolio basics

Investors need to build diversified portfolios of income-producing assets. Later in this section on portfolio basics we'll look at what that diversification might begin to look like. But to build a portfolio needs some careful thought and well-founded principles. Most of what follows is just as true for portfolios designed to produce a capital gain as it for those aiming to generate an income. The key is to build a sustainable portfolio that will stand the test of time and produce a useful stream of income net of costs.

Costs kill your returns

Most investors understand the simple concept that extra costs destroy your returns. If you pay too much for investment advice, be it from an adviser or a fund manager, you'll probably be paying for many years hence in terms of reduced future returns. And just in case you desired any more evidence for this it's probably worth looking back at the hard, concrete numbers shown in Table 7.4.

The bottom line? There are lots of uncertainties in the world of investing but there is one great dependable fact, proved by mountains of research. Costs destroy your returns over time and every 0.5% extra in fees or expenses compounds over time to reduce your potential rate of return. You can't control the future but you can cut your costs by being discriminating and careful!

Think about rebalancing your portfolio

When you decide upon your mix of income-producing assets, don't just assume that the combination is immutable and will never ever change. Investors do need to frequently check up on the state of their portfolio and analyse how it's changing over time. But how should one cope with changes in the mix of assets over time? What happens if some investments shoot ahead, while others fall by the wayside? To understand this challenge let's imagine the portfolio of my good old Uncle Fred with his simple holding of three index funds tracking UK equities, UK bonds and gold (he's a cautious type). He invests £100 in each fund and within six months his equity investment has doubled whereas his bonds have gone down by 5% and his gold holdings have dropped by 20%.

At the end of six months – an eventful six months it must be said – his portfolio looks something like this

- UK equities £150
- bonds £95
- gold £80.

In total Uncle's portfolio is now worth £325 but equities account for 46% of total holdings against the original 33% allocation, whereas gold has sunk to just under 25%. What should he do? Should he take his profits on equities and then reinvest in gold, or stick with the asset mix?

Uncle Fred decides to play 'Steady Eddie' and decides not to do anything until the end of this first year. By that point his equities have come down a little to £130, his bonds are back at £100 and his gold has rallied back to £90 – implying a total portfolio that's worth £320. Equities are still worth 40% of his portfolio but at least gold is back up to 28% of total holdings. Uncle Fred decides that he's now going to rebalance, and sells some of his equity holdings (just over £23) and invests just over £16 back in gold and another £6 in bonds.

According to advisers like Paul Merriman and Richard Buck – based in the US – Uncle Fred was spot on because he managed his returns to control his risks. In a paper entitled 'One portfolio for life?', the American-based advisers suggest that although 'annual rebalancing is not absolutely necessary, if it's neglected, the portfolio's risk can start creeping up. To maintain the proper amount of risk, you should keep the portfolio within reasonable distance of its… target allocation. When the stockmarket is hot, as it was in the 1990s, the equity part of a balanced portfolio can quickly creep up' (www.fundadvice.com).

To back up their conclusions the authors studied a hypothetical portfolio, without rebalancing, that began with a 60% holding in US equities and 40% in bonds at the start of 1990 through to 2005. By the end of 1999, 78% of the portfolio was in equities and only 22% in bonds. Investors might have been very satisfied with the total returns but Merriman and Buck remind us that 'that was just in time for the bear market of 2000 through 2002 to come along and teach unwary investors about the dangers of being over-exposed to equities. The portfolio that had never been rebalanced lost 22.2 per cent of its value from the end of 1999 through 2002. But if that portfolio had been rebalanced every year, the loss was only 12.6 per cent' (www.fundadvice.com).

Merriman and Buck adhere strongly to the view that rebalancing on annual basis is the right thing to do if only because it's so counterintuitive, forcing you punish the winners to reward the losers. 'A more productive attitude is to think of rebalancing as a mechanical way to require investors to buy low and sell high,' suggest the authors. And Merriman and Buck are far from being the only advocates of a regular rebalance. A recent study from US brokers Smith Barney concluded that:

> Rebalancing also tends to reinforce one of the main benefits of portfolio diversification: the tendency of returns on different assets to offset each other over time. By remaining close to their target allocations, investors should be able to reduce portfolio volatility. This allows the magic of compound growth to work more quickly, boosting long-term returns.[1]

American fund management group Vanguard has also weighed in to this debate looking at returns from both a rebalanced portfolio and one that's unbalanced. Their conclusion:

> If a portfolio is never rebalanced, it will gradually drift from its target asset allocation to higher-return, higher-risk assets. Compared with the target allocation, the portfolios expected return increases, as does its vulnerability to deviations from the return of the target asset allocation.[2]

To demonstrate what can happen if you ignore 'best practice', the Vanguard researchers looked at a very boring and standard split of 60% stocks and 40% bonds that was never rebalanced. According to the Vanguard study, 'Because stocks have historically outperformed bonds, the portfolio's asset allocation gradually drifts towards 90% stocks and 10% bonds', i.e. your portfolio becomes too risky because the allocation of risky equities becomes dominant.

If anyone deserves the last word on this subject, it's probably John Bogle, one of the most articulate American-based investment thinkers and writers – he also founded the massive fund management group Vanguard. He's recently completed an analysis for the *New York Times* on the subject of rebalancing. Controversially, he's not convinced by most forms of rebalancing, annual or otherwise. According to a report on Bogle's blog:

---

[1] *The Art of Rebalancing: How to tell when your portfolio needs a tune-up* (www.asaecenter.org/files/ArtofRebalancing.pdf).

[2] *Portfolio Rebalancing in Theory and Practice* (https://institutional.vanguard.com/lip/pdf/ICRRebalancing.pdf).

Fact: a 48% S&P 500, 16% small cap, 16% international, and 20% bond index, over the past 20 years, earned a 9.49% annual return without rebalancing and a 9.71% return if rebalanced annually. That's worth describing as 'noise,' and suggests that formulaic rebalancing with precision is not necessary. We also did an earlier study of all 25-year periods beginning in 1826 (!), using a 50/50 US stock/bond portfolio, and found that annual rebalancing won in 52% of the 179 periods. Also, it seems to me, noise. Interestingly, failing to rebalance never cost more than about 50 basis points, but when that failure added return, the gains were often in the 200–300 basis point range; i.e. doing nothing has lost small but it has won big.[3]

Bogle's conclusion?

Rebalancing is a personal choice, not a choice that statistics can validate. There's certainly nothing the matter with doing it (although I don't do it myself), but also no reason to slavishly worry about small changes in the equity ratio... I should add that I see no circumstance under which rebalancing through an adviser charging 1% could possibly add value.[4]

Don't try to time the markets – stick to your principles

Investors looking for an income need to be aware that their behaviour really matters, i.e. that many investors display a series of alarming characteristics that can destroy a well-balanced portfolio. In particular they assume that they can sit in front of a computer screen or read a paper and make a judgement as to whether an asset – shares, bonds or anything that moves up and down in price – is cheap or 'worth a punt'. Sadly the ability of most investors to time their 'entry' and 'exit' points in bond or equity markets is hopeless. Most investors would be better off not trying to over-trade – jumping in and out quickly – and simply stick with a buy and hold strategy, i.e. buy for the long term, annually rebalance and then sit tight.

> most investors would be better off not trying to over-trade

Researchers at The Schwab Center for Investment Research in the USA have put some hard numbers on the cost of this curious behavioural vice of over-confidence in judging the direction of markets. They looked at four buy and hold investors who each received $2,000 annually for 20 years to invest in the markets – a grand total of $40,000. Two decades later here were the results:

---

[3] http://johncbogle.com/wordpress/category/ask-jack/
[4] Ibid.

- The Perfect Timer – $387,120. Strategy? The money's put into the market at the monthly low point every year.
- Treasury Bill (government gilt) Investor – $76,558. Strategy? Terrified of shares, the investor only puts their money into Treasury Bills.
- Autopilot Investing – $362,185. Strategy? This investor automatically invests the money on the day received and then leaves it alone.

And the Schwab study is just the tip of the research-based iceberg that suggests that poor market timing is incredibly costly. Back in 1998, for instance, academics at the University of Utah and Duke University reviewed 132 investment newsletter portfolios involving some form of market timing, over the period between 1983 and 1995. The average return from these 'timed' portfolios was 12% with 11.9% volatility. An S&P portfolio with the same volatility returned 16.8% for the same period.

Embarrassingly the researchers suggested that the more famous the market timer, the worse the results. A newsletter called *Granville Traders Portfolio* lost 2.2% annually and the *Elliot Wave Theorist Traders Newsletter* portfolio was down 10.1%. The academics' withering analysis was backed up by investment research outfit, the Hulbert Financial Digest, which also reviewed 25 newsletters with 32 portfolios and found that none of the newsletter timers beat the market. With the ten years ending 31 December 1997, market timers averaged from 5.84% to 16.9% – the average being 11.06%. However the S&P 500 index earned 18.06% and the Wilshire 5000 value weighted total return index returned 17.57%. Another ten-year study showed averages from 4.4% to 16.9% a year with the average of 24 market timers at 10.9 %. Even when adjusting for something called the risk return average, these expert 'market timers' were still far below the average of the buy and hold.

And just in case you thought it was only academics who suggest that market timing is for mugs, it's worth listening to the man who mightily influenced the great Sage of Omaha – Warren Buffett – on the subject of market timing. Buffett's great hero Benjamin Graham was one of the most famous timing sceptics, declaring in his book *The Intelligent Investor* that: 'We are sure that if [the investor] places his emphasis on timing, in the sense of forecasting, he will end up as a speculator and with a speculators' financial results.'[5]

Benjamin Graham, *The Intelligent Investor* ([1949] HarperCollins, 2003).

What about using index tracking funds

Many investors may be dimly aware that there's a big debate going on within the investment industry. On one side is a revolutionary new bunch of advisers and fund providers who reckon that the future is in index tracking funds. These are sometimes called passive funds and they're built on a simple idea, namely that the cheapest and easiest way of trying to follow the market is to 'track' the market via an index of some sort, i.e. the FTSE 100. In effect when you buy an exchange traded fund that follows this index, it's buying you lots of little stakes in the companies that comprise the index. In an ideal world the composition of your FTSE 100 should mirror in percentage terms the composition of the FTSE 100.

Ranged against this index tracking school is the orthodox mainstream who maintain that indices are useful but only as benchmarks, i.e. something to measure your fund against. They think the best idea is to hire a fund manager who looks at the index or asset class and makes lots of trading decisions about what to buy and sell. This active approach costs more money in terms of fees but opens up the possibility of greater returns if they buy and sell the right things at the right times. Sadly this approach also introduces the very real risk that the active fund manager will fail to make those right decisions, hitting the private investor with not only those extra expenses but the unintended consequences of their poor judgement.

The academic evidence against actively managed funds and in favour of index tracking funds is pretty overwhelming. Research study after research study has shown that cutting costs and cutting the risk of managers getting it wrong produces superior returns over time. We think that index funds should sit at the heart of any modern portfolio, but note the use of that term 'sit at the heart'. A sound portfolio is probably one that uses a core of well-diversified index funds around which circles a 'satellite' of slightly more unusual funds and shares that may involve some active fund management. That acceptance of some role for actively managed funds, especially in imperfect markets, is in part motivated by the recognition that there are successful fund managers who do indisputably add value some of the time – they frequently work in those more inefficient bits of the market and they can produce excellent returns for a substantial period of time.

Our general concern with active fund management is that most investors don't actually use the very best managers – they use below average
managers suggested to them by fund wrap platforms, and financial advisers motivated by news stories and commission kickbacks rather than true
long-term excellence. If you had some magic ability to spot the successful
managers, time and time again, we might concede that active fund management might be worth the greater risk, most of the time. Sadly, that
isn't the case: most private investors have absolutely no objective way of
knowing whether a fund manager is delivering on their huge salary.

We'd also suggest that another argument offered by the fans of active
fund management isn't borne out by the research. Some fund managers say that a good active manager can really work wonders in a bear
market, i.e. a market where prices are falling fast. They can get out of the
bad stuff, hold cash and invest only in the quality stuff. Research from
Vanguard in the USA suggests otherwise. In a paper entitled 'The active
passive debate: bear market performance' (in the *Australian Journal of
Financial Planning*, May 2010) analyst Christopher Philips looks at how
active fund managers performed in bear markets using the Morningstar
Direct database of equity mutual funds in the USA and Europe. His results
fit in with the general rule that active fund managers tend to underperform, even in bear markets:

> We observe that a majority of active managers outperformed the market in
> just 3 of 6 U.S. bear markets and in 2 of 5 European bear markets. To be
> sure, in each bear market, funds existed that successfully outperformed the
> broad market. However, these results clearly indicate a lack of consistency
> with respect to the success of active funds in general...
>
> (www.jofp.com)

Philips looked in particular at the 2000–03 bear market and found that
although 60% of all active funds outperformed the US stockmarket, only
23% of active funds outperformed the European stockmarket over the
same period. His conclusion? Although some fund managers can outperform in a bear market, there's no real consistency overall – in some
bear markets they do, but for most of the time, most managers don't. 'As
a result, it should not be assumed that an indexed investor is at an immediate disadvantage during a bear market relative to an actively managed
fund, despite the opportunity for the manager to add value,' Philips says.

Table 8.1 Performance of active funds during bear markets

Bear market – years of low or negative returns	Number of funds	% out-performing market benchmark
US funds versus Dow Jones Wilshire 5000 Index		
1973/1974	110	43
1980/1982	167	78
1987	291	57
1990	405	44
1998	1082	39
2000/2003	1405	60
European and offshore funds versus MSCI Europe		
1990	37	57
1992	81	33
1994	128	66
1998	378	39
2000/2003	796	23

Source: Vanguard

But look closely enough at the Vanguard data in Table 8.1 and you'll see two interesting themes. First that in Europe, as the number of funds grows their success in beating the markets falls. In the USA, by contrast, active fund managers seem to have been more successful and to have worked their way through the bear markets moderately well.

Is there any bottom line? Some active fund managers indisputably do add value some of the time and there is evidence to suggest that active funds managers in inefficient markets can add value for certain periods of time. Also if you find a good fund of funds managers who are good at consist-ently picking the good managers of the future, stick with them! Their skill and clairvoyance is going to deliver your above average returns, but ask yourself how they spot these investment ideas in advance. And even if they've been successful in the past, will that winning streak/consistent analysis and research hold for the future as well? Last but by no means least, be aware of the index you're tracking and understand the risks you're taking. Many big indices can perform truly badly in a bear market as momentum-based stocks take a hit. Don't blithely assume that the bigger the index, the less risky it is.

And one last crucial observation on this debate: remember that the average active fund manager charges more than 1.6% in costs for their expertise whereas most index tracking funds charge around 0.5% p.a. A superb manager might deliver some extra value but that extra 0.9% per annum in lower fees via a tracker for instance adds up to a lot of money over the very long term. Also you'll find that index tracking fund managers offer a huge range of funds, especially in the bonds space. In Table 8.2 we've listed the full range of index tracking bond ETFs (Exchange Traded Funds) from the main provider Blackrock iShares, all of which can be purchased through any stockbroker. Of the 28 ETFs in this list, all but two charge less than 0.3% in annual costs whereas most actively managed bond funds charge around 1% in fees plus extra dealing costs.

So ETFs do make sense, but we've also said that some active fund managers can add value, especially if they have a good record and sound principles. It's also true that this huge range of ETFs shown in Table 8.2 might be very confusing for some investors. They might not have the slightest clue as to the differences between an index-linked bond fund from America and a high yield corporate bond fund from Europe. Great choice is only useful if you have some real understanding of the differences between products. Investors might consider picking just one of the bigger, 'catch-all' ETFs such as the Global bond funds or the UK All Stocks Gilt index tracking fund (all conventional gilts).

Alternatively an investor might consider spending the extra money and investing in a fund manager who will make the decisions for them. That extra 50 to 90 basis points in cost – 0.5% to 0.9% – might be worth it for expertise. If you do decide to make this move into actively managed funds Table 8.3 might be of some use. It shows a selection of top managers identified by an online service called Trustnet – available at www.trustnet.com. This Alpha Managers list identifies some of the sharpest minds in the business by looking at past returns and portfolio characteristics. The analysis is run across the huge range of fund sectors but we've narrowed the list into two main groups, managers in the equity and income space and specialist bond managers.

this Alpha Managers list identifies some of the sharpest minds in the business

We've also shown their annual management charge (in nearly every case the total expense ratios of all costs is a lot higher) and given some idea of current running yields (based on the Autumn of 2010). If you have to hunt for a really superb active fund manager you'd probably do well to start with this list and then run your own research.

Table 8.2 iShares Funds overview

Fund name – All Irish Funds	Flat yield %	Yield to maturity (%)	Ticker	Base currency	Total expense ratio (%)	Total net assets in relevant local currency (millions)
US Treasury						
iShares Barclays Capital $ Treasury Bond 1–3	1.71	0.73	IBTS	USD	0.20	505
iShares Barclays Capital $ Treasury Bond 7–10	1.21	0.54	IBTM	USD	0.20	487
Index-linked Bonds						
iShares Barclays Capital £ Index-Linked Gilts	3.22	2.44	INXG	GBP	0.25	503
iShares Barclays Capital Euro Inflation Bond	1.77	0.76	IBCI	EUR	0.25	17.6
Euro Government Bonds						
iShares Barclays Capital Euro Aggregate Bond	0.95	0.39	IEAG	EUR	0.25	240
iShares Barclays Capital Euro Government Bond 1–3	1.64	1.10	IBGS	EUR	0.20	599
iShares Barclays Capital Euro Government Bond 10–15	4.24	3.44	IEGZ	EUR	0.20	24
iShares Barclays Capital Euro Government Bond 15–30	4.19	3.69	IBGL	EUR	0.20	154

Fund name – All Irish Funds	Flat yield %	Yield to maturity (%)	Ticker	Base currency	Total expense ratio (%)	Total net assets in relevant local currency (millions)
iShares Barclays Capital Euro Government Bond 3–5	2.78	1.74	IBGX	EUR	0.20	397
iShares Barclays Capital Euro Government Bond 5–7	3.44	1.93	IEGY	EUR	0.20	42
iShares Barclays Capital Euro Government Bond 7–10	3.35	2.33	IBGM	EUR	0.20	390
iShares Barclays Capital Euro Treasury Bond	3.74	2.43	SEGA	EUR	0.20	11
iShares Barclays Capital Euro Treasury Bond 0–1	3.98	1.02	IEGE	EUR	0.20	17.5
Corporate Bonds						
iShares Barclays Capital Euro Corporate Bond	3.76	2.50	IEAC	EUR	0.20	1008
iShares Barclays Capital Euro Corporate Bond 1–5	4.61	2.77	SE15	EUR	0.20	45
iShares Barclays Capital Euro Corporate Bond ex-Financials	4.59	2.72	EEXF	EUR	0.20	92
iShares Barclays Capital Euro Corporate Bond ex-Financials 1–5	4.63	2.26	EEX5	EUR	0.20	61
iShares Markit iBoxx $ Corporate Bond	5.22	4.20	LQDE	USD	0.20	928

Table 8.2 Continued

Fund name – All Irish Funds	Flat yield %	Yield to maturity (%)	Ticker	Base currency	Total expense ratio (%)	Total net assets in relevant local currency (millions)
iShares Markit iBoxx £ Corporate Bond	5.82	5.21	SLXX	GBP	0.20	1243
iShares Markit iBoxx £ Corporate Bond ex-Financials	5.35	4.34	ISXF	GBP	0.20	133
iShares Markit iBoxx Euro Corporate Bond	4.36	2.39	IBCX	EUR	0.20	3773
iShares Markit iBoxx Euro High Yield	6.71	6.97	IHYG	EUR	0.50	46
Global Government Bonds						
iShares Citi Global Government Bond	2.53	1.48	IGLO	USD	0.20	350
UK Government Bonds						
iShares FTSE Gilts UK 0–5	4.14	1.02	IGLS	GBP	0.20	233
iShares FTSE UK All Stocks Gilt	4.16	2.60	IGLT	GBP	0.20	386
Global Emerging Markets Bonds						
iShares JPMorgan $ Emerging Markets Bond Fund	6.19	5.33	SEMB	USD	0.45	884
Covered Bonds						
iShares Markit iBoxx Euro Covered Bond	3.72	2.83	ICOV	EUR	0.20	61

Table 8.3 The Alpha Managers

		Yield (%)	AMC (%)
	Bond funds		
John Anderson	Gartmore Corporate Bond	5.50	1
Stephen Bailey	CF Walker Crips Corporate Bond	5.30	1
Gordon Brown	Baillie Giff Gilt (B)	2.90	1
Stewart Cowley	Old Mutual Global Strategic Bond (A)	2.25	1
Kevin Doran	IFDS Brown Shipley Sterling Bond	5.80	1
Ian Fishwick	Fidelity Long Bond	4.33	0.25
Quentin Fitzsimmons	Threadneedle Sterling Bond	2.70	1
David Hooker	Insight UK Index-linked Bond	1.29	0.25
Gareth Isaac	GLG Total Return Bond	2.14	1
Philip Payne	Henderson Sterling Bond	5.00	1.25
Alex Smitten	Cazenove UK Corporate Bond	5.70	1
Richard Woolnough	M&G Strategic Corporate Bond	4.11	1
	Equity and income funds		
Stephen Bailey	CF Walker Crips Equity Income	3.71	1.5
Greg Bennett	Marlborough UK Equity Income	2.60	1.5
Adam Cordery	Schroder Monthly High Income	8.39	1.25
Robin Geffen	Neptune Income	4.90	1.6
John Hamilton	Jupiter Distribution	4.10	1.25
James Harries	Newton Global Higher Income	5.26	1.5
Leigh Harrison	Threadneedle UK Equity Income	4.80	1.5
Robert Hay	Newton Global Higher Income	5.26	1.5
Rob Hepworth	Ecclesiastical Higher Income	3.96	1.25
Richard Hodges	L&G Managed Monthly Income	4.50	1
Christopher Metcalfe	Newton Income	3.50	1.5
Bill Mott	PSigma Income	4.40	1.5
Anthony Nutt	Jupiter Income	4.10	1.5

▶

Table 8.3 continued

		Yield (%)	AMC (%)
Nick Purves	SJP Equity Income	3.20	n/a
Ian Spreadbury	Fidelity Money Builder Income	4.16	0.8
John Stopford	Investec Monthly High Income	7.85	0.95
Victor Wood	McInroy & Wood Income	3.10	1.5
Neil Woodford	Invesco Perp Income	3.93	1.5
Bob Yerbury	Pru Invesco Perpetual Managed	3.27	1.5

Source: Trustnet (www.trustnet.com)

How do I change the mix of assets in my portfolio over time?

As we've examined a series of basic portfolio ideas, it's become clear that the passage of time makes a huge difference. We've already examined the idea that portfolios might need some form of rebalancing over time. But what about your own changing attitude towards risk and return as you grow older: how does that change over time and what effect does it have on your portfolio of income-producing investments?

Imagine you're 25 years old. You've just landed a job managing the night shift at a major UK superstore in south London and the world is your oyster. You're earning just enough money to put aside say £100 a month in a fund that you'll stick with for the next 40 years of your working life but for now you want lots and lots of growth in your underlying investments. That means you're willing to take on some risk – now – and the long-term data on returns suggests that the riskiest, most rewarding of the major asset classes are equities. Bonds by contrast are a bit boring and safe and although you're probably never going to lose more than 20% in any one year (that's called your maximum drawdown in the trade) you're equally never going to bag any huge tenbaggers that make your fortune. In summary our 25-year-old thrusting young buck quite sensibly tells his adviser that his risk tolerance is high and that he wants to stack up on equity exposure and 'go for it' in terms of risk.

Flash forward 30 years. Our young buck is now a considerably older 55-year-old who's just ten years away from retirement (still with the major superstore now owned by a Mongolian coal conglomerate!) working in

Department 23 at Head Office examining Sigma Six Efficiency. He can just about put up with the boredom of the job because he knows that retirement is only ten years away (although he's heard rumours that the retirement age might increase to 85 soon). That means capital preservation is all important. He absolutely cannot afford a 'drawdown' of something like 20% in one year – that means he takes a very negative view of equities and he's a big fan of bonds.

This transition we've just described sits at the heart of something called lifecycle analysis. Over those 30 years (from 25 to 55), our private investor changes – both physically and in his tolerance of risk – and over time that translates into a big change in his choice of assets. Early on he's sensibly interested in equities and probably no bonds, in his mid-forties he's probably making the shift away from equities into some bonds and by his mid-fifties he's probably biased towards bonds. Curiously once he gets to retirement at 65, the consensus on the 'correct' balance becomes a little muddier. On paper, retirees should be ultra cautious – they have to preserve their pensions pot for a retirement that could last 30 or more years. But they also require an income to live on and the assets with the safest profile – bonds and especially government bonds or gilts – tend to pay the lowest yield. Also pensioners have to be cautious about another major risk – inflation. Sticking all your money in conventional bonds in high inflationary times might mean you preserve your nominal (before inflation) returns, but the real value after inflation might be diminishing rapidly. Some academics and economists maintain that pensioners should be willing to take on extra risk, to grow their income and to grow their capital sum in inflationary times. The *Investors Chronicle* economist Chris Dillow has suggested that pensioners shouldn't really be paranoid about preserving all their capital until death primarily because they can't benefit from that wealth when they're six feet under. His strategy? Possibly consider taking on extra risk via equities and especially those equities that pay a dividend, and reducing your bond exposure.

Regardless of this post-retirement debate, the simple process of constructing a mix of assets that can be used as the building blocks of a single portfolio and can change over time has evolved into a complex research literature at whose heart sits something called the glidepath. Figure 8.1 is from one of the largest investment research organisations called Ibbotson Associates in Chicago, but most other outfits' glidepaths look pretty similar. This glidepath starts with high risks assets, transitions through a balanced approach in mid-life and ends with a mixture of assets with a bias towards bonds later in life.

Every provider and analyst will have their own starting and ending points and relative combinations but they all feature the exact same blended glidepath. The only substantive debate seems to be whether a very young person has some limited bond exposure and whether a retired person should have some equity exposure and at what level.

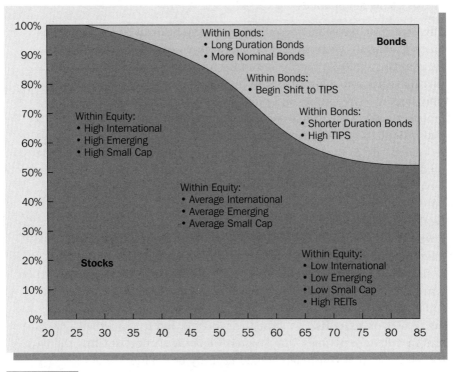

Figure 8.1   Generalised Ibbotson target maturity glidepath

Source: Ibbotson Associates (www.ibbotson.com)

This blindingly simple analysis has evolved into something called a target date fund. This involves you sitting down, working out your planned retirement age (which will nearly always be massively wide of the mark given changing longevity patterns!) and then finding a fund that sports the closest equivalent to that year, called a target date. Given that its 2010 as this book is being written, and if you're 30 now, you'll probably be looking at retiring in 35 years time in which case your 'target date' is probably around 2045.

The Ibbotson Associates research notes that: 'Target maturity investment solutions should help investors through the investment phases of accumulation, transition, and retirement' (www.ibbotson.com). A second variation on the same model can also be found called target risk funds which don't specify an actual year but take a measured risk approach, suggesting a transition from ultra-high risk to ultra-low risk and all shades of risk control in between. This new niche is growing fast. According to Ibbotson's research at the end of 2007, there were approximately 38 registered target maturity fund families in the US representing 256 individual target maturity funds with assets under management of $178 billion. In 2008 two major UK providers – Fidelity and ABN Amro – also launched their own versions of the lifecycle approach and over the next few years investors can expect a plethora of new launches as asset managers wake up to the huge marketing opportunity.

How much should I diversify?

So far in this section we've mentioned diversification but never really detailed exactly what we mean by building a portfolio full of diverse income producing assets. To understand how you might go about this exercise it's probably worth touching on the slightly arcane world of portfolio theory. This hugely extensive and influential body of work was pioneered by a certain Harry Markowitz, an economist. The body of theory isolates all the key elements of a well-diversified portfolio and then guides investors through an optimum portfolio construction process and how to build an efficient frontier. We're not going to bore you with a lengthy exposition of the ins and outs of this academic field of study but suffice to say that there are three building blocks that comprise total return.

THE THREE BUILDING BLOCKS

■ **The risk free return.** This is usually the rate of return you get from cash although economists like to use terms like 'the rate that best neutralises your risks'.

■ **Return from beta.** Technically speaking this is the return you get above the risk-free rate of return from holding an asset class like equities or a market. So if the risk-free rate of return is 2% and you buy a tracker for the FTSE All Share index that gives you 8% pa, your beta is 6%.

■ **Return from alpha.** This is the tricky one as it's the value added by a manager which is derived by the manager moving away from the beta

---

The key to understanding diversification is that lots of different kinds of markets and assets – bonds mixed with equities and say an alternative asset such as commodities – can give you lots of different betas and if you're lucky those different betas don't move as one, i.e. they're not correlated. Thus if equities go down, bonds might rise in value along with say commodities like gold. The key is that mixing up different betas might give you added benefits and improve returns. In fact economists are so smitten with the idea of diversification – some call it the diversification premium – that they suggest it is the one free lunch left in investing. Markowitz's ideas have also been used and developed by a wide range of professional economists – Yale University's fund manager David Swensen for instance has spent decades running hugely diversified portfolios investing in everything from forests through to private equity funds and hedge funds.

For Swensen, the key insight is that you can now juggle all these different betas in an accessible manner using actively managed funds and index tracking ETFs. Swensen in particular has gone on the record and said that his hugely diversified portfolio is expected to return about 10.1% per year, with expected standard deviation of 11.8% per year, and that for most private investors the only sensible way of achieving that diversification is through index tracking funds. In an interview in the March/April 2009 issue of the *Yale Alumni Magazine* Swensen proclaims that:

> With all assets, I recommend that people invest in index funds because they're transparent, understandable, and low-cost... Almost everybody belongs on the passive end of the continuum. A very few belong on the active end. But the unfortunate fact is that an overwhelming number of investors find themselves betwixt and between. In that in-between place, people end up paying high fees whether to a mutual fund or a stockbroker or another agent. And they end up with disappointing net returns.
>
> (www.yalealumnimagazine.com)

But Swensen's work is not the most influential recent academic study. That title belongs to an analysis from 1991, by three academics – Brinson, Singer and Beebower[6] – which looked at what really contributes towards the performance of a portfolio. They looked at fund managers' market timing skills, their ability to pick shares or their ability to diversify assets. They studied the largest 91 pension plans in the USA over a ten-year period, with portfolio sizes reaching to $3 billion. Yet again the virtues of traditional active fund management were found to be wanting: the academics calculated that only 6% of total returns could be attributed to

---

[6] Gary P. Brinson, Brian D. Singer, and Gilbert L. Beebower (1991) 'Determinants of Portfolio Performance II: An Update', *The Financial Analysts Journal*, 47(3); an update of work by Brinson, Hood and Beebower in 1986.

just allocate across different asset classes in an intelligent, diversified manner

market timing and stock selection. A massive 94% could be explained by the careful use of diversification and the use of varying asset classes and markets over time. In fact the study found that traditional active fund management skills like timing and stockpicking produced negative returns over time after they'd been adjusted for risk. The bottom line – don't bother picking shares or trying to time the market, just allocate across different asset classes in an intelligent, diversified manner. By now you'll be able to see that diversification can work wonders if done properly, especially if you're willing to stack up your portfolio with different types of asset classes. US stockmarket analyst Geoff Considine has even gone so far as to put a number on the value of the diversification premium – between 2 and 2.5% per annum.

So much for the theory – what does this body of analysis suggest that an investor actually do with their portfolio? It will come as no surprise that a huge number of incredibly complex computer-based tools have been developed that tell you the 'optimal' mix of assets. Many advisers use derivations of these models and they are undoubtedly helpful if you understand what's really going on with the maths.

But back in the real world there are some much simpler answers to our question of what a diversified portfolio might actually look like. Take this illuminating episode. Professor Markowitz was asked at a conference in Chicago what he invested in: 'I should have computed co-variances of the asset classes and drawn an efficient frontier – instead I split my contributions 50/50 between bonds and equities.' Just to ram the point home, it's also worth quoting Eugene Fama, the father of the index funds movement who, when asked by a publication called *Investment News* what he invested in, replied by detailing a mixture of funds that invested in a very broad-based US index called the Wilshire 5000, plus a little in small cap and international index funds, and a little bit over a third in value oriented stock indexes and short-term bond funds.

That's it. Professor Fama – along with Professors Markowitz and Sharpe – did what so many people have done in the past, namely mix and match a small number of key asset classes, cheaply and efficiently. They could have made the exercise enormously efficient and endlessly optimised the mix of asset classes to build their own efficient frontier (which in turn defines the optimum efficient frontier) but they kept it simple and intuitive, and mixed and matched a bit of equity and a bit of bonds. This consensus in favour of simple diversification is also in evidence when talking portfolios with most British investment academics: most of these 'experts' personally stick to a simple, classic, split, namely 60% equities (broad equity market indices) and 40% in government bonds.

US-based analysts Paul Merriman and colleague Richard Buck have tried their best to put some more flesh on the bone of this simple 60/40 idea. Back in September 2005 they attempted to answer the struggle of how to go about building one portfolio for life. Using the database of Dimensional Fund Advisors, their research department looked at returns between 1955 and 2004, a 50-year period that included lots of bear, bull and sideways tracking markets.

They looked at three potential portfolios:

- the S&P 500 tracker
- another variant invested 60% in the S&P 500 Index and 40% in five-year Treasury bond notes (very easy for any investor to replicate)
- another 60/40 split made up of 40% Treasury Bills and 60% equity but this time the equity was split four ways between US-based large-cap stocks, large-cap value stocks, small-cap stocks and small-cap value stocks.

According to Merriman and Buck's analysis (www.fundadvice.com/index.php) the 'all-equity S&P 500 Index portfolio had an annualized return of 10.9 percent over that 50-year period' while the '60/40 version's annualized return was 9.6 percent'. Surely the average private investor would have always plumped for this all-equity version? Merriman and Buck aren't so sure – though the mixed 60/40 equities/bond mix returned less than the pure equities approach it did so with a much lower level of risk. 'Statistically, you could say the 60/40 portfolio reduced return by 12 percent while reducing risk by 42 percent,' say Merriman and Buck. 'Or you could say the 60/40 portfolio provided 88 percent of the return with only 58 percent of the risk.'

The best performer by far though came in the shape of the third mixture – the 60/40 portfolio with greater equity diversification. 'Over the 50 years in our study,' Merriman and Buck report, 'this diversified 60/40 portfolio produced a return of 11.4 percent, with a maximum drawdown of 25 percent. Compared with the all-equity portfolio, this diversified mix raised the return by an extra 0.5 percentage point while it reduced the risk by 44 percent'. That 0.5% per annum difference may not seem that great but the authors remind us that over 50 years $100 invested at 10.9% would grow to $17,643. The same $100 invested at 11.4% would grow to $22,093, a difference of $4,450, or an increase of 25%! 'In dollar terms,' they add 'that difference alone is equal to more than 44 times the entire original investment of $100.'

But what about going global? Merriman and Bucks' original analysis only looked at US investments but surely there must be some benefit from investing internationally as well? The authors agreed and subsequently looked at year-by-year returns from 1970 through to 2004 if an investor had stuck with the diversified option (the third on the above list with no international stocks) or invested in an alternative strategy which consisted of a 60%/40% equity split but with that equity portion split 50% into US-based stocks of varying sizes (large-cap stocks, large-cap value stocks, small-cap stocks and small-cap value stocks) and 50% international (split five ways this time to include large-cap stocks, large-cap value stocks, small-cap stocks, small-cap value stocks and stocks in emerging markets). The returns then increased by more than forty-fold! The bottom line – the more you diversify internationally, the greater your potential returns!

THE VIRTUES OF BONDS IN THE MIX

Readers should hopefully be convinced by now that bonds have lots of positives going for them when it comes to building a diversified portfolio of income-producing assets. Perhaps the most obvious is that they produce a decent income! Crucially there's also a great deal of evidence to show that bonds are less *volatile* than other assets, especially equities – and volatility matters because large capital losses can destroy your total returns. Figure 8.2 is from an analysis run by ETF firm iShares in June 2010 and looks at the volatility – the changeability around a mean or average – of European fixed income bonds and European shares.

The conclusion is fairly obvious, namely that bonds are less volatile. Here's the iShares analysis (www.iShares.com):

> Over the past seven years fixed income volatility has been substantially lower than for equity benchmarks. At the same time, if one considers the average historical performance of European fixed income benchmarks versus equity benchmarks one can observe steady returns for bonds versus stocks over time. On a cumulative basis Barclays Capital Euro Aggregate Index has on average delivered a 41.2% return while the EURO STOXX 50 Index has delivered a 33.3% return for the period from December 2002 to end April 2010.

The key observation here is that over the past few years in Europe bonds have not only been less volatile but they've also produced better returns!

There's an additional positive for bonds (much ignored) when compared against other income-producing assets including high yielding equities that pay a dividend – the volatility of income payments is also much lower with bonds. According to iShares (www.iShares.com):

> Over time the coupon payments of the bonds have been relatively stable, for example, for the Aggregate Bond Index the coupon ranged from 4.28% to ▶

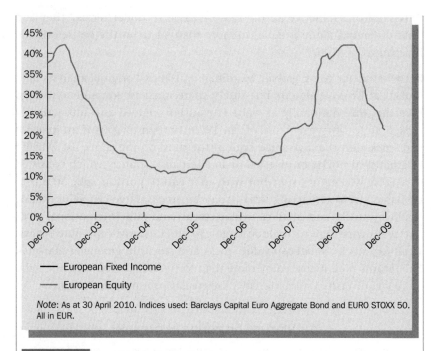

European Fixed Income
European Equity

Note: As at 30 April 2010. Indices used: Barclays Capital Euro Aggregate Bond and EURO STOXX 50.
All in EUR.

Figure 8.2   **Historical fixed income and equity volatility**

Source: iShares

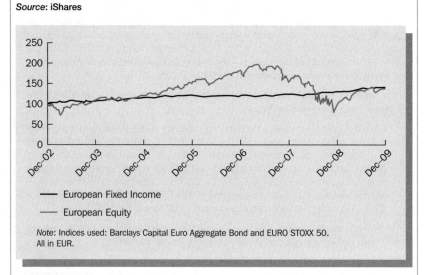

European Fixed Income
European Equity

Note: Indices used: Barclays Capital Euro Aggregate Bond and EURO STOXX 50.
All in EUR.

Figure 8.3   **Historical fixed income and equity volatility**

Source: iShares.

5.66% over a 10-year period, while for the corporate bond index from 4.76% to 5.54% respectively.

Table 8.4 shows the full range of income yields over time for a range of European assets.

Table 8.4 Income yields for a range of European assets

	Barclays Capital Euro Aggregate Bond Index (coupon %)	Barclays Capital Euro Corporate Bond Index (coupon %)	Barclays Capital Euro Treasury Bond Index (coupon %)	EURO STOXX 50 Index (dividend yield)	DAX Index (dividend yield)
Maximum	5.66	5.54	5.92	8.75	6.94
Minimum	4.28	4.76	4.23	1.37	1.35
Difference	1.38	0.78	1.69	7.38	5.59
Current	4.28	5.01	4.23	3.63	3.13

Note: Bloomberg, Barclays Capital, Datastream. As at 30 April 2010. Coupon and gross dividend yield data.

Source: iShares.

The risk bundles

With these basic portfolio principles firmly in the front of our mind, it's time to scan the full array of income-producing investments examined so far in this book and try to build a rough categorisation of the different options available to investors based largely on an understanding of risk. This is bound to be a 'rough and ready' exercise and some asset classes can and do cross over between different risk levels, but the idea here is to suggest three distinct bundles of risk-based, income-producing assets. In time honoured style we'll break these bundles into the following:

▪ **lower risk** – ideal for the very cautious investor who doesn't want to risk losing very much capital, and many older pensioners

▪ **medium risk** for those who want some possibility of capital growth as well as the potential for a higher return – this extra potential return in both capital and yield terms comes with an inevitable price in terms of extra risk

▪ and finally our **higher risk** portfolio for those more adventurous types looking to lock in the potential for some capital gains as well as an above average income.

All things being equal we'd suggest that older investors with a conservative attitude towards risk stay away from anything in the higher risk bundle, although if you are in your early sixties and beginning to worry about a long retirement that stretches out for 20–25 years and you have some extravagant tastes that require a big income, you might want to consider taking on some extra risk. We'd also strongly suggest that if you feel your risk level fits the lower risk bundle mix, you shouldn't attempt to buy any assets sitting in the higher risk category.

Before we dive into the risk bundles let's remind ourselves of some of the principles and insights examined in this book as we've moved through the spectrum of income-producing assets.

The risk–reward trade off is crucially important

In simple language the riskier an asset, the higher its potential return or yield. A simple way of understanding this is to look at sovereign debt – governments with a fantastic long-term record for reliability (like our own) can get away with paying a fraction of the rate charged to riskier emerging market governments. That risk spread can amount to many hundreds of basis points (basis points are one hundredth of a single percentage point). At the height of the market panic back in 2008, risky corporate debt (also known as high yield) was trading at a difference of more than 10% per annum or 1,000 basis points in yield terms over safe, investment grade corporate debt. That margin – like that for developed/emerging sovereign debt – has now narrowed very appreciably with some analysts worrying that the 'spread' has become much too narrow considering the extra risk.

Frequency of payment is hugely important

One of the great attractions of many high street savings accounts is that they can pay interest monthly, although monthly frequency often comes at a cost with slightly lower interest rates. Many dividends are also paid quarterly or twice-yearly while most bonds only pay annually.

The tax treatment and the wrapper used also matter hugely

Readers will probably remember preference shares (commonly called prefs) from earlier chapters. These are issued by various financial institutions and they traditionally pay out more in income than government bonds (also known as gilts) and investment grade corporate bonds. Crucially these prefs also pay tax before they issue a payment to investors – for basic rate taxpayers that means that any income you receive is net of tax unless you are a higher rate taxpayer. If you invest in an ISA this is all a little besides the point as all income you receive in your tax wrapper comes free of tax, be it from a pref or from a PIBS (Permanent Interest Bearing Share) issued by a building society or a mainstream corporate bond (although you can't reclaim any tax paid at source via prefs).

Understand the difference between the current value and the redemption value

Many investors prefer high street savings accounts because of their simplicity. You invest £100 and when you close the account you get your £100 back. With many fixed income securities the current value of the bond could be more or less than the final value you receive when the bond winds up or redeems. This matters hugely as it affects the yield you receive. The temptation for instance is to look at a long-dated bond – say a gilt or corporate bond – and then compare the current price with the interest coupon or yield. But in some cases the current bond purchase price is *more* than the final redemption price if you hang about until the bond winds up and is repaid (hopefully!). If the fixed income security trades at above the redemption price and you hold to maturity you might trigger a capital loss and that needs to be accounted for in the yield return. Thus you'll see a difference between the flat or running yield (the current share price versus the interest coupon) and the redemption yield (the yield versus the current share price adjusted for any losses at redemption). This can work both ways of course: many building society PIBSs and banking group preference shares for instance trade at below the issue (par) price at which they will be redeemed or called. If you held them to redemption and that security was called and repaid in full, you'd make money from both the running yield and the capital gain.

The pecking order and counterparty risk

Many of the most interesting income-producing assets tend also to be more risky – an echo of our first point. They also tend to occupy a fixed place in the hierarchy of payments in the event of a bankruptcy. PIBS and Prefs for instance rank behind corporate debt but rank *ahead* of equity. This pecking order – the queue to be repaid assets in event of default – is also applicable to collective fund assets but in a different way. Some exchange traded fund providers for instance

> many of the most interesting income-producing assets tend also to be more risky

offer exposure to an index via derivatives-based structures that guarantee to make the capital payment from both change in the index and the yield. It's a respected structure that 99.99% of the time presents no real risk, except when markets are in meltdown and you discover that the 'counterparty' guaranteeing that payment is actually Lehmans!

The time span for investing in an income-based product is hugely relevant

The general rule is that the shorter the period of time that you lend your money out, the lower the required interest rate or yield and vice versa, i.e. you'd expect the rate of return on government debt due to be repaid in six months to be less than the yield paid on debt not due to be repaid for 30 years. This rule generally holds true but every once in a while the markets warp and an inverse relationship takes over. Also be aware that some fixed income securities can be perpetual i.e. they have no due date for redeeming or being called and can carry on forever. Governments have been at this particular game for hundreds of years – UK Consuls (originally issued in 1752 with the current 2½% Consolidated Stock issued in 1923) are perpetual government loan stock and have no set repayment date.

Inflation is deadly

Later on in this chapter we'll look at the varying impact of inflation on income-producing assets but as a general rule increasing prices, as measured by a major index like the RPI, destroys the present-day value of your income, which is bad news for bonds. In most circumstances investors would want to be rewarded for higher inflation with higher yield. In the case of index-linked certificates and government bonds that relationship is an explicit part of the structuring of the bond and its payout. But most fixed income securities have no explicit relationship to inflation although you might generally expect floating rate securities (those without fixed coupon payments) to increase their payout as inflation increases. Equities have a slightly different relationship with inflation. Most big companies with pricing power are able to increase their dividend payout as inflation increases, and equities as an asset class tend to perform very reasonably on inflationary epochs except when hyperinflation breaks out, in which case many assets rapidly become worthless.

Value matters

Most investors understand the concept of value in equities – cheap stocks with decent asset backing can make a good investment over the very long term, and usually pay out a very high income as dividend. But bonds are no different – some bonds can be cheap and good value based on the reliability of their asset backing. Investors tend to forget that the capital price of gilts and bonds can vary enormously over time and that you can buy income-producing bonds at the *wrong* price even if they are producing the right yield. Equally though some assets like high yield bonds do trade at a sensible low price precisely because some companies do go bankrupt and fail to pay their lenders. Default is an ever present and real risk in the world of bonds!

Nothing in the world of income-based investments is entirely risk-free!

Economists love to play around with the concept of the risk-free asset such as cash or bonds. They compare the likely returns on these assets with those from risky stuff such as equities to establish the premium we're willing to pay to buy extra risk and returns. But government bonds are not risk-free – governments have and will continue to default on their debts. Even very established, respectable governments have been known to resort to inflationary policy to whittle away the long-term value of their liabilities. Equally, many investors thought that money market funds were risk-free until they discovered that their funds had invested in supposedly easy to access, short-term commercial paper issued by... Lehmans. More than a few safe money market funds 'broke the buck,' i.e. couldn't pay out $1 for every $1 invested. High street savings are guaranteed by the government but only up to a limit. Many wealthy investors in the Icelandic banks for instance lost their savings above that limit.

All these factors should remind you that investing for an income is every bit as difficult as investing for a capital gain. You need to consider a range of factors, diversify risk and returns and do your research on the underlying structure that you're investing in. There is no 'one size fits all' approach to deriving an income – except perhaps if you have to invest in a single annuity at retirement in which case you're legally obliged to focus on one structure. Yet you can also have your cake and eat it – you can invest in a range of assets that produce a much higher income without commensurately higher risk to your capital.

To help you navigate your way through the maze of income-producing assets it's worth thinking about them as being composed of three risk-based bundles. Be prepared to mix and match assets within and between the bundles and see what works for you. See Tables 8.5–8.7.

Table 8.5 The lower risk bundle – 0.5% to 4.50% per annum

Asset	Likely yields (as of Autumn 2010)	Comments	Biggest danger
Conventional government bonds	0.5% to 4.50%	UK, US and continental European gilts are almost risk-free although nominal prices can move up and down. The longer the duration, the higher the interest rate in most cases.	In a higher inflation world investors abandon bonds, triggering a sell-off.
Inflation-linked government bonds	0.5% to 2%	Again almost risk-free but could be very low return in a low inflation environment.	A deflationary environment will produce very low real returns. Also beware changes in the real yield.
Annuities	1% to 4.5%	As safe as the insurance companies that issue them, which means they are very secure. But rates can be very low if you want an annuity stream for a long time.	Changes in gilt rates have a major impact on income payments.
High street savings accounts	0.5% to 4.5%	Very safe and backed by the government in many different ways – the FSCS as well as implicit government guarantees to back retail banks.	Beware all the terms and conditions and sudden changes in interest rates.
High street long-term fixed rate bonds	3.5% to 4.5%	Great for locking in a high fixed rate over a period as long as five years.	

Table 8.5 Continued

Asset	Likely yields (as of Autumn 2010)	Comments	Biggest danger
Investment grade corporate bonds	3.5% to 5%	Some of the very highest grade corporate bonds are now regarded as almost as safe as government bonds.	There is still corporate risk especially if the global economy takes a big tumble.
Premium bonds	1.5%	You could win a million and even smaller amounts of money could produce a win; tax-free.	In reality you are unlikely to earn the equivalent of 1.5% in income.
Money market funds	0.5% to 2%	Run by large asset management groups and banks these are a great home for cash.	Very low rates and always some minimal risk of bank failure.

Table 8.6 The medium risk bundle – 3.5% to 7% per annum

Asset	Likely yields (as of Autumn 2010)	Comments	Biggest danger
Corporate bond funds	4% to 7%; usually around the 4.5% to 5.5% range	Both ETFs and unit trust funds offer a diversified mixture of riskier corporate bonds and decent yields.	If the economy stalls and equity investors flee risk, these could sell off quickly.
Emerging market bonds	5.5% to 7%	Most emerging markets governments have low debt levels and a lot of conventional bond money is flowing East and South.	Emerging market governments are not as safe as the UK and mainstream Europe. They can and do default, and if investors flee risk these could be regarded as too risky. ▶

Table 8.6 Continued

Asset	Likely yields (as of Autumn 2010)	Comments	Biggest danger
Equity income unit trust funds and dividend weighted equity index funds	3.5% and 7%; most around the 4% to 6% range	Many established companies have a very solid reputation for paying dividends they can easily afford and these yields are frequently well above those on offer from equivalent bonds. These funds can also do well in inflationary eras.	Equities – shares – are riskier than bonds and in a bear market can fall in value.
Structured products	4% to 7%	Many mainstream structured products can offer a decent yield of around 5% with downside conditions that would recall a catastrophic fall in equity markets before capital values take a hit.	There's always the risk that your counterparty could default, leaving your investment worthless. Also these products still carry equity risk. Many also require you to lock your money away for years.
Infrastructure funds	4.5% to 6%	These own solid, dependable income streams from government-run infrastructure schemes. Many of these schemes are very long term with some inflation protection added in as well.	They are still equity-based products, with all the obvious risks. Government's might also change their mind about schemes and can cancel contracts in extreme circumstances.
Some PIBSs and PSBs	6% to 8%	Some fixed income securities from relatively secure financial institutions such as the Nationwide Building Society and the Co-op, can offer very decent yields with little credit risk.	Poor liquidity in the market can produce some fairly nasty bid offer spreads. There's also the chance that the financial institution might run into financial problems.

Table 8.7 The higher risk bundle – 5% to 12% per annum

Asset	Likely yields (as of Autumn 2010)	Comments	Biggest danger
Equity income investment trusts	5% to 8%	Structurally these are rather similar to mainstream equity income unit trusts but extra gearing on the balance sheet and discounts can substantially increase the yield.	These are subject to the obvious equity risk, liquidity can dry up, and gearing is a double-edged sword.
Real estate investment trusts	6% to 12%	These diversified portfolios of commercial real estate assets can produce very reliable income streams, most of which is paid straight to the investor. Until recently real estate has been regarded as relatively lower risk.	Real estate has recently proved to be very volatile, especially as debt levels have risen. The underlying market in buildings is also relatively illiquid. And these stockmarket-based structures are also subject to all the risks of owning equities.
Listed structured products	7% to 12%	These equity-based structures are aimed at wealthier investors and can pay out some very high coupons, paid by relatively secure institutions.	You need to understand the structure, the risks attached to the issuer and the payout profile. These can also be difficult to trade in.
PSBs, PIBSs and other bank hybrid debt structures	6% to 15%	There's a huge range of structures available at all levels of risk from many different financial institutions (but mainly the banks).	Can be illiquid, volatile and subject to bank risk. Also bid offer spreads can be vast!

The inflation factor

Before we take a closer look at some model or idealised portfolios it's worth examining one last absolutely crucial phenomenon that affects the pricing of all income-producing assets. Inflation is hugely important in determining your outlook on different classes of investments. In the next section we'll look at a few portfolios that attempt to mix and match different asset classes. But to build this diversified portfolio we've made some very simple assumptions about inflation – that it's neither too low (slipping into deflation) or too high. Most of the time inflation does fit this ideal pattern – for much of the past few decades inflation in the developed western world has stayed within a 1–5% range. But there's always a very good chance that in the future matters may be very, very different. If inflation does shoot up, or we tumble into severe deflation, what impact will there be on different income-producing asset classes? Table 8.8 tries to give some clues as to what might happen with both scenarios.

Table 8.8 Two scenarios and possible outcomes

Asset class	Low inflation/deflation – low interest rates	High inflation – increasing interest rates
Conventional government bonds	Will probably see yields drop to very low levels and capital prices increase.	Expect a big sell-off as interest rates rise.
Inflation-linked government bonds	Yields will tumble and overall returns will be also be very low.	As inflation rises both the coupon (the yield) and the final redemption price (the capital price) should increase unless real yields take a big tumble.
Investment grade corporate bonds	Should behave like conventional government bonds and rise in value with yields tumbling.	Might perform better than some government bonds as successful companies tend to have strong pricing power in an inflationary environment.
Corporate bonds	As long as the economy doesn't tumble into recession, prompting massive bankruptcies, these should rise in value with yields following gilts.	As interest rates rise, expect values to fall away as investors flee all fixed rate coupons.

Table 8.8 Continued

Asset class	Low inflation/deflation – low interest rates	High inflation – increasing interest rates
Savings accounts	Interest rates will probably stay very low unless banks and building societies decide to compete for savings.	Expect rates to rise but probably at a lower rate than inflation.
Annuities	Bad news as gilt yield rates will be unusually low – payouts will suffer.	As interest rates rise, gilt yields will have to rise as well, producing higher payouts.
Structured products	Low interest rates generally produce lower yields because the product providers have to use bonds within their structures.	Yields should start rising.
Equity-based products	In general equities tend to underperform bonds in very low inflation environments.	Most equity markets tend to perform better than equivalent bonds as inflation increases but hyperinflation is bad for virtually all forms of capital. Dividends tend to rise at a slightly higher rate than inflation.
Infrastructure funds	Should produce a stable but sub-6% yield.	There is inflation protection built into most PFI/PPP contracts so should perform well.
Real Estate Investment Trusts (REITs)	Landlords can't keep hiking up rents in a low inflationary world but they should still be able to pull in a stable 4–8% yield depending on risk.	Landlords should be able to increase rents as inflation rises but there's likely to be a lag and over time REIT yields will underperform.

Three model income portfolios

It's now time to take our principles focused on building a diversified, robust portfolio and mix them up with our bundles of risk to produce model portfolios that combine different assets and ideas. We've detailed three different idealised, model portfolios: a cautious income portfolio for middle-of-the-road investors; an adventurous one for investors looking for capital gain and a big yield; plus one final, simple, ultra-defensive portfolio for investors looking for rock solid capital preservation and no meaningful equity risk.

The cautious income portfolio

Our cautious income portfolio is ideal for cautious investors looking for an income but also some possibility of moderate capital gains in the future. In portfolio terms there's a strong bonds bias, and it's focused on capital preservation but also offers some limited exposure to equities. In overall terms the mix is 60% in bonds and 40% in equities but we've carefully weighted the equity portion towards more conservative ideas such as infrastructure funds that produce an income. The top line composition is as follows:

- equities – 24.5%
- infrastructure and real estate – 15.5%
- bonds including corporate bonds – 60%.

In Table 8.9 we've broken down these top lines into a series of distinct asset classes and markets with their accompanying index. Your choice is whether to use an ETF to buy this exposure or to use an active manager.

Table 8.9 Distinct asset classes and markets

Asset class and index/market	% of total portfolio
Mainstream blue chip equities – FTSE 100 Index or equivalent fund	5.0
World equities – MSCI WORLD exc UK	2.0
High yielding UK equities – FTSE UK Dividend Plus or equity income fund	6.5
High yielding European equities – DJ EURO STOXX Select Dividend 30 index	6.0
Utility and infrastructure shares – MacQuarie Global Infrastructure 100 index	12.5
Real estate funds – EPRA/NAREIT Developed World Property Dividend Plus	3.0
Corporate bonds – iBoxx Sterling Corporate index	5.0
Conventional UK bonds – FTSE All Stocks Gilt index	40.0
Index-linked UK Gilts – Barclays UK Index-linked index	20.0
Total %	**100.0**

All these asset classes or indices produce a stream of income either through coupons paid by bonds or through dividends. Using our allocations we've then looked at current running, flat yields and detailed them in Table 8.10. As you can see the blended average yield of the portfolio is about 3% per annum.

Table 8.10 Yields at 9 September 2010

Index	Yield % (flat yield where appropriate)
FTSE All Stocks Gilt	4.16
Barclays UK Index-linked Gilts	0.95
FTSE NAREIT/EPRA Global Property Dividend Plus	2.84
FTSE MacQuarie Global Infrastructure 100	3.18
DJ EURO STOXX Select Dividend 30 index	3.92
UK Dividend Plus	4.57
FTSE All	2.98
FTSE World exc UK or MSCI World exc UK	1.45
Blended overall yield	**3.00**

What's the thinking behind our blend of asset mixes? In our model portfolio we've tried to reflect the huge variety of debates about risk and reward, future inflation and current low interest rates. Overall we have weighted the portfolio 60% towards safer bonds and 40% towards riskier assets. If you were to invest in ETFs that followed the main indices used in our model portfolio, you'd be receiving a total portfolio return of around 3% at the moment, with much the largest component of income coming from the biggest holding in the main conventional gilts index, the FTSE All Stocks Gilt. We think that gilts are still, probably, the safest place to be over the next few years or so and would suggest that talk of a massive bubble in prices is currently misplaced, but if inflation were to raise its ugly head in the future we'd suggest switching aggressively into index-linked gilts. As matters stand at the moment, though, we still think that the balance of probabilities leans towards deflation and continued gilt price stability.

We have though suggested putting 20% of the portfolio into those index-linked gilts as a safety policy. If the RPI started climbing back towards 4% per annum we'd suggest switching around the current 40% conventional gilts/20% index-linked ratio. Our 5% in corporate bonds is probably the most controversial idea: many, many advisers think that corporate bonds with their current high yields are the best place to derive an income. One major benchmark index – the iBoxx Sterling Liquid Corporate Long-Dated Bond index – is currently yielding a very high 5.5% flat yield. But we're cautious about any future slowing down in recovery rates and mindful of the possibility of not too distant double or even treble dip recessions. We're also concerned that volatility might stay high and we wouldn't rule out a sudden increase in corporate defaults. All in all we're more cautious of corporate bonds than many advisers and would recommend only a small exposure relative to government bonds.

> we're more cautious of corporate bonds than many advisers

In the equity portion of the portfolio we've deliberately tilted the holdings towards infrastructure assets such as utility companies and PFI investment funds. These are producing historically high, and relatively safe yields. We've also recommended some exposure to higher yielding equity indices and shares. We think that finding some way of tracking an index like the Dow Jones Global Select Dividend index or the DJ Eurostoxx 50 Euroland Equity index might be a good idea. These indices follow some of the world's largest companies that pay out an above average dividend yield.

Our most controversial idea is to invest 6.5% in high yielding UK stocks, either via an index like the UK Dividend Plus index or through an established equity income fund. Again these high yielding, value stocks have had a very tough few years and the UK Dividend Plus index has turned in some dreadful results, but there is reason to think that now the pain is being recognised in dividend cuts, the remaining high yielders might prove a better bet.

The adventurous income portfolio

Our next portfolio is for more sophisticated investors willing to hunt down much more exotic investment funds and take some risks. The key point in this portfolio is that many of the assets are producing super-sized income yields but there's still the possibility that you'll make some strong capital gains if the equity markets power ahead. Asset classes such as convertibles and our two specific listed structured product ideas – both from Bank of America Merrill Lynch – will make capital gains if the stockmarkets bounce upwards. Equally, though, we've also included some more cautious bond investments such as mainstream UK gilts via an index such as the FTSE All Stocks Gilt index. See Table 8.11.

Table 8.11 Spread of the adventurous income portfolio

Fund/ETF	Asset class	Yield	% of portfolio
SPDR Barclays Capital Convertible Securities ETF (CWB)	US convertibles	3.15	5%
iShares iBoxx Euro High Yield Corporate Bond ETF	High yield corporate bond	6.71	5%
iShares iBoxx Euro Covered Bond Fund ETF	Covered bonds	3.72	5%
Nationwide 7¼% PIBS (call 5/12/2021 @ 100p)	PIBSs	7.55	15%
Co-operative Bank 13% Perp. Sub Bonds (CPBC)	PSBs	8.39	10%
Merrill Lynch 7% Fixed Income (24B)	Structured product	8.78	10%
Fixed Coupon Dow Jones EURO STOXX 50 Index Certificate	Structured product	8.60	10%
iShares UK All Stocks Gilt ETF	Conventional gilts	4.16	20%
iShares iBoxx £ Corporate Bond exc Financials ETF	Conventional UK corporate bonds	5.35	10%
iShares JPMorgan $ Emerging Markets Bond Fund	Emerging markets bond fund	6.19	10%

Blended average % yield 6.37

In overall terms the blended yield of this mix of assets is 6.37 per annum. It's important to understand the mix of assets within this portfolio and where they sit on the risk/return spectrum – and whether you stand any chance of making a capital gain! Starting at the beginning of the list of assets the SPDR Barclays Capital Convertible Securities ETF – ticker CWB – is an American exchange traded fund that invests in the largest convertible stocks on the US markets. This is a very broad market with lots of choice and quality providers but the yield is relatively low at 3.15% – that's because you're also getting some opportunity to make a capital gain if equities in aggregate terms move upwards. The fund actually invests in a wide range of convertibles that pay an income and also give investors the option to convert into underlying shares if certain price targets are met. A bullish market will unleash a wave of options redemptions which might make investors more money – in the meantime they get the coupon payments. It's also crucially important to understand that this ETF is American listed and thus can only be bought in dollars – although most mainstream UK brokers are more than happy to trade US shares for a small premium in dealing costs. That extra risk in terms of exchange rates is not to be ignored and investors also have to remember to fill in a form that lets them recoup any withholding taxes paid on owning US securities.

Our next two fund ideas are also ETFs but this time they're from a UK-based issuer called iShares. The first focuses on European high yield bonds – in effect junk bonds – which pay out a high yield compared to investment grade corporate bonds. As we discussed earlier in this book the term 'junk' tends to imply that a security or share has no value but this is far from being the case most of the time. Junk bonds simply sit at the bottom of a long list of corporate credit ratings and many, if not most, of the bonds traded pay out in full with no interruption to their coupons. This ETF trades in the European pool of bonds and as with our convertible idea earlier, there's a series of obvious risks. The first is that underlying securities are denominated in euros and any big moves either way in FX rates could have a major impact. The underlying bonds are also riskier than ordinary corporate bonds, which is why you receive an extra yield. If the economies of Europe avoid a deep and prolonged recession, there's probably very little risk of default but if Europe does lunge into recession these junk bonds will be punished. Equally investor's need to be alert to the fear of moving into a slowdown – as opposed to the actual reality! If investors suddenly become deeply risk averse, junk bonds could be sold off aggressively. But as of writing you are being rewarded mightily for the extra risk compared to other safer forms of bond investment, with a yield of over 6.7%.

The iShares covered bond fund is an altogether safer proposition. Covered bonds are mortgage-based securities where the issuer pays out a stream of coupons based on a pool of mortgage-backed securities but also takes the risk on to their balance sheet of default. Unlike many US-based residential mortgage-backed securities the risk is thus not based on defaults by homeowners within the pool but default by the bank as well. That makes covered bonds a much more secure AAA rated set of securities and on the continent covered bonds are hugely popular as a source of income for private investors. Yet again, though, there are some clear and obvious risks – mainly that the underlying securities are euro denominated.

Next up on our list of investment ideas are two hybrid bonds issued by a building society and a mutual respectively. As we discussed in Chapter 5 on hybrid structures many investors have run scared from financial services bonds and especially PIBSs issued by building societies and PSBs issued by ex-building societies. Liquidity has been a real concern, spreads have shot up and some building societies have restructured their balance sheets, forcing PIBS-holders to move over to riskier CoCo structures where some form of virtual equity risk is involved in the payout. More importantly, some ex-building societies swallowed up by banks have stopped paying their coupons whilst their new parent groups restructure their debts. As a consequence prices have slumped and many investors now make a point of avoiding all PIBSs and PSBs. We'd suggest that sell-off has been something of an over-reaction – there are still some quality issuers of bonds that do warrant further investigation. Both the Nationwide and the Co-op have rock solid balance sheets and avoided any major problems during the recent global financial crisis. More to the point, both gobbled up smaller issues with the Co-op buying the Britannia Building Society and the Nationwide scooping up a range of smaller, local building societies. Both of these very large and well-funded outfits now boast a range of financial bond structures but we've identified two in particular – the Nationwide's 7¼% PIBS (call 5/12/2021 @ 100p) and a perpetual subordinated bond called Co-operative Bank 13% Perp. Sub Bonds (CPBC). Both structures pay between 7% and 8.5% and should be fairly accessible via a good stockbroker, although we'd strongly suggest making sure your broker talks to the market makers to see whether the bid offer spread can be narrowed down! The risks? The most obvious potential challenge is another financial crisis – at which point investors could dump any financial services asset perceived to be vulnerable. Default in either case is hugely unlikely but there is always a chance that the issuers could force the hybrid investors into one of these new CoCo structures where they have to take on some risk of conversion into equity if the financial institutions' reserves fall to very low levels. We think the chances of that are low but not insignificant which is why you're being paid a very substantial yield for taking on the extra risk.

Our list also features two highly unusual listed structured products from Merrill Lynch, now part of the Bank of America Group – these are the Merrill Lynch 7 % Fixed Income (24B) and the Fixed Coupon Dow Jones EURO STOXX 50 Index Certificate. Investors can find out more details relating to the former security by going to www.definedfunds.ml.com while details on the latter structure are at www.londonlisted.ml.com. Before we explain the risk–reward payoff within these structures it's hugely important to understand that these are primarily aimed at the more adventurous investor who has a broker willing to make the extra effort to source stock – these funds are not really accessible via an ordinary mass market online broker.

Both are structured in a fairly innovative way with some very clear counterparty risk structures. The 7% income fund is in effect a tracker on the FTSE 100 with no capital protection. In March 2013 it will pay out based on where that index is standing at the time, with the issue index level of 6116 as the reference. So, if the FTSE 100 is 10% below this initial level – at around 5500 – you'll get back 90p per 100p share. If the FTSE rises to 6116 you get 100p, but if the index rises above this level, you still only get back 100p. In effect this is a tracker fund up to a certain level at which point any capital gain is capped, but you carry on receiving that coupon all the way through to redemption. That income payment is 7p per annum per 100p share, paid half yearly.

The EURO STOXX 50 index is based on a similar idea – you are tracking up to a certain point but you also receive an income along the way. In this case you receive an annual income payment through to May 2013 of 7p per share with the underlying index being something called the Dow Jones EURO STOXX 50 index. At issue this index was trading at 3750 and so the final payout will be based on a formula using this initial level. If the Dow Jones Euro STOXX 50 trades at 10% lower than that initial index level (i.e. 3375), you get back 90p in the £; if it shoots past this level, you still only get back 100p per share.

These structured products do not offer any capital protection – your final payout is effectively tracking upto a certain level what the index is giving you. That means based on current prices – 81p for the 7% Fixed Income and 79.63p for the Euro version – you'll only ever make a maximum capital gain of 25% from current levels. But along the way you also receive an income that's over 8% per annum. There's also a clear counterparty risk – your return on the Euro product is based on Merrill Lynch risk. If Merrill goes bust, you might not get back your money! With the UK 7% Fixed Income fund your payout is based on a series of bonds issued by building societies including Bradford and Bingley and an Irish outfit called EIB. These are all structured as senior debt and to date there doesn't appear to be any threat to the payout but, if the credit crisis were to deepen, those bonds might be under threat. The key with both products is to do your own research and talk to an adviser.

Our three portfolio investments are all ETFs issued by iShares, now part of Blackrock. They track three very different bond markets – emerging markets, mainstream UK government gilts and UK corporate bonds. We've discussed these markets in much greater detail in Chapter 3 on bonds but the invest-ment rationale for each is clear – both the UK corporate bond fund and its emerging markets sibling pay out a much higher yield with the obvious greater level of risk. That extra risk is balanced off with an ETF that tracks the full spectrum of UK government gilts (with the exception of index-linked gilts). Combine these three very different risk and return profiles and investors should be receiving well over 5% per annum in income.

Stepping back from all the different investment ideas, it's essential to make one important caveat. This portfolio of income-producing investments does boast some relatively solid, lower risk ideas including UK government gilts, but overall this is not a portfolio for the risk averse, and especially not an investor fearful of a great depression! There are some fairly obvious equity risk-based products in the mix of ideas and so this is a portfolio only for the more adventurous.

Our simple, ultra-defensive portfolio

Our last portfolio is our simplest – just four ideas with a heavy bias towards lower risk government and covered bonds producing a blended or average yield of 3.25% per annum. Crucially the first three bond funds – all struc-tured as ETFs from iShares – charge well under 0.4% per annum in total expenses and can easily be purchased through a mainstream stockbroker. This portfolio of four ideas is very defensive in flavour with quite a bit of inflation proofing (the index-linked gilt fund and the infrastructure fund) and solid asset booking in all four funds. This portfolio absolutely won't make huge capital gains moving forward and is clearly vulnerable to any government bond sell-off but could be useful as a model for investors fright-ened by equity risk but looking for a simple to implement set of ideas.

Table 8.12 Spread of the ultra-defensive portfolio

Index (ETF)	Asset class	Yield	% of portfolio
iShares Barclays Capital £ Index-Linked Gilts (INXG)	Inflation-linked Bonds	0.96%	30%
iShares FTSE UK All Stocks Gilt (IGLT)	UK conventional gilts	4.16%	50%
iShares Markit iBoxx Euro Covered Bond (ICOV)	European covered bonds	3.7%	10%
HSBC Infrastructure (HICL)	Infrastructure assets	5%	10%
Blended yield 3.24%			

Investing for an income

Our model portfolios outlined above all come with lots of obvious risk warnings and caveats but perhaps the most important one is that they contain yields and prices that are in essence a snapshot in time. By the time this book is actually published we can, with some certainty, say that all the yields will have changed as will the prices! Crucially, sentiment towards different asset classes and structures can change radically over time. As of writing, government bonds seem to be a sensible safe haven, especially UK and US government debt, but that could change almost overnight if the markets believe that inflationary forces are starting to build. Perception of future risk is constantly evolving and mutating and this is bound to have an effect on absolutely every income-producing investment listed in this book.

perception of future risk is constantly evolving and mutating

Luckily the web is full of wonderful resources where you can check on current prices, work out yields and generally gauge sentiment. My personal online favourites include www.ft.com, www.yahoo.co.uk (their finance section), www.advfn.co.uk and www.totalinvestor.co.uk. But searching through all these different websites can be time consuming and not a little tiring which is where www.investingforanincome.com comes in. We've taken all the ideas in this book and built them into a simple downloadable snapshot called Income Alert. This pdf-based document (there's also a free online section as well) contains all the different income investing categories and is updated every month. The PDF also contains pithy, succint commentary on everything from individual corporate bonds through to news on the latest savings accounts. There is a small charge but there's also a free alternative for those who register. More details at www.incomealert.co.uk.

9

Investing in shares through a dividend index

by Jeremy Schwartz

Introduction

In this final chapter we're going to dig a little deeper into the returns on offer from investing in equities. In particular we're going to focus on why dividends are so crucial, how they can be used by an investor to build a portfolio of stocks and why an index tracking approach to investing might be a smart move. We've already established that dividends matter and that over time the humble dividend cheque amply rewards most investors for the risk of investing. But how can investors capture this simple idea, cost effectively and in an accessible manner. WisdomTree, a US fund manager that offers index tracking funds, has pioneered an unusual approach which consists of focusing down on those dividend cheques and building funds that track an easy to understand index. In this chapter WisdomTree's Director of Research, Jeremy Schwartz, explains their novel approach and why both index tracking and dividends really should sit at the centre of any investment portfolio targeting an income.

In an earlier chapter we established the merits of high dividend investment strategies with a focus on research covering the UK equity markets. In this chapter, we first review some of the research behind high dividend yield strategies for the US equity markets. We discuss reasons why high dividend investment strategies have added value over time.

Then we establish why dividend weighted indexes are efficient tools to execute a high dividend investment strategy. We quantify the impact dividend weighting has on a portfolio of stocks, and illustrate how dividend weighted indexes can be used as a guide to asset allocation strategies.

Higher dividend yields and excess returns

Numerous academic studies have demonstrated that high dividend yielding stocks have out-performed the broader markets over long periods of time.

Jeremy Siegel's research on dividends and S&P 500

Wharton Professor and WisdomTree Senior Investment Strategy Adviser Jeremy Siegel evaluated the link between dividend yield and stock returns for the S&P 500 in his book *The Future for Investors* (Crown Business, 2005). Professor Siegel conducted a study that annually, as of 31 December, would sort the S&P 500 by its dividend yield, ranking each stock into a quintile. The result of Professor Siegel's study showed that the lowest yielding stocks underperformed the market, and did so with significantly higher volatility, while the highest yielding stocks out-performed the market, with similar volatility as the market. While the S&P 500 and the two highest yielding quintiles had volatility shy of 18% per year, the two lowest yielding quintiles had volatility north of 21% per year.

When compounded over the 50 years of Professor Siegel's study, those seemingly small differences in annual returns led to substantial divergences in wealth accumulation. The two highest yielding quintile stocks compounded to a wealth accumulation five times as large as the two lowest yielding quintile stocks: a hypothetical $1,000 invested in the two highest yielding quintiles would have accumulated to $434,424, while $1,000 invested in the two lowest yielding quintiles would have accumulated to $83,367.

Fama–French research

Eugene Fama a professor at University of Chicago, and Kenneth French a professor at Dartmouth, report returns on various investment factors, one of which involves sorting the market by dividend yield. The Fama–French research breaks out the zero dividend yield companies separately from the dividend yield quintiles. We compare the Fama–French research on divi-

both studies find very similar results

dend yields to Professor Siegel's research to show both studies find very similar results.

The zero dividend yielding portfolios had the lowest return, less than 9% annualised from 1958–09, with the highest volatility, above 24%. The two highest yielding quintiles offered returns in excess of 12% per year, approximately 3 percentage points ahead of the zero-yielding stocks and approximately 2.5 percentage points per year of the lowest and low yielding stocks, and they did so with the lowest volatility of the quintiles (see Figure 9.1).

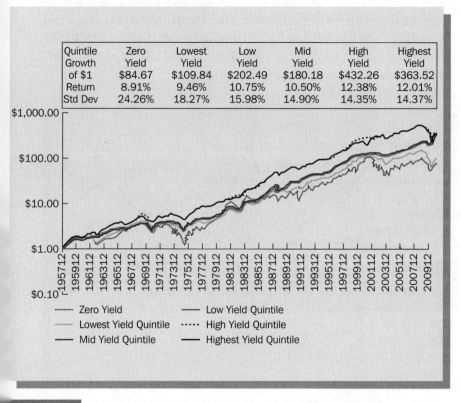

Figure 9.1   Fama–French dividend yield and returns, 1958–2009

Source: http://mba.tuck.dartmouth.edu/pages/faculty/ken.french/data_library.html

In addition to their importance in selecting among stocks within a certain market, dividend yields can be useful metrics to base relative allocation decisions among countries or regions of the world.

The importance of dividend yields as valuation risk indicators: a case study

A country's dividend yield can serve as an important valuation indicator of how expensively priced stocks are in that country. In fact, some powerful long-term trends can be viewed from the prism of whether a country's dividend yields are more or less than those of the broader market averages.

Australia and Japan are two countries that are currently at the opposite ends of the spectrum of their dividend yields: Australia has above average yields and Japan below average yields. This has been true for each of these countries for a number of years, but was not always true, particularly about 40 years ago when Japan had higher dividend yields than the MSCI EAFE (Europe, Australasia and Far East) and Australia had lower dividend yields (see Figure 9.2).

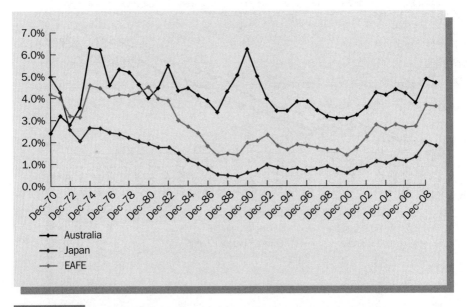

Figure 9.2   Annual dividend yields on MSCI Indexes, 1969–2009

Source: MSCI

During the late 1970s and throughout the 1980s, Japan's dividend yields continually sunk as its equity markets rose. From an initial yield above 5%, Japan's dividend yield plunged to just a half of 1% in 1989 at the peak of its market. Meanwhile, EAFE's dividend yields cratered along with Japan's, as Japan eventually came to dominate EAFE, and more than 60% of the weight of the MSCI EAFE was in Japan in 1989.[1] While EAFE's dividend yield reached a low of 1.4% in 1989, Australia's was over 5%.

Future returns from various starting dividend yields

Over the 20 years following the bottom of Japan's dividend yields in 1989, the returns were –2% per year, while MSCI EAFE had returns of 4.4% per year. Contrast those paltry returns with those from Australia, which had average annual returns of 10.7% per year, more than 600 basis points per year better than EAFE and nearly 13 percentage points per year better than Japan. The starting dividend yield in Australia in 1989, at 5%, was literally ten times higher than the dividend yield in Japan (see Figure 9.3). That means that to receive the same dividend income from a stock, Japanese investors were willing to pay ten times as much as investors in Australia. The depressed relative valuations for Australia in 1989, combined with its above average dividends from 1990–09, set the stage for its strong relative performance. Japan's miniscule dividend yield, by contrast, of less than 1%, was an ominous sign that Japan was in a bubble.

Meanwhile, the 40-year returns on Japan actually kept pace fairly well with EAFE, although Australia edged it out slightly because of its lengthy period of time with above average dividends. Japan's dividend yield 40 years ago was above 5%, higher than that of the broader international markets, and that initial starting level made up for its future below average yields.

The 20-year aftermath of the Japan bubble

The aftermath of the Japan bubble in 1989 had long-lasting implications for the most popular international benchmark, the MSCI EAFE index. For 20 years, those negative Japan returns weighed on the returns of the MSCI EAFE index. To quantify Japan's impact, one just needs to compare returns of the MSCI EAFE ex Japan, which returned nearly 4 percentage points per year more than the MSCI EAFE for the next 20 years from 1 January 1990 to 31 December 2009.

Laurence Siegel, 'International Equity Benchmarks', CFA Institute, Level 3, Volume 4, 3rd edn. Pearson Custom Publishing 361.

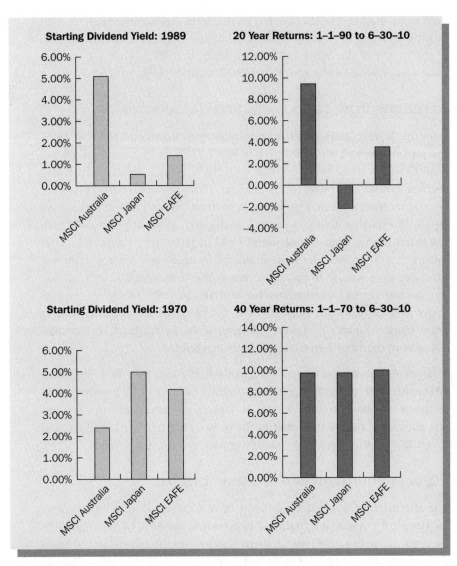

Figure 9.3   Dividend yield as a valuation indicator: Japan vs Australia

Source: WisdomTree, MSCI

Dividend weighted indexing: neutralising the impact of 'expensive' countries

A dividend weighted index mitigates the negative drag of countries with expensive valuation multiples (below average dividend yields). A dividend weighted approach therefore was less susceptible to the Japan bubble that plagued the MSCI EAFE index for 20 years.

Specifically, by setting the weights of index component securities by their contribution to the total dividend stream (defined as the total dividends paid over the prior 12 months of each company), valuation levels are removed from the index weighting equation. For two companies with the same dividend levels, a market cap weighted index such as the MSCI EAFE index, will give more weight to the company with the higher valuation multiple, while dividend weighted indexing does no such thing. Recall that in 1989, Japan had a valuation multiple that was ten times as large as that of Australia and therefore its weight in a market cap weighted approach was magnified by those high valuations. Clearly removing the valuation multiple from the global indexing equation can lead to different mixes of stocks. This mostly manifests in different country allocations in a global setting but can also have sector implications.

Dividend stream weighting: introducing a tilt to highest yielding stocks

While some investors will look at the results of the studies by Professors Siegel, Fama and French, and suggest the only stocks they want to hold in their portfolios are these highest yielding stocks, these strategies involve more concentrated portfolios that can subject themselves to greater volatility over short horizons.

A dividend weighted index tilts the weight to higher yielding stocks in a broadly diversified portfolio while tilting the weight away from stocks with the lowest dividend yields. When rebalanced annually, this dividend stream weighted indexing strategy automatically adjusts the exposures for changes in valuation metrics.

Of course, subsets of the total dividend universe can be formed to focus specifically on stocks selected from the highest yielding quintiles, as illustrated in Siegel's and Fama and French research – WisdomTree does so and calls them 'Equity Income Indexes'.

How dividend indexes are built

Dividend stream weighted indexes are built by summing up the total dividend stream of each respective market, and allocating the weight to each company according to its contribution to the total dividend stream of that region. For instance, as of the latest rebalancing of a Global Dividend Weighted index in May 2010, the largest dividend payer in the world was AT&T, which paid $9.8 billion of dividends over the prior 12 months, followed by Total SA, which paid $9.7 billion of dividends over the prior 12 months. The total dividends paid of the global index of stocks was $808 billion, and AT&T's and Total SA's weight is their contribution to the total $808 billion, or approximately 1.2% allocated to each (see Table 9.1)

Just as with traditional index families, sub-indexes can be derived from the broadest global dividend index including segments based on regions that typically include the United States, Developed International Markets, and the Emerging Markets (see Table 9.2).

Because WisdomTree starts with a very broad universe of over 4,300 global securities and nearly $30 trillion of market capitalisation coverage, it is able to create sub-indexes that mirror the traditional asset allocation strategies across size segments (large/mid/small cap) and regions of the world.

Figure 9.4 illustrates the size segment breakdown of a broader regional index. This segment breakdown is replicated across the USA and the developed international world, with small cap cuts also available in the emerging markets.

Dividend weighted indexes and country allocations

One of the primary questions equity investors must answer is how they will determine their allocation of capital across countries. Research shows many investors exhibit a home country bias, where they are under-diversified on a global basis. There are a myriad of explanations that have been given to explain investors' home bias, including more confidence in knowledge of stocks in home countries, it is more expensive to invest in foreign securities, and foreign investing involves additional currency risk. However, new investment tools like exchange traded funds have made it far simpler to achiever global diversification at fairly low execution costs – some of which now even include currency hedging strategies. So how should one decide how much to allocate on a global basis?

many investors exhibit a home country bias

WisdomTree believes that the best way to allocate a global index portfolio is according to the Global Dividend Stream, the sum total of all dividends paid over the prior year. By contrast, currently the most common way to allocate globally across countries is to use each country's market capitalisation – or free-float market capitalisation – while another popular benchmark weighting methodology utilises a country's global GDP contribution.

Table 9.1 Largest global dividend payers – WisdomTree Global Dividend index

Ten largest companies by cash dividends

Rank	Ticker	Name	Country	Trailing 12m dividend per share	Shares outstanding in billions	Company dividend stream ($ billions)	Percentage of dividend stream
1	T	AT&T Inc	United States	$1.66	5.90	$9.80	1.21%
2	FP FP	Total SA	France	$4.13	2.35	$9.69	1.20%
3	XOM	Exxon Mobil Corp	United States	$1.72	4.72	$8.14	1.01%
4	VOD LN	Vodafone Group PLC	Britain	$0.14	52.63	$7.57	0.94%
5	TEF SM	Telefonica SA	Spain	$1.60	4.56	$7.29	0.90%
6	FTE FP	France Telecom SA	France	$2.64	2.65	$6.99	0.87%
7	941 HK	China Mobile Ltd	Hong Kong	$0.34	20.06	$6.90	0.85%
8	SAN SM	Banco Santander SA	Spain	$0.83	8.23	$6.86	0.85%
9	HSBA LN	HSBC Holdings PLC	Britain	$0.37	17.42	$6.49	0.80%
10	GSZ FP	GDF Suez	France	$2.70	0.44	$6.11	0.76%
Top 10						**$75.84**	**9.38%**
WisdomTree Global Dividend Index Total						**$808.47**	**100.00%**

Source: WisdomTree, S&P

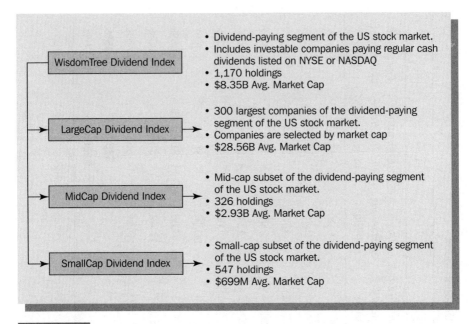

WisdomTree Dividend Index	• Dividend-paying segment of the US stock market. • Includes investable companies paying regular cash dividends listed on NYSE or NASDAQ • 1,170 holdings • $8.35B Avg. Market Cap
LargeCap Dividend Index	• 300 largest companies of the dividend-paying segment of the US stock market. • Companies are selected by market cap • $28.56B Avg. Market Cap
MidCap Dividend Index	• Mid-cap subset of the dividend-paying segment of the US stock market. • 326 holdings • $2.93B Avg. Market Cap
SmallCap Dividend Index	• Small-cap subset of the dividend-paying segment of the US stock market. • 547 holdings • $699M Avg. Market Cap

Figure 9.4   **Example of sub-index breakdown – United States size segments**

Source: WisdomTree, S&P

In contrast to statistical methodology differences across countries for calculating GDP measures or other fundamental accounting-based metrics like different accounting treatments for earnings, a dividend paid in one country is essentially identical to a dividend paid in another country, and it serves as a useful benchmark for allocating capital across the world.

Weighing a global index by each country's dividend stream creates a diversified and differentiated set of country exposures. As of 31 May 2010, the WisdomTree Global Dividend Stream was in aggregate $808 billion US dollars, of which the United States was the biggest contributor to global dividends with $226.5 billion dollars in dividend payments, or 27.9% of the aggregate global dividend stream.

The top five countries in a global dividend stream weighted index as of 31 May 2010 were: USA (27.9%), France (8.5%), the UK (8.4%), Japan (6.3%) and Australia (6.0%).

By contrast, a market capitalisation weighted approach would allocate more to the USA (approximately 43.4%), noticeably more than the dividend weighted allocation (see Figure 9.5). The implication of the dividend allocation being much less to the USA is that the US is an expensive country when one considers the total market capitalisation one is paying to access a given dividend stream.

Table 9.2 Regional dividend indexes

Rank	United States			Developed international			Emerging markets		
	Name	Company dividend stream ($ billions)	Percentage of dividend stream	Name	Company dividend stream ($ billions)	Percentage of dividend stream	Name	Company dividend stream ($ billions)	Percentage of dividend stream
1	AT & T Inc	$9.80	1.21%	Total SA	$9.69	2.18%	Petrobras	$2.77	2.45%
2	Exxon Mobil Corp	$8.14	1.01%	Vodafone Group PLC	$7.57	1.71%	China Construction Bank-H	$2.48	2.19%
3	Johnson & Johnson	$5.54	0.69%	Telefonica SA	$7.29	1.64%	Banco Do Brasil SA	$2.48	2.19%
4	Chevron Corp	$5.54	0.68%	France Telecom SA	$6.99	1.58%	Taiwan Semiconductor Manufacturing	$2.33	2.06%
5	Verizon Communications Inc	$5.35	0.66%	China Mobile Ltd	$6.90	1.55%	Industrial & Commercial Bank of China - H	$1.86	1.64%
6	Pfizer Inc	$5.28	0.65%	Banco Santander SA	$6.86	1.55%	Gazprom Oao-Spon Adr	$1.85	1.63%
7	Procter & Gamble Co	$5.25	0.65%	HSBC Holdings PLC	$6.49	1.46%	Lukoil Oao	$1.50	1.33%
8	Microsoft Corp	$4.61	0.57%	GDF Suez	$6.11	1.38%	Vale SA	$1.47	1.29%
9	Wal-Mart Stores Inc	$4.42	0.55%	Glaxosmithkline PLC	$5.68	1.28%	Bank Of China Ltd-H	$1.40	1.24%
10	Philip Morris International	$4.38	0.54%	Royal Dutch Shell A Shares	$5.67	1.28%	CEZ As	$1.35	1.19%
Top 10		$58.30	25.74%		$69.26	15.61%		$19.48	17.21%
Total dividend stream		$226.53	100.00%		$443.72	100.00%		$113.20	100.00%

Source: WisdomTree, S&P

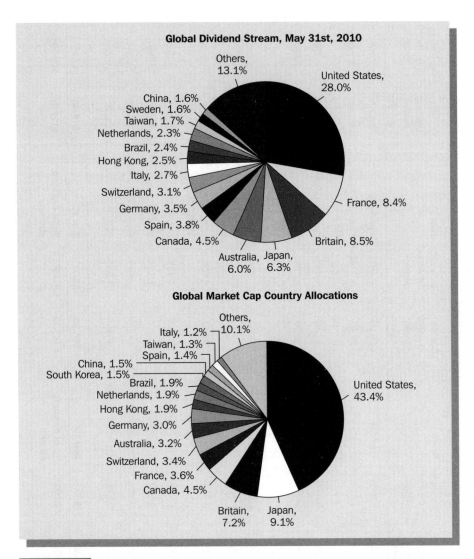

Global Dividend Stream, May 31st, 2010

Others, 13.1%
United States, 28.0%
China, 1.6%
Sweden, 1.6%
Taiwan, 1.7%
Netherlands, 2.3%
Brazil, 2.4%
Hong Kong, 2.5%
Italy, 2.7%
Switzerland, 3.1%
Germany, 3.5%
Spain, 3.8%
Canada, 4.5%
France, 8.4%
Britain, 8.5%
Australia, 6.0%
Japan, 6.3%

Global Market Cap Country Allocations

Others, 10.1%
Italy, 1.2%
Taiwan, 1.3%
Spain, 1.4%
China, 1.5%
South Korea, 1.5%
Brazil, 1.9%
Netherlands, 1.9%
Hong Kong, 1.9%
Germany, 3.0%
Australia, 3.2%
Switzerland, 3.4%
France, 3.6%
Canada, 4.5%
United States, 43.4%
Britain, 7.2%
Japan, 9.1%

Figure 9.5   WisdomTree Global Dividend Stream vs MSCI ACWI Market Cap Weighted Countries

Source: WisdomTree, S&P, Bloomberg

Dividend weighted indexing and relative value rebalancing

It is common practice for investors to take stock of their portfolios and decide to rebalance allocations that have moved astray from target allocations. Some take 'chips off the table' in areas of their portfolio that performed well and add some exposure in places that may have lagged and fallen in relative weight. If this type of rebalancing makes sense for portfolios as a whole, WisdomTree believed it also would make sense for indexes. Relative value rebalancing is one of the prime distinguishing characteristics of a dividend stream weighted index and it is notably lacking from market cap weighted index methodologies.

Although many concede that stock prices can deviate from fair value, they generally believe that costly research and security analysis are required to find these divergences. But with dividend weighted indexing this is not the case. Dividend weighted indexing provides a simple, cost-efficient strategy, designed to exploit the inefficiencies and mispricings in the market by weighting individual stocks by the total dividends companies pay. Critically important to this strategy is a relative value rebalancing process that adjusts weight in the index based on annual price change measures relative to annual dividend changes and adds (or subtracts) weight based on price falls (or rises) measured relative to their dividend change (see below).

Stock price during year	Dividend change	Weight change at rebalance
⬆	Up	Depends which rose more
	Flat	Decrease
	Down	Decrease
⬌	Up	Increase
	Flat	Unchanged
	Down	Decrease
⬇	Up	Increase
	Flat	Increase
	Down	Depends which fell more

Why choose dividend weighing to measure value?

The amount of cash a company can distribute to its shareholders gives a clear picture of the profitability of that firm regardless of the country or sector in which it operates. One could view market cap weighting as exposure to total value and dividend weighted methodology as exposure to the cash flows from owning global equities.

What dividend weighting introduces that market cap weighted indexing does not is a form of relative value rebalancing. Market cap weighted indexes are designed to be very low turnover, but in so doing they never rebalance based on relative value: market cap indexes give stocks greater weight when their prices rise and lower weight when they fall. Market cap weighted indexes have no adjustment mechanisms to say a stock has moved 'too much' relative to some market fundamental metric.

The advantages of using dividends to weight and rebalance stock indexes include:

- Dividends provide a compelling theoretical basis for stock values. Basic finance teaches us that asset prices are the present value of future cash flows. For stocks, cash flows are dividends.

- No other metric has the transparency and comparability across markets.

- Historically, reinvested dividends have provided the lion's share of the stockmarket's long-term real return. Reinvested dividends accounted for 97% of the long-term wealth accumulation in stocks from 1926–09.[2]

- Dividend weighted indexes can potentially raise the dividend yield on an index compared to a market capitalisation weighted index.

- Dividends may offer more protection during bear markets because as stock prices fall, investors can buy more shares at cheaper prices with reinvested dividends, a factor that can boost long-term returns.

- Cash dividends are an objective measure of a company's value and profitability — one that cannot be manipulated by accounting schemes.

The dividend approach repositions the index to avoid having exposure in companies that may have become dramatically overvalued. This is particularly true in market bubbles like the Japan bubble illustrated earlier and the information technology bubble experienced in 1999 and 2000. This bubble pushed the sector to have 30% of the weight in the S&P 500 at the peak and then lost 80% in value. A dividend weighted methodology would have pared back exposure to this dangerously overvalued sector and thus diminished the effects of that sector's decline when the bubble burst.

---

[2] Jeremy Siegel (2005) *The Future for Investors: Why the Tried and the True Triumph Over the Bold and the New*, with updates to 2009, Crown Business.

The dividends of dividend weighted indexes

The most common weighting metric in traditional indexes like the S&P 500, the MSCI EAFE Index and the MSCI Emerging Markets Index is market capitalisation. Market capitalisation is a measure of the total value of companies and is one measure of company size.

A dividend stream weighted index tilts the weight to the higher yielding stocks (when compared to a market cap index) and can really be considered a modified market cap weighted index – with market cap modified (multiplied) by dividend yields. The maths that implements the dividend tilts in a dividend weighted index works as follows:

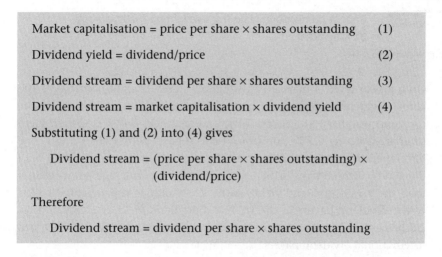

Market capitalisation = price per share × shares outstanding   (1)

Dividend yield = dividend/price   (2)

Dividend stream = dividend per share × shares outstanding   (3)

Dividend stream = market capitalisation × dividend yield   (4)

Substituting (1) and (2) into (4) gives

Dividend stream = (price per share × shares outstanding) × (dividend/price)

Therefore

Dividend stream = dividend per share × shares outstanding

A drawback of the traditional market cap weighted indexing approach is when there are two stocks that pay the same level of dividend income. A market cap weighted index gives more weight to the company selling at the higher valuation multiple – the one with a lower dividend yield. In WisdomTree's view, this is not the optimal way to maximise dividend income for a basket of stocks, as it means giving more weight to companies where one has to pay more to get a certain level of dividend income.

Figure 9.6 illustrates the difference dividend weighting makes at the latest annual rebalance in May 2010, in raising the dividend yield for the same basket of stocks when contrasted with using a market cap weighted approach.

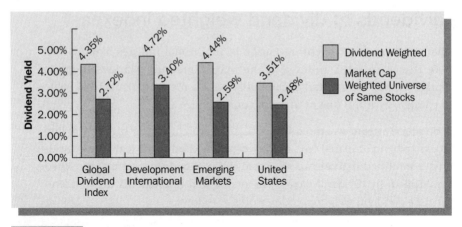

Figure 9.6   **Impact on dividend yield from weighting methodology, 31 May 2010**

Source: WisdomTree, S&P

On a global level, a market cap weighted index of approximately 4,300 global dividend payers would have a dividend yield of 2.72%, while the dividend weighted alternative of the same stocks had a dividend yield of approximately 4.35%, or around a 160 basis points differential. The developed international index had the highest dividends of 4.72% on a dividend weighted basis, which was just about 2 percentage points greater than the 3.51% dividend yield for the US. A market cap weighted basket of the dividend payers in the US had a dividend yield of 2.48%, almost 2.3 percentage points less than the dividend weighted index of developed international dividend payers.

EXAMPLE

The example illustrated by Table 9.3 shows how different stocks might be weighted using market cap weighting and dividend weighting. As you can see, the dividend weighted portfolio generates approximately 32% more dividend income and almost 1 percentage point of additional dividend yield than the market cap weighted option.

Increasing interest in dividends

Motivating interest in higher income dividend investment strategies is the relatively low level of real interest rates available in 2010 across the globe. The USA is a prime example of the low levels of global interest rates.

Table 9.3 Dividend weighting vs. market cap weighting

Company	Market Cap (Billions)	Dividend Stream (Billions)	Dividend Yield	Market Cap Weight	Investment	Dividend Income	Dividend Weight	Investment	Div Income
A	$400.0	$10.00	2.50%	50.00%	$500,000	$11,200	40.00%	$400,000	$10,000
B	$200.0	$3.00	1.50%	25.00%	$250,000	$4,350	12.00%	$120,000	$1,800
C	$200.0	$12.00	6.00%	25.00%	$250,000	$15,250	48.00%	$480,000	$28,800
Totals	$800.0	$25.0			$1,000,000	$30,800		$1,000,000	$40,600

Interest rates on US bonds are essentially as low as they have been in the past 40 to 50 years, leading many to believe that interest rates on bonds have nowhere to go but up. If that happens, return to bonds, which have seen an influx of capital in recent years, may suffer. Compounding worries about this recent 'bond bubble' are fears of government debt and deficits driving up future inflation. Inflation erodes the purchasing power of bonds and leads to higher interest rates, which would be a doubly whammy for bond investors.

> inflation erodes the purchasing power of bonds and leads to higher interest rates

Dividend-paying stocks are often considered one strategy to provide inflation hedging characteristics. Since the S&P 500 index inception in 1957, S&P 500 dividends have grown at a rate of 4.98% per year, which is about 100 basis points higher than the inflation rate, which averaged 3.98% per year (see Table 9.4). Note, during the 1970s and 1980s – when inflation rates averaged 6.22% – dividend growth averaged 6.46%, still outpacing inflation.

Table 9.4 Dividend growth and inflation (data as of 31 December 2009)

	S&P 500	
	Dividends	*Inflation*
1960s	4.88%	2.94%
1970s	5.98%	7.36%
1980s	6.94%	5.10%
1990s	4.08%	2.93%
2000s	3.12%	2.52%
	S&P 500	
	Dividends	*Inflation*
1957–2009	4.98%	3.98%
1970–1989	6.46%	6.22%
1990–2009	3.60%	2.73%

Source: Bob Shiller website: http://www.econ.yale.edu/~shiller/[3]

---

[3] Performance information prior to 1 June 2006 presented herein for the WisdomTree Dividend Indexes is based on hypothetical back tested data for the specified time period(s) shown and was not calculated in real time by an independent calculation agent. A back test is an indication of how an index would have performed in the past if it had existed. Hypothetical back tested performance has inherent limitations.

WisdomTree narrowed the gap between dividend yields and bond rates

WisdomTree launched its family of dividend indexes in June 2006. At the time, the ten-year US bond interest rate was 5.0%, the S&P 500 had a trailing 12-month dividend yield of 2.0% and the WisdomTree Dividend Index had a trailing 12-month dividend yield of 3.1%.

Interest rates on bonds have declined considerably from when WisdomTree launched in June 2006. The interest rates on the ten-year bond were close to 3% in June 2010.

Average index dividend yields and bond rates (30 June 2006 to 30 June 2010)

■ S&P 500: 2.19%

■ WT Dividend: 3.75%

■ 10-Year Bond: 3.90%

See Figure 9.7.

Average index dividend yield v. bond spread (30 June 2006 to 30 June 2010)

■ S&P 500: −171 basis points

■ WT Dividend Index: −15 basis points

See Figure 9.8.

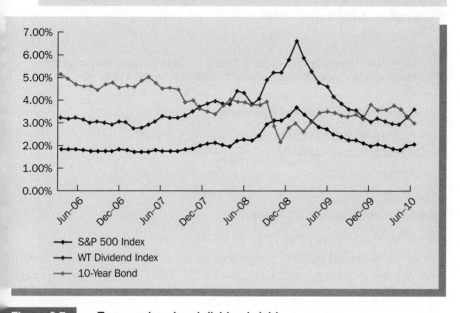

Figure 9.7   Ten-year bond and dividend yield

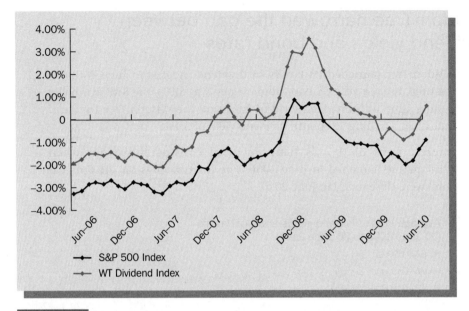

Figure 9.8   Spread: index dividend yield – 10-year bond

One reason WisdomTree created sub-indexes of its broadest index is that certain segments of the market have even higher dividend yields than the index of all the dividend payers. The two US-based indexes with the highest dividends are the WisdomTree SmallCap Dividend index and WisdomTree Equity Income index.

> WisdomTree SmallCap Dividend & Equity Income indexes had higher average dividend yields than 10-year bonds (30 June 2006 to 30 June 2010)
>
> **Average dividend yields and bond rates**
>
> - WT SmallCap Dividend: 5.57%
> - WT Equity Income: 5.23%
> - 10-Year Bond: 3.90%
>
> See Figure 9.9.
>
> **Average dividend yield v. bond spread**
>
> - S&P 500: –171 basis points
> - WT SmallCap Dividend Index: +167 basis points,
> - WT Equity Income Index: +132 basis points
>
> See Figure 9.10.

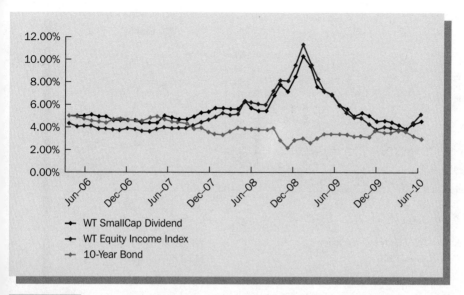

Figure 9.9   Ten-year bond and dividend yield minus 10-year bond

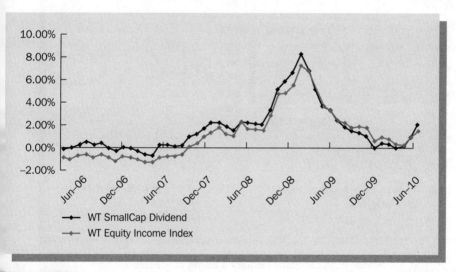

Figure 9.10   Spread index dividend yield

WisdomTree also focuses on high dividend stocks globally (see Figure 9.11).

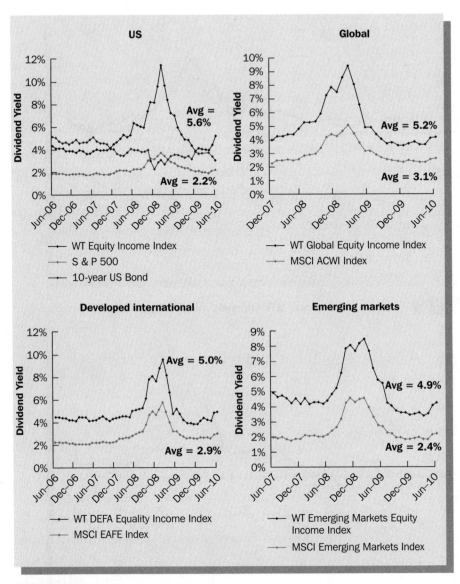

Figure 9.11   Global high dividend ('Equity Income') indexes

How long and how much growth is required for lower current dividends to catch up?

One often heard criticism of high dividend investment strategies in that companies are paying out their earnings and not reinvesting for future growth. WisdomTree believes that dividend weighted indexes, which historically increased the dividend yields on its indexes compared to similar market cap weighted indexes, had similar or even higher growth than the lower-yielding strategies. WisdomTree thus does not believe its dividend weighted indexes should have slower dividend growth over time.

However, if you're not convinced that dividend weighted, higher yield-ing indexes can achieve the same dividend growth as lower yielding, higher dividend growth strategies, let's analyse how long it takes higher growth dividend strategies to have dividend levels catch up to the higher yielding strategies.

In Figure 9.12, we illustrate how long it takes for varying growth rates of dividends to make up for a starting dividend yield deficit by comparing hypothetical dividend levels for a 2% starting dividend yield – where divi-dends grow at various growth rates – compared to higher starting dividend yields of 3% or 4% initially with no growth.

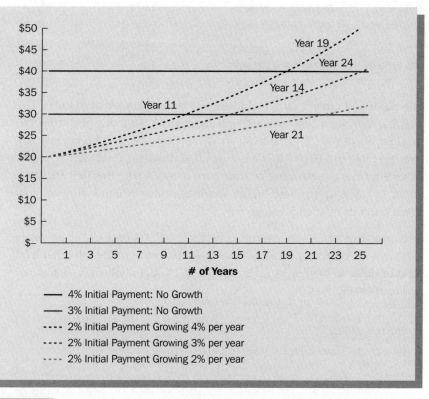

- 4% Initial Payment: No Growth
- 3% Initial Payment: No Growth
- - - - 2% Initial Payment Growing 4% per year
- - - - 2% Initial Payment Growing 3% per year
- - - - 2% Initial Payment Growing 2% per year

Figure 9.12   Hypothetical dividend yield levels for various starting yields and growth rates.

Note that Figure 9.12 only displays the *annual* income deficits. Because in each of the early years there is an income deficit, it takes longer for the cumulative distributions of the lower yielding, higher growth stocks to catch up in cumulative distributions.

Table 9.5 illustrates for each of these scenarios how long it would take for the various higher growth rate strategies to catch up to the no growth, higher yielding options.

Table 9.5 Time it takes for annual/cumulative dividends to catch up (for 2% initial payment growing faster than higher yield no growth)

Growth for 2% initial yield	Starting dividend yield/ no growth	Number of years for annual dividends	Number of years for cumulative dividends
2% initial/ 2% growth	3% initial/no growth	21	40
	4% initial/no growth	35	65
2% initial/ 3% growth	3% initial/no growth	14	27
	4% initial/no growth	24	44
2% initial/ 4% growth	3% initial/no growth	11	21
	4% initial/no growth	19	33

The yields and growth rates in Table 9.5 were not selected at random. The S&P 500 as of June 2010 had a 2% dividend yield. An index of all the dividend payers in the USA has dividend yields above 3%, and higher yielding strategies like the Equity Income index had dividend yields north of 4%. Table 9.5 thus gives a sense of how long it could take the S&P 500 dividends to catch up to these higher yielding strategies depending on how much faster its dividends can grow.

Note, the 'rule of 72' (see over) is generally a helpful back-of-the-envelope method for evaluating dividend strategies that have double the dividend yield of other strategies. In Table 9.5, the 2% initial dividend vs 4% initial dividend exemplifies this.

The rule of 72

The rule of 72 states that the number of years it takes for a number to double is 72 divided by a growth rate – at a 2% higher growth rate the rule of 72 says it would take approximately 36 years, while at a 4% higher growth rate it would be approximately 18 years. But remember those are only *annual* income deficits, the cumulative dividend differential will take longer since the income deficits from early years needs to be made up.

Conclusion

The most critical question for income oriented investors is how much capital is required to generate a given income stream. If one had a goal of generating dividend income of $50,000 a year, and there were two alternatives – Stock A, with a dividend yield of 2%, and Stock B, with a dividend yield of 3% – then it takes a $2.5 million investment in Stock A to generate $50,000 of dividend income, but only $1.67 million investment in Stock B to get the same $50,000 of income. Certainly the $1.67 capital requirement is easier to fulfil than a $2.5 million requirement.

Table 9.6 illustrates the various capital requirements to generate $50,000 of dividend income.

Table 9.6 Dividend yield and capital requirements to generate $50,000 of income

Dividend yield (%)	Capital required ($)
2.0	2,500,000
3.0	1,666,667
4.0	1,250,000
5.0	1,000,000
6.0	833,333
7.0	714,286
8.0	625,000

Market cap weighted indexes give greater weights to companies with lower dividend yields, raising the capital requirements to generate given income streams. WisdomTree's global dividend stream weighted approach produces broadly diversified portfolios that can be used to focus on higher dividend strategies from any region of the world that have potential to lower the capital requirements necessary to generate a given income stream.

The breadth of dividend weighted index strategies that have been developed allow one to target strategies as specific and narrow, or as broad and diversified, as one desires – from United States large cap dividend payers to emerging markets small cap dividend payers or global equity income (highest dividend yielders), there are now a multitude of investment benchmarks that can be tracked.

WisdomTree believes that the investment environment is likely to support the case for dividend strategies over the coming years. The demographic situation in the USA, Western Europe and Japan, with all the baby boomers entering retirement, is apt to place a premium on income oriented investments. Dividend stream weighted strategies provide a number of options that can potentially help investors achieve their income oriented goals.

Index